■

"If you're interested in the mobsters, grifters, showgirls, corrupt cops, and crooked judges of New York in the 1920's (and it's hard not to be), *Gangsterland* is for you. David Pietrusza's tour of the bars and nightclubs, the floating crap games and the bucket shops, the whorehouses and courtrooms and gambling dens brings the era's underworld into vivid light. And you can tell that Pietrusza had a blast writing it!"

—DANIEL OKRENT,
author of *Last Call: The Rise and Fall of Prohibition*

"When David Pietrusza walks down the sidewalks of New York, he doesn't see modern skyscrapers and Starbucks coffee shops. Reading *Gangsterland*, you will see what he sees: hideouts, speakeasies, murder sites, and theater stages where the mistresses of both mob bosses and the city's good-time mayor trod the boards. His book gives a literary tour of New York when the Twenties were roaring and reminds us that a single building can have many lives. Fascinating and fun!"

—KATHRYN SMITH, author of *Baptists & Bootleggers: A Prohibition Expedition Through the South . . . with Cocktail Recipes*

"David Pietrusza is a national treasure. Few historians can match his one-two punch of gorgeous prose and deep insight. This combo delivers the kind of haymaker that would have made Jack Dempsey proud. *Gangsterland* is a true crime heavyweight champ, filled with stories of New York's seedy past and a must-read for anyone interested in the murder and mayhem of the Roaring Twenties—and who isn't?"

—**BOB BATCHELOR,**
cultural historian, author of *The Bourbon King:
The Life and Crimes of George Remus, Prohibition's Evil Genius*

"David Pietrusza brings history alive like very few authors can. Weaving journalistic accounts together with meticulous research and lively prose, Pietrusza makes it feel as though you're on a tour right through the heart of Jazz Age Manhattan. I plan to take the book with me next time I'm in Midtown and follow in David's footsteps, reading each story as I go and imagining the scene from a century ago."

—**KEVIN BALFE,** founder of CrimeCon

GANGSTERLAND

GANGSTERLAND

A TOUR THROUGH
THE DARK HEART OF JAZZ-AGE
NEW YORK CITY

DAVID PIETRUSZA

DIVERSION
BOOKS

■

Dedicated to
VINCE GIORDANO
whose wonderful band, The Nighthawks,
has brought 1920s Times Square back to life
for so many fun years.

■

For more information, email info@diversionbooks.com.

Diversion Books
A division of Diversion Publishing Corp.
www.diversionbooks.com

First Diversion Books Edition: November 2023
Paperback ISBN 9781635769890
Ebook ISBN 9781635768787

Times Square Postcard (p. iii) Courtesy of Columbia University Libraries

Printed in the United States of America
10 9 8 7 6 5 6 5 4 3 2 1

CONTENTS

CAST OF CHARACTERS

PEARL "POLLY" ADLER (1900–1962) Russian-born proprietor of a string of celebrity-patronized brothels. George McManus is a repeat (and violent) customer.

JULIUS WILFORD "NICKY" ARNSTEIN (née Arndstein) (1879–1965) Berlin-born con man and bond hijacker. Associate (and admirer) of Arnold Rothstein. And most significantly: Mr. Fanny Brice.

ABRAHAM WASHINGTON "ABE," "THE LITTLE CHAMP," or "THE LITTLE HEBREW" ATTELL (1883–1970) World featherweight champion. Longtime associate of Arnold Rothstein—his accomplice in fixing 1919's World Series.

GEORGE YOUNG BAUCHLE (1879–1939) Wealthy grandson of George Young, a founder of the Y&S licorice company—and Arnold Rothstein's blue blood front man in the high-stakes, high-society floating gambling society, the Partridge Club. Neither his fortune nor his respectability survives.

LT. CHARLES BECKER (1870–1915) Corrupt and brutal NYC cop. An ally of "Big Tim" Sullivan. Fried in the chair for gambler Beansie Rosenthal's 1912 murder.

MIKE BEST (née William Besnoff or Bestoff) (?–1947) Prominent New York gambler. Part owner of the Cotton Club. Wounded in a 1937 West 53rd Street shooting.

HYMAN "GILLIE" BILLER (1888–?) George McManus's Russian-born bagman. Indicted for the Rothstein murder. Never brought to trial.

FANNY BRICE (née Fania Borach) (1891–1951) The *Ziegfeld Follies'* immortal "Funny Girl." Wife (though not at the same time) to gambler Nicky Arnstein and showman Billy Rose. A rival in love to Lillian Lorraine. Not a fan of Arnold Rothstein.

"PEACHES" BROWNING (née Frances Belle Heenan) (1910–1956) Teenaged bride of wealthy real estate man Edward West "Daddy" Browning (1875–1934). Their juicy divorce triggers a frenzy of tabloid headlines.

NATHAN BURKAN (1879–1936) Romanian-born attorney. A prominent Tammany official and the nation's foremost entertainment and copyright attorney. Assigned to vet the late Arnold Rothstein's embarrassing private papers.

WILLIAM THOMAS "SLEEPY BILL" BURNS (1880–1953) Former major league pitcher. A prime fixer of 1919's "Black Sox" World Series—thanks to Arnold Rothstein's big bankroll.

RICHARD ALBERT CANFIELD (1855–1914) Manhattan and Saratoga Springs proprietor of opulent (though still illegal) gambling houses. A hero and role model to Arnold Rothstein.

MAURICE FREEMAN CANTOR (née Morris Cantor) (1895–?) Tammany-backed Upper West Side New York State assemblyman. Arnold Rothstein's—and Inez Norton's—grasping attorney.

PRIMO "THE AMBLING ALP" CARNERA (1906–1967) Huge but not very talented Italian-born heavyweight champion, significantly boosted to the crown through his mob connections.

EARL CARROLL (1893–1948) Pittsburgh-born producer of *Earl Carroll's Vanities*—a scantily clad rival to Flo Ziegfeld's *Follies*. Sentenced to Atlanta penitentiary for an incident involving a tub full of illegal champagne—and the naked seventeen-year-old showgirl Joyce Hawley.

RENÉE CARROLL (née Rebecca Shapiro) (1907–2000) The world's most famous (maybe the world's *only* famous) hatcheck girl. A fixture at Vincent Sardi's famed West 45th Street restaurant and a surprisingly respected reviewer/critic of prospective scripts.

WILLIAM "RED" CASSIDY (c. 1893–1929) Waterfront hoodlum and speakeasy owner. He made the mistake of annoying Legs Diamond at Legs's Hotsy Totsy Club.

LOU CLAYTON (née Louis Finkelstein) (1890–1950) Jimmy Durante's partner in his famed nightclub/speakeasy "Clayton, Jackson, and Durante" act. One tough customer.

VINCENT "MAD DOG" COLL (1908–1932) Brazen (or just plain crazy) Irish-born mobster. A Dutch Schultz rival. Kidnapper of Frenchy DeMange. Machine-gunned on orders from Owney Madden.

"DAPPER DON" COLLINS (née Robert Arthur Tourbillon) (1880–1950) Con man, badger game operator (with the beautiful Buda Godman), and rum-runner (with the less beautiful Arnold Rothstein). On familiar terms with Lillian Lorraine and Inez Norton. Died at Attica.

BETTY COMPTON (née Violet Halling Compton) (1904–1944) British Wight-born *Ziegfeld Follies* showgirl and the mistress (and later wife) of disgraced Gotham mayor James J. Walker.

JOHN L. "DASHING JACK" CONAWAY (1881–1911) Blue-blooded Philadelphia broker and champion polo player and fox hunter, and billiards player. His thirty-two-hour-long 1909 billiards match against the young Arnold Rothstein generates national headlines.

GEORGE F. CONSIDINE (1868–1916) Part-owner of the Metropole Hotel with brothers John R. and William F. Considine. Partner (with Arnold Rothstein) in Maryland's Havre de Grace racetrack. Co-manager with brother John R. of prizefighting champs James J. Corbett and Kid McCoy.

JOHN W. CONSIDINE SR. (c. 1883–1943) "Big Tim" Sullivan's partner in the West Coast's Considine-Sullivan vaudeville circuit. Father of John W. Considine Jr., an Oscar-nominated Hollywood producer (*Boys Town*), and Bob Considine, a very popular Hearst newspaper columnist and author.

JOHN R. CONSIDINE (1861 or 1862–1909) Part-owner of the Metropole Hotel. Co-manager of James J. Corbett and Kid McCoy. Brother of George F. and William F. Considine.

WILLIAM F. CONSIDINE (c. 1870–1932) Part-owner of the Metropole Hotel. Brother of George F. and John R. Considine.

FRANK "THE PRIME MINISTER OF THE UNDERWORLD" COSTELLO (née Francesco Castiglia) (1891–1973) Calabria-born early associate of Lucky Luciano and Meyer Lansky. Their bootlegging activities will be backed by Arnold Rothstein. With help from "Dandy Phil" Kastel, Costello eventually dominates illegal gambling nationwide.

JUDGE JOSEPH FORCE CRATER (1889–vanished in 1930) Corrupt, philandering Tammany New York City magistrate. His 1930 disappearance remains one of the great mysteries of all time.

MARION DAVIES (née Marion Cecilia Douras) (1897–1961) Brooklyn-born showgirl and later a silent film star. William Randolph Hearst's long-time mistress.

ELAINE DAWN (?–?) Club Abbey dancer. Also in 1927's Broadway hit musical *Show Boat*. Roommate of dancer Sally Lou Ritz—and another of Judge Crater's mistresses.

WILLIAM HARRISON "JACK" or "THE MANASSA MAULER" DEMPSEY (1895–1983) World heavyweight champion. Once managed by "John the Barber" Reisler. Broadway restaurateur. Did Abe Attell and Arnold Rothstein help fix his 1926 title loss to Gene "The Fighting Marine" Tunney?

GEORGE JEAN "BIG FRENCHY" DEMANGE (1896–1939) Beer baron Owney "The Killer" Madden's best friend—and partner in Harlem's Cotton Club.

Kidnapped at West 54th Street's Club Argonaut in 1932 by Vincent "Mad Dog" Coll.

ALICE KENNY SCHIFFER DIAMOND (c. 1900–1933) Long Island-born former secretary. Legs Diamond's adoring and much-forgiving second (and final) wife. Rendered penniless following his murder, the 5'7" Alice worked in burlesque and at Coney Island side shows. Shot to death at her Brooklyn apartment.

EDDIE DIAMOND (1902–1930) Legs Diamond's tubercular younger brother and partner-in-crime. Nearly rubbed out in Denver in 1930.

JACK "LEGS" DIAMOND (1897–1931) Particularly brutal Philadelphia-born hoodlum, bootlegger, liquor hijacker, and Rothstein bodyguard. Many a time, rivals filled Legs's lanky body with lead—but (up to a point) never killed him, thus generating Diamond's less-desired nickname, "The Clay Pigeon of the Underworld." Finally murdered in his sleep in upstate Albany.

DEMARIS "HOTSY TOTSY" DORE (c. 1910–?) A friend of "Peaches" Browning. A dancer at Broadway's Club Frivolity. Later hostess at Frankie Marlow's Silver Slipper cabaret. Rothstein bodyguard "Fatty" Walsh's not particularly loyal girlfriend. An uncooperative witness to his 1929 murder.

JOHN THOMAS "JACK" DOYLE (1876–1942) Betting commissioner. Proprietor of 42nd Street's Doyle Billiard Academy. Onetime billiard hall partner of John McGraw.

WILLIAM J. "BIG BILL" OR "BROADWAY BILL" DUFFY (c. 1883–1952) Brooklyn-born pal of Owney "The Killer" Madden and "Frenchy" DeMange. Reform school and Sing Sing graduate. Partner in the Club La Vie, the Silver Slipper, and Rendezvous speakeasies. Heavyweight champ Primo Carnera's manager. Convicted of tax evasion in 1934.

JAMES FRANCIS "SCHNOZZOLA" DURANTE (1893–1980) Frenetic, bulbous-nosed lead entertainer with the team of "Clayton, Jackson, and Durante." Proprietor of West 58th Street's Club Durant, whose basement garage hosts Arnold Rothstein's floating craps games.

ISIDORE "IZZY" EINSTEIN (1880–1938) and MOE W. SMITH (1887–1960) The era's most successful (and roly-poly) Prohibition agents. Sacked by the Bureau in 1925 largely for their success—and their fame.

CHARLES ENTRATTA (aka "Charles Green") (1904–1931) Legs Diamond henchman. Involved in the fatal Hotsy Totsy Club shooting. Fatally shot from behind at a Brooklyn bottling plant.

SAMUEL "SAMMY THE HOOK" ENTRATTA (née Sam Ippolito) (c. 1910–1932) Buda Godman's ill-fated accomplice in 1932's $305,000 Glemby jewel robbery. Fearing justice, he commits suicide.

WILLIAM "THE GREAT MOUTHPIECE" FALLON (1886–1927) Former Westchester County prosecutor turned brilliant mob-connected Manhattan defense attorney specializing in jury tampering. His clients include Arnold Rothstein, Charles Stoneham, John McGraw, and Isidore Rapoport. His girlfriends include showgirl Gertrude Vanderbilt.

LARRY FAY (1888–1933) Horse-faced bootlegger and speakeasy operator. Taxicab and milk trade magnate. Facing declining fortunes, he is shot dead by a disgruntled employee.

HILDA FERGUSON (née Hildegarde Gibbons) (1903–1933) Dot King's blonde, leggy former showgirl roommate. Atlantic City boss "Nucky" Johnson's once well-provided-for mistress. A witness to her later boyfriend "Tough Willie" McCabe's 1931 East 52nd Street's Sixty-One Club 1931 knifing. An alcoholic, she dies penniless and friendless.

FRANCIS SCOTT KEY (F. Scott) FITZGERALD (1896–1940) Jazz Age novelist whose *The Great Gatsby* immortalizes Arnold Rothstein as the crass "Meyer Wolfsheim," the "one man [who] could start to play with the faith of *fifty million people.*"

JULES "BIG JULIUS" FORMEL JR. (1876–1950) Saratoga gambler who fingers Rothstein corruption in the spa city. Protagonist of 1901's heroic rescue of Miss Anita Gonzales from a runaway carriage and of a 1903 Wild West–style West 28th Street gun battle.

GLADYS GLAD (1907–1983) *Ziegfeld Follies* showgirl. Married to columnist Mark Hellinger in 1929.

BUDA GODMAN (née Helen Julia Godman) (aka Helen Strong) (1888–1945) Chicago-born beauty. Badger game operator with "Dapper Don" Collins. Jewel thief. Charles Stoneham's mistress.

VIVIAN GORDON (née Benita Franklin) (1891–1931) Cocaine-addicted prostitute and brothel operator. Bankrolled by Rothstein. Badger game partner of Legs Diamond. Found beaten and strangled in the Bronx's Van Cortlandt Park.

"WAXEY" GORDON (née Irving Wexler) (1888–1952) Lower East Side–born hoodlum. Rothstein-connected bootlegger and rumrunner. Died at Alcatraz.

FREDERICK W. GRESHEIMER (aka "Freddie Gresham") (1880–?) Stockbroker and jailbird. Husband of Lillian Lorraine—responsible for the broad daylight beating of her former lover Flo Ziegfeld.

MARY LOUISE CECILIA "TEXAS" GUINAN (1884–1933) Flamboyant ("Hello, suckers!") speakeasy hostess (at multiple locations including Larry Fay's El Fey Club, the 300 Club, the Club Moritz, the Salon Royale, and the Club Argonaut). Former Western genre silent movie star.

THOMAS "TOMMY" GUINAN (1897–1967) Texas Guinan's younger brother. Operator of West 48th Street's Club Florence—site of the 1928 brawl that cost W. C. Fields's former girlfriend Bessie Poole her life.

JOYCE HAWLEY (née Theresa Daugelos) (1909–?) The seventeen-year-old showgirl in Earl Carroll's champagne-filled bathtub.

MILLICENT VERONICA WILLSON HEARST (1882–1974) Former Broadway showgirl. Cheated-on wife of William Randolph Hearst.

WILLIAM RANDOLPH "THE CHIEF" HEARST (1863–1951) Powerful (and fabulously wealthy) press baron. Foe of Tammany Hall. Actress Marion Davies's paramour.

MARK JOHN HELLINGER (1903–1947) *New York Daily News* and (later) *Daily Mirror* columnist. Married to showgirl Gladys Glad.

CHARLES "VANNIE" HIGGINS (1897–1932) Brooklyn-based gangster. Shot to death following his daughter's tap dance recital.

JAMES JOSEPH "JIMMY" HINES (1876–1957) Tammany boss of West Harlem. Patron of the burgeoning illegal numbers racket, Dutch Schultz, and George "Hump" McManus. Convicted of bribe-taking and racketeering in 1939.

PHILIP "DANDY PHIL" KASTEL (1893–1962) Shady bucket shop operator. Later, a key to The Syndicate's gambling operations. Doris Sheerin's sugar daddy. A suicide.

BERTHA KATZ (c. 1894–1922) Attractive (*too* attractive) sister-in-law to "John the Barber" Reiser. Murdered by her outraged and unattractive (*too* unattractive) sister Bertha Reiser and Berthas's son Morris.

BENNIE MICHAEL "BENNY" KAUFF (1890–1961) New York Giants outfielder. Accused of auto theft and of knowledge of the Black Sox World Series fix. Banned from baseball for life.

JOHN O. "HONEST JOHN" or "KICK" KELLY (1856–1926) Times Square gambling house operator. Former major league umpire. Famous for never paying—or accepting—a bribe.

DOT "THE BROADWAY BUTTERFLY" KING (née Dorothy Keenan) (1896–1923) Suffocated in her Rothstein-owned apartment while being robbed of her $30,000 jewelry collection—jewels insured by A. R.

FIORELLO HENRY "THE LITTLE FLOWER" LA GUARDIA (née Fiorello Raffaele Enrico La Guardia) (1882–1947) Greenwich Village–born former East Harlem congressman. Later New York mayor. A foe of Tammany, Rothstein, and all things corrupt—including artichokes.

WILLIAM FRANCIS "BILLY" LAHIFF (1883–1934) Much-loved Times Square chophouse proprietor. In 1928, Arnold Rothstein will sell his Woodmere, Long Island's 260-acre Cedar Point Golf Club to a LaHiff-headed syndicate.

MEYER "LITTLE MAN" LANSKY (née Meier Suchowlański) (1902–1983) Russian-born protégé of Arnold Rothstein who will teach him the secrets of attracting (and retaining) suckers to his Las Vegas and Havana casinos.

DIANA LANZETTA (c. 1900–?) Florida-born *Ziegfeld* girl who became the sister-in-law of former Jimmy Hines–backed congressman James J. Lanzetta (he defeated Fiorella La Guardia in 1932). Later president of the Women's National Democratic Club. Robbed of cash and jewels in 1937 by Jimmy Meehan.

LOUISE LAWSON (c. 1899–1924) Texas-born gold digger. Slain during a jewel robbery at her West 77th Street apartment. Arnold Rothstein had previously insured her jewels.

ISAIAH LEEBOVE (1895–1938) Pittsburgh-born attorney for such hoods as Arnold Rothstein, Legs Diamond, Owney "The Killer" Madden, Salvatore Spitale, Sidney Stajer, and gamblers Nick "the Greek" Dandalos and Nigger Nate Raymond. Murdered after relocating to Michigan.

LILLIAN LORRAINE (née Ealallean De Jacques) (c. 1892–1955) Beautiful but volatile showgirl. A steerer for Arnold Rothstein's gambling house. Flo Ziegfeld's mistress.

CHARLES "LUCKY" LUCIANO (née Salvatore Lucania) (1897–1962) Italian-born drug peddler and pimp. A Rothstein protégé—but still a suspect regarding his murder. Convicted by Tom Dewey on pandering charges in 1936, he cooperated with U.S. officials in their wartime World War II efforts and died an exile back in Naples.

OWNEY "THE KILLER" MADDEN (1891–1965) British-born, Manhattan-raised all-around criminal. Jailed for murder in 1915. Bootlegger and nightclub owner. Partner of Big Bill and George Jean "Big Frenchy" DeMange. Patron of dancer/hoodlum/actor George Raft.

WILLIAM JOSEPH "BILLY" MAHARG (1881–1953) Former lightweight prizefighter and very briefly a major league ballplayer. "Sleepy Bill" Burns's partner in fixing 1919's World Series.

GENE MALIN (née Victor Eugene James Malinovsky) (aka Jean Malin and Imogene Wilson) (1908–1933) Openly flamboyantly gay Club Abbey MC.

FRANKIE MARLOW (née Gandolfo Civito) (?–1929) An all-around mobster—a prizefight manager and speakeasy owner "who for more than a score of years had had a finger in every enterprise of Broadway's underworld." Lured to his death from in front of West 52nd Street's La Tavernelle.

TONY MARLOW (?–1928) Former Chicago bootlegger. A Joey Noe hench-man. Murdered by Diamond Brothers goons while standing in front of West 54th Street's Harding Hotel. His death triggers Noe's own death.

WILLIE "TOUGH WILLIE" or "THE HANDSOMEST MAN ON BROADWAY" McCabe (?–1953) Former Chicago bootlegger and one-time Rothstein bodyguard. Stabbed (non-fatally) in 1931 at East 52nd Street's Sixty-One Club. Later, Lucky Luciano's boss of Harlem's lucrative numbers rackets. Nonetheless, he died at Roosevelt Island's City Hospital for the indigent.

JOHN JOSEPH "MUGSY" or "THE LITTLE NAPOLEON" MCGRAW (1873–1934) Longtime manager of Horace Stoneham's baseball New York Giants. Billiard hall partner of Arnold Rothstein. Drunken brawler at West 44th Street's Lambs Club.

ANDREW J. "THE LONE WOLF" MCLAUGHLIN (?–?) Vice squad patrolman. A potential key to 1931's Vivian Gordon murder mystery.

FRANCIS "FRANK" MCMANUS (c. 1892–?) George McManus's brother. Proprietor of West 77th Street's Blossom Heath Inn, site of 1931's Legs Diamond–Vannie Higgins knife-wielding brawl.

GEORGE A. "HUMP" MCMANUS (1893–1940) Prominent gambler. Hard-drinking and violent. Tried (and acquitted) for Arnold Rothstein's 1928 murder.

JIMMY MEEHAN (née Raffaele Marino) (c. 1904–?) Small-time gambler. His apartment hosted the high-stakes poker game that led to Arnold Rothstein's slaying. Jewel thief.

WILSON MIZNER (1876–1933) Famed raconteur and phrase-maker. Instrumental to 1909's famed Rothstein–Conaway marathon billiards match.

EUGENE "RED" MORAN (1894–1929) Rothstein $1,000-per-week body-guard. Involved in 1922's $300,000 Schoellkopf jewel robbery. Suspected of trying to kill Eddie Diamond. Found dead in a Newark dump.

HELEN MORGAN (née Helen Riggins) (1900–1941) Perhaps the Jazz Age's premier torch singer. Opening in 1927's groundbreaking musical *Show Boat*, how-ever, failed to prevent the Feds from raiding her West 54th Street speakeasy, Chez Morgan, three nights later. Also proprietor of West 54th Street's Helen Morgan's Summer Home. She sang perched from atop her accompanist's piano—some said because she was invariably too soused to stand up.

JOSEPH "JOEY" NOE (c. 1903–1928) Bronx bootlegger. Boyhood friend and boss of Dutch Schultz. Fatally ambushed by a trio of Legs Diamond's gunmen outside West 54th Street's Chateau Madrid. Remarkably also a Bronx deputy sheriff.

INEZ NORTON (née Inez Smythe) (c. 1903–?) Blonde Florida-born showgirl. Arnold Rothstein's last mistress.

GALINA "GAY" ORLOVA (c. 1914–1948) Lucky Luciano's Russian-born girlfriend. An eventual suicide.

BESSIE CHATTERTON POOLE (1895–1928) The heavy-drinking showgirl mother of W. C. Fields's illegitimate son. Died of injuries suffered at Tommy Guinan's Chez Florence. Quickly forgotten by Fields.

GEORGE RAFT (née George Rauft) (1901–1980) Speakeasy dancer. Owney Madden's friend and chauffeur. Later a prominent Hollywood "tough guy" actor.

ISADORE RAPOPORT (c. 1891–?) Saratoga speakeasy operator, illegal brewery operator, "mastermind" of 1946's $734,000 Mergenthaler Linotype Co. robbery in Brooklyn—among numerous other nefarious activities.

NATHAN LENNET "NIGGER NATE" RAYMOND (aka Nathan Sedlow) (1891–?) San Francisco–based gambler. Banned from baseball's Pacific Coast League for fixing games.

JACOB "JOHN THE BARBER" REISLER (née Jacob Reisler) (c. 1877–1930) Austrian-born Broadway barber and Jack Dempsey's early manager. A witness to the Rosenthal slaying. His marital unfaithfulness leads to familial gunplay.

MINNIE REISLER (?–1952) "John the Barber" Reisler's aggrieved wife. Bertha Katz's even more aggrieved sister.

MORRIS REISLER (1897–1966) Son of John and Minnie Reisler. Convicted burglar. Outraged by his father's all-in-the-family infidelity.

GEORGE GRAHAM RICE (née Jacob Simon Herzig) (1870–1943) Inventor of the horse racing tip sheet. Pioneering stock swindler. Tenant and friend of Arnold Rothstein.

GEORGE RINGLER (née Abe C. Ringel) (1890–1956) Arnold Rothstein's cousin—and, perhaps, a connection to Rothstein's Oriental drug trade. An intimate of Mayor Walker.

SALLY RITZ (aka Sally Lou Ritz or Sally Lou Ritzi) (1903–?) Club Abbey dancer. Another Judge Crater girlfriend.

MARION "KIKI" ROBERTS (née Marion Strasmick) (c. 1910–?) Boston-bred showgirl; *Ziegfeld* showgirl mistress of Legs Diamond. Save for his killers, she is the last to see him alive.

BILLY "THE BANTAM BARNUM" ROSE (née William Samuel Rosenberg) (1899–1966) Songwriter, speakeasy operator (with Arnold Rothstein as an unwanted "partner"), Broadway producer, and theater owner—and the 5'6" Fanny Brice's 4'11" third husband.

"BALD JACK" or "BILLIARD BALL JACK" ROSE (née Jacob Rosenzweig) (1876–1947) Polish-born East Side gambler. Former prizefight promoter and minor league baseball manager. Pimp and Lt. Charles Becker's bagman. Indicted but never tried for Herman Rosenthal's murder.

HERMAN "BEANSIE" ROSENTHAL (1874–1912) Lower East Side and Times Square gambling house operator. A favorite of Tammany's "Big Tim" Sullivan. His exposé of NYPD Lt. Charles Becker's shakedown sparks Rosenthal's Hotel Metropole drive-by assassination.

SAMUEL LIONEL "ROXY" ROTHAFEL (1882–1936) German-born, ex-Marine theater impresario responsible for Manhattan's most opulent motion picture palaces, including Radio City Music Hall.

ARNOLD "THE BRAIN" or "THE BIG BANKROLL" ROTHSTEIN (1882–1928) Gambler. Loan shark. Stolen jewel fence. Bootlegger. Drug smuggler. Casino and racing stable owner. You name it. He did it. 1919 World Series fixer. Murdered following his refusal to pay a dubious $300,000 gambling debt.

CAROLYN GREEN ROTHSTEIN (1888–?) Former Broadway showgirl. Arnold Rothstein's long-suffering, free-spending (and cheated-on) wife. She sues for divorce just before his 1928 murder.

ALFRED DAMON RUNYON (1880–1946) Manhattan (Kansas)-born newspaper columnist—and creator of a series of short stories depicting Broadway's underworld—tales that eventually inspired Broadway's *Guys and Dolls*.

VINCENT SARDI SR. (née Melchiorre Pio Vincenzo Sardi) (1885–1969) Italian-born proprietor of West 45th Street's famed Sardi's restaurant.

ARTHUR "DUTCH" SCHULTZ (née Arthur Simon Flegenheimer) (1901–1935) Bronx-based bootlegger and numbers racket mobster. A protégé of Joey Noe and a rival to Legs Diamond. Murdered by fellow mobsters at a Newark chophouse after he vowed to kill racket-busting prosecutor Tom Dewey.

MARY "MICKEY OF THE RENDEZVOUS" SEIDEN (née Betty Farley) (c. 1910?) Silver Slipper dancer. Frankie Marlow's girlfriend—and a witness to his fatal 1929 kidnapping.

ARCHIBALD "ARCHIE" SELWYN (née Archibald Simon) (1877–1959) A co-founder with his brother Edgar of Goldwyn Pictures.

EDGAR SELWYN (née Edgar Simon) (1875–1944) Arch Selwyn's brother and business partner.

DORIS SHEERIN (aka Mrs. Mary Elizabeth Dilson) (c. 1899–?) Broadway, vaudeville, and motion picture actress. Stock market fraudster "Dandy Phil" Kastel's gold-digging girlfriend.

CHARLES "CHINK" SHERMAN (née Charles Shapiro) (?–1935) Rothstein- and Owney Madden–connected mobster and gambler. A Dutch Schultz foe. Knifed at the Club Abbey in 1931. Found dead upstate in 1935.

HARRY SITAMORE (alias Charles Kramer, Harry Sitner, Irvin Siegel, Harry Sidamore, Thomas Green, Jerry Lietel et al) (c. 1895–?) Longtime high-end jewel thief. A suspect in showgirl Louise Lawson's 1924 slaying.

SALVATORE "SALVY" SPITALE (1897–1979) Palermo-born Legs Diamond ally. Co-owner of West 46th Street's Hotel Richmond. A suspect in Vannie Higgins's 1932 execution.

SIDNEY STAJER (1894–1940) Arnold Rothstein's drug-addicted pal. A key component of Rothstein's massive international drug-smuggling operation.

CHARLES ABRAHAM STONEHAM (1876–1936) Crooked stockbroker. Rothstein-backed New York Giants owner. Polygamist. Paramour of badger game operator and jewel thief Buda Godman.

TIMOTHY DANIEL "BIG TIM" SULLIVAN (1862–1913) Lower East Side Tammany boss. State senator and congressman. Father of modern gun control—New York State's 1911 "Sullivan Act." Patron of gamblers Beansie Rosenthal and Arnold Rothstein—and Lt. Charles Becker. Suspected of involvement in Rosenthal's slaying. Ravaged by syphilis, he dies suspiciously.

TIMOTHY P. "LITTLE TIM" or "BOSTON TIM" SULLIVAN (1870–1909) Lower East Side bootblack who rose to city alderman. Tammany ally (and cousin) of "Big Tim" Sullivan.

HERBERT BAYARD SWOPE SR. (1882–1958) Pulitzer Prize–winning *New York World* editor. Best man at Arnold Rothstein's Saratoga Springs 1909 wedding. A key figure in the leadup to gambler Beansie Rosenthal's 1912 murder.

CIRO "THE ARTICHOKE KING" TERRANOVA (1888–1938) Palermo-born racketeer. Connected to the most highly suspicious robbery at Judge Albert Vitale's 1929 testimonial dinner. A tenant of Arnold Rothstein. Mayor La Guardia will ban artichokes to break his power. He dies penniless.

FRANK ALOYSIUS ROBERT TINNEY (1878–1940) Star vaudeville and Broadway blackface comedian. Charged with beating his mistress, showgirl "Bubbles" Wilson, as well as *Daily News* photographer Nicholas Peterson.

GEORGE D. UFFNER (1895–1959) Rothstein drug-smuggling henchman. Jailed for forgery in 1931. Paramour of Edith Wheaton.

HARRY VALLON (c. 1878–?) New York–born hoodlum and faro dealer. Bridgie Webber's partner in various stuss parlors. He helps hire Beansie Rosenthal's assassins—but escapes prosecution for murder.

GERTRUDE VANDERBILT (1896–1960) Broadway actress and *Ziegfeld Follies* showgirl. Bill Fallon's loyal mistress.

JUDGE ALBERT H. VITALE (1887–1949) Tammany magistrate. His $19,940 loan from Arnold Rothstein and his role in a bizarre 1929 Bronx stickup helps unravel Tammany Hall power.

JAMES JOHN "GENTLEMAN JIMMY" WALKER (1881–1946) New York's songwriting, high-living Jazz Age mayor. Paramour of showgirl Betty Compton. Forced to resign in 1932.

THOMAS "FATS" or "FATTY" WALSH (c. 1895–1929) Former Rothstein bodyguard. Rubbed out during a Coral Gables, Florida card game.

LOUIS WILLIAM "BRIDGIE" WEBBER (1877–1936) Forty-Second Street poker room operator and Pell Street opium den proprietor. Herman Rosenthal's rival in the gambling trade—and part of the plot to kill him.

MARY JANE "MAE" WEST (1893–1980) Author, producer, and star of 1926's controversial Broadway show *Sex*. Jailed at Welfare Island for obscenity.

EDNA WHEATON (c. 1902–1965) Paramount Studios beauty contest winner and *Ziegfeld* showgirl—and Rothstein drug henchman George Uffner's mistress.

GEORGE WHITE (née Eassy White) (1891–1958) Producer of popular Broadway Jazz Age reviews ("George White's Scandals"), the first of which will be bankrolled by Arnold Rothstein.

IMOGENE "BUBBLES" WILSON (1902–1948) (née Mariam Imogene Robertson) (aka Mary Nolan) *Ziegfeld* showgirl. Later a movie actress under the name "Mary Nolan." Blackface comedian Frank Tinney's mistress. A suicide from barbiturate overdose.

WALTER WINCHELL (née Walter Winchel) (1897–1972) Former vaudevillian turned pioneering tabloid gossip columnist. A pal of Owney Madden, he will help arrange Lepke Buchalter's dramatic 1939 surrender to J. Edgar Hoover.

BOBBIE WINTHROP (née Roberta Kenney) (1890–1927) *Ziegfeld* showgirl. Arnold Rothstein's alcoholic mistress—and, perhaps, his one true love. A suspected suicide. A. R. went to her funeral—and then to the track.

WILLIAM WOLGAST (c. 1890–1929) A Hotsy Totsy Club waiter who had the fatal misfortune to witness Legs Diamond's rub-out of fellow mobster William "Red" Cassidy.

FRANKIE YALE (née Francesco Ioele) (aka Frankie Uale) (1893–1928) Italian-born Brooklyn mobster. Reputedly machine-gunned to death on orders from Al Capone. His funeral was rather large.

FLORENZ EDWARD ZIEGFELD JR. (1867–1932) Legendary Broadway producer whose series of reviews, the *Ziegfeld Follies*, presented such stars as Fanny Brice, Will Rogers, and W. C. Fields—plus a host of mob-connected chorus girls such as Lillian Lorraine (also his own mistress), Bobbie Winthrop, Kiki Roberts, Gertrude Vanderbilt, Edna Wheaton, "Bubbles" Wilson, and Grace LaRue, as well as two prominent jewel robbery victims: Diana Lanzetta and the murdered Louise Lawson.

INTRODUCTION

Once upon a time, in an enchanted realm we hereby dub Jazz Age Manhattan, there reigned a very smart and wealthy monarch . . .

. . . a very, very *bad*, smart and wealthy monarch . . .

. . . a very, very, *very* bad, smart and wealthy monarch named Arnold Rothstein.

And once upon another time, yours truly penned A. R.'s royal four-flusher biography.

Which is why the blood-and-peroxide-drenched cement shoes walking tour before you will largely center upon his enterprises, crimes, and exploits.

But don't worry: there's plenty of room for other villains and villainesses.

Plenty.

History, literature, and Hollywood have all immortalized Mr. Rothstein as the shady moneyman who bankrolled baseball's infamous 1919 World Series fix, the underworld virtuoso, who as F. Scott Fitzgerald so famously declared, toyed "with the faith of fifty million people — with the single-mindedness of a burglar blowing a safe."

Which—I more than readily concede—is hardly an unalloyed compliment. But A. R. was so much more—*and less*—than even that. So, let us dissect said Big Bankroll's serpentine curriculum vitae.

He was (in no particular moral order): a high-stakes gambler, loan shark, pool shark, casino and racetrack impresario, bookmaker, thief,

Arnold Rothstein in 1921
(AUTHOR'S COLLECTION)

fence of millions in stolen jewels and bonds, perjurer and suborner of perjury, political fixer, Wall Street swindler, real estate speculator, labor racketeer, and rumrunner. And, worst of all—mastermind of the modern American drug trade.

Welcome to Arnold Rothstein's kaleidoscopic netherworld. Welcome to the seedy underbelly of Roaring Twenties Manhattan. Welcome to the crazy quilt that F. Scott Fitzgerald cataloged as an "an age of miracles . . . an age of art . . . an age of excess," garishly lit by Times Square's neon glare and boisterously choreographed by high-kicking chorus lines of jazz-baby gams and glitter.

"The Big Bankroll" made the Roaring Twenties roar. Sir Arthur Conan Doyle needed to invent his own evil genius, that veritable "Napoleon of Crime," Professor Moriarty, "the organizer of every deviltry, the controlling brain of the underworld." Arnold Rothstein concocted himself and made mere fiction pale in the bargain.

Shake hands with Arnold Rothstein—but count your fingers afterwards. Shake hands with Arnold Rothstein for an introduction to the darker legends of America's wildest days and nights:

- Con artists Nicky Arnstein, Wilson Mizner, and "Dapper Don" Collins.
- Legal eagles (or vultures) Bill "The Great Mouthpiece" Fallon and Maurice Cantor.
- Crooked cops like the NYPD's Lt. Charles Becker and vice squad patrolman Andrew J. "The Lone Wolf" McLaughlin.

- The unlikely—but amazingly effective—Prohibition Bureau team of "Izzy and Moe"—agents Izzy Einstein and Moe Smith.
- Baseball's John J. "Mugsy" McGraw, New York Giants owner Charles A. Stoneham, Giants outfielder (and possible car thief) Benny Kauff, and the 1919 Black Sox.
- Boxers Abe "The Little Champ" Attell, Jack "The Manassa Mauler" Dempsey, and Primo "The Ambling Alp" Carnera.
- Politicians "Gentleman Jimmy" Walker, "Big Tim" Sullivan, "Little Tim" Sullivan, Fiorello "The Little Flower" La Guardia, and James J. Hines.
- Jewel thieves Harry Sitamore and Eugene "Red" Moran.
- Ganglords Lucky Luciano, Meyer Lansky, Legs Diamond, Louis "Lepke" Buchalter, Dutch Schultz, Waxey Gordon, and Frank Costello.
- Master drug smugglers George Uffner and Sidney Stajer.
- Topflight newsmen Damon Runyon, Mark Hellinger, and Herbert Bayard Swope.
- Showbiz legends Florenz Ziegfeld, Fanny Brice, Lillian Lorraine, George M. Cohan, Irving Berlin, Arch and Edgar Selwyn, and Fats Waller.
- Speakeasy operators Larry Fay, Jimmy Durante, Billy Rose, and siblings "Texas" and Tommy Guinan.
- Shoot-the-limit gamblers Richard Canfield, "Titanic" Thompson, "Nigger Nate" Raymond, Joe Bernstein, George "Hump" McManus, "Bridgie" Webber, Joseph J. "Sport" Sullivan, and "Honest John" Kelly.

Arnold Rothstein, the "Respectable Businessman"
(AUTHOR'S COLLECTION)

Rothstein's unsavory world centered in Manhattan, but the center within the center spun dizzily round Broadway and Times Square. Here, he ran his first gambling house, hobnobbed with the rich and powerful, bankrolled hit Broadway shows and opulent legitimate theaters, spent his nights at fabled Lindy's restaurant—and on a dreary November 4, 1928, Sunday evening, calmly walked to a conference in Room 349 of Seventh Avenue's Park Central Hotel—and to his own mysterious murder.

Also noshing at Lindy's that fateful evening was fabled Hearst columnist Damon Runyon. Later that night, hearing the news of his acquaintance's demise, Runyon sped to his typewriter to pen a lengthy and perceptive Rothstein obituary. It read in part:

> He had few friends, and many enemies. Some of the latter were of years standing. But they were not enemies calculated to do a foe bodily harm. They took it out in hating him and execrating his name....

Rothstein at the Track

Rothstein had plenty of physical courage, make no error there. Also he had enormous vanity. "I'm a hundred per cent right," was his favorite expression. He was one of the strangest men that ever stepped in shoe leather.

He was rich beyond dreams of avarice. He had a lovely wife, a magnificent home. He had Rolls Royces, every form of luxury. He had his health, and he was in his thirties when he got hold of his first big money. He could go anywhere, do anything.

But he never went anywhere. He barely took a pleasure trip. He seemed to have no pleasures.

He could have associated with fine people, visited nice homes, been a man of consequence, for all his gambling career. Other men have risen above these things.

But Rothstein chose, instead, to hang out with fellow gamblers of high and low degree, to remain a citizen of the underworld. He couldn't get away from his old life.

(AUTHOR'S COLLECTION)

Back in 2003, I published a best-selling biography of Mr. Rothstein. Delving into his tangled history, I uncovered a veritable road map of physical sites linked to his life and times, his extensive high crimes and misdemeanors, his dubious "gonnections," as *The Great Gatsby* dismissively dubbed them. A few years afterwards, I conducted a walking tour of Rothstein's Times Square locales. In 2022, I found myself being interviewed on New York City radio regarding those sites. Only then—bingo!—did the light go on: I should posthaste compile a properly comprehensive walking tour covering the era's high crimes and misdemeanors. I am still amazed at just how extensive this subject is—and how very much more I have only recently discovered.

But, then again, *everything* about Arnold Rothstein is amazing.

So, here—heading north—is essentially Arnold Rothstein's Times Square, a Runyonesque mix of gamblers and gangsters, crooks and cops, showgirls (a *lot* of showgirls, indeed, a veritable bleached bevy) and speakeasies. Here in the belly of the big city resided a very small world of power and vice, of bright lights and big money, circling itself like a venomous snake. Names intersect. Places intersect. Rackets intersect. Gambling and bootlegging; Tammany Hall and City Hall; Wall Street and sports and the theater are all joined at the hip—or, rather, the hip flask. And at the heart of all this darkness nested our own Prince of Darkness, Mr. Rothstein.

At day's end, the wages of sin really is death. Certainly, death was the hand Arnold Rothstein finally drew.

Few of the characters we meet here end well. Fewer deserve to.

But meet them we will.

Street by street, block by block, building by building.

So, hop on board.

Just don't turn your back on anyone.

GANGSTERLAND SOUTH
Times Square

1. **LORBER'S RESTAURANT** 1420 Broadway (Between West 39th and West 40th Streets) Situated across Broadway from the old Metropolitan Opera House, this elegant establishment provides a convenient entryway into a look at Rothstein's less-well-known—but, nevertheless, highly lucrative—enterprises: fencing stolen jewelry.

Any aficionado of early cinema knows quite well just how many tuxedo-clad plots revolved around stolen jewels—whether it's John Barrymore heisting Greta Garbo's gems in 1932's *Grand Hotel* or William Powell lusting after Kay Francis's valuables (and her) in the same year's rather unimaginatively titled *Jewel Robbery*, and so on, and so on.

In fact, jewel robberies *were* big business. And Arnold Rothstein was big in that business. Providing expert testimony regarding Arnold's role as a premier fence for purloined baubles was Mildred Sitamore, wife of master jewel thief Harry Sitamore (aka "Harry Sidamor," among other aliases). Following her husband's 1933 Miami arrest, Mildred penned a series of articles for the Hearst press explaining how he operated. In one she wrote:

Few people were in better position to know Arnold Rothstein than I was. My husband, Harry Sitamore, known to police of this country and Europe as the world's cleverest jewel thief, sold more than $10,000,000 worth of stolen gems to Rothstein between 1921 and 1928. It was those stolen jewels and dope peddling not the rackets that gave Rothstein his millions, not his highly publicized love for gambling. Arnold Rothstein did make millions of dollars out of crime, without ever being molested by the law. . . .

[P]etty larceny crooks don't buy stolen jewels to the tune of millions of dollars a year. Rothstein did. I know that because, as I said, he bought $10,000,000 worth of jewels from my husband alone. . . . And Harry Sitamore was only one of many jewel thieves who took their loot to Rothstein. The racketeer had only one limitation so far as his purchase of stolen jewels went. He would not buy any lot of gems worth less than $50,000.

"It isn't worth my time," he told Harry.

Among the many jewel heists fenced by Rothstein, according to Mildred Sitamore, one involved a theft designed to cover a $50,000 gambling debt owed to Rothstein. As she explained:

Rothstein sent for my husband. He explained the situation, but said he didn't want to penalise this man's wife any more than was necessary for him to get his own $50,000 back. "You get the jewels after her husband tips us off that the time is right, and I will sell them back through the company which insures them. I'll make them pay $65,000—that is $50,000 for me and $15,000 for your trouble." That was the racketeer's proposal. Sitamore laughed at him. "When I steal a $750,000 bunch of 'ice,' it won't be for $15,000," Harry said, and he stuck to it, despite Rothstein's efforts to change his mind.

Some other crook stole the jewels for Rothstein. They were sold back to the insurance company for $65,000, just as Harry had been told they would be, and the husband's gambling debt to Rothstein was marked paid. The "mystery" was never solved, because the wife didn't want it solved.

But now back to Lorber's. There, one night, Sitamore cagily schmoozed with the blonde secretary of a downtown (16 Maiden Lane) diamond merchant. His goal: to obtain as much inside information as possible regarding her boss's huge diamond shipments. Expending a relatively modest $19 for "two dinners . . . ; a two-dollar tip to the waiter, two five-dollar-and-a-half tickets to see the world's most beautiful girl, Gladys Glad (*see* **THE GLOBE THEATER 205 West 46th Street**), then appearing at the New Amsterdam Roof, and two dollars more for a taxi ride to Brooklyn after the show," he eventually obtained information crucial to what quickly emerged as his largest heist: a $500,000 haul of uncut Belgian diamonds originally destined

Diminutive restaurateur Adolf Lorber had originally commenced his trade back in 1897 at 274 Grand Street ("the Delmonico's of the east side") before moving uptown to Broadway in 1912, where his $2.00 dinners earned him the sobriquet "The Napoleon of the Table d'Hôte," Caruso being among his regular patrons. Prohibition, however, cut into Lorber's business, destroying his cabaret trade, but he soldiered on, relying more and more on his reputation with out-of-town visitors, until finally shutting his doors in November 1930. (COURTESY OF COLUMBIA UNIVERSITY LIBRARIES)

for a St. Louis buyer. As Mildred Sitamore later revealed, her hubby's caper went down like this:

> Around noon . . . Harry called the secretary, and in the course of his conversation she volunteered the information that the jeweler and the buyer had just left to have the gems appraised, and that her employer, expecting an important telephone call at 1:30, had left word with her to tell the caller to phone him at a well-known restaurant in the district.
>
> The scheme was working out just as my husband had believed it would, and he went to the restaurant she had named to await the coming of the jeweler and the buyer. Harry sat at a booth where he could see whoever came in, without being seen himself. A few minutes after one o'clock, the two men came in.
>
> One of them carried a bright black leather brief case that held a fortune in jewels. Harry looked carefully at the brief case, and then left the place. He took a taxicab to a leather goods store and bought another like it. Then he returned to the restaurant, avoided recognition by the jeweler by sitting some distance from his table, and waited his chance.
>
> At one-thirty a waiter walked up to the jeweler's table and spoke to him. The man got up and walked toward a telephone in a line of booths along the back wall of the place. Harry followed, stepped into another booth, and called the number of still another of the restaurant phones. When a waiter answered, he asked for the St. Louis buyer, whose name he had learned from the secretary.
>
> Before the men could get to the phone, Harry was out of the booth and close to his table. Both men were away from the table in the telephone booths, but they had left that brief case loaded with jewels on a chair. Harry picked up the brief case full of jewels, put the one he had purchased in its place, and walked out of the restaurant.
>
> Those diamonds were sold to Arnold Rothstein the next day. Rothstein paid my husband $110,000 for them. A few days later the jeweler got them back, after the insurance company, through

negotiations with go-betweens, paid $200,000 to Rothstein's agent. Harry was responsible for many of the greatest jewel thefts this country has known in the last fifteen years, but never before nor since did he have an opportunity to steal $500,000 worth of jewels so quickly and easily.

As we shall see, it was not the last of either Sitamore's—or Rothstein's—misdeeds.

2. "BIG TIM" SULLIVAN'S OFFICE 1440 Broadway (Between West 40th and West 41st Streets) Lower East Side Tammany

boss "Big Tim" Sullivan was not only a mentor to such rising star professional gamblers as Arnold Rothstein and Herman "Beansie" Rosenthal, he was a vaudeville impresario, a partner in the West Coast's Considine-Sullivan Circuit, a state senator, and briefly a U.S. congressman—though,

not at all impressed by the latter office. "There's nothing in this Congressman business," he complained. "They know 'em in Washington. The people down there use 'em as hitchin'-posts. Every time they see a Congressman on the streets they tie their horses to him."

Technically, he ruled over Tammany only on the Lower East Side. In reality, mustering hordes of immigrant Irish, Jewish, and German votes, he wielded city-wide influence. "What did his power amount to?" asked a muckraking journalist in *McClure's Magazine*. "More than any one ever exactly measured. Every time

"Big Tim" Sullivan (center, in straw hat) (AUTHOR'S COLLECTION)

he entered Tammany Hall all hands stood aside that he might not be delayed.

"Tammany Hall dared not nominate a mayor who was disliked by Sullivan, a judge who had slighted him, a senator who had voted the wrong way on a Sullivan measure, or a sheriff who would not appoint a bunch of Sullivan deputies. Three recent sheriffs of the county of New York were of Big Tim's choosing. He named three of his following for justice of the Supreme Court. One of these choices was so rank that the whole town rose at it."

While a state senator, Sullivan also authored the nation's first significant gun control law, New York State's "Sullivan Act." Contradicting such statesmanship, it's very likely that he was involved in ordering the July 1912 murder of "Beansie" Rosenthal—also another first: history's initial "drive-by" murder. (*See* **THE HOTEL METROPOLE 142-149 West 43rd Street.**)

Sullivan's vaudeville partner, John W. Considine Sr., was the father of John W. Considine Jr., an Oscar-nominated Hollywood producer (1938's *Boys Town*), and Bob Considine, a very popular Hearst newspaper columnist and author. Sullivan went insane from tertiary syphilis in 1912 and died under mysterious circumstances in August 1913, his body found on railroad tracks in the Eastchester area of the Bronx.

His life was memorialized in the Gotham Film Company's 1914 silent film *The Life of Big Tim Sullivan; or, from Newsboy to Senator*.

3. ■ **THE BROADWAY THEATER 1445 Broadway at West 41st Street** Here on the Thursday evening, January 3, 1901, twenty-six-year-old Jules Formel ("a commission merchant at 10 Barclay Street") and his fiancée, Miss Anita Gonzales of Havana, Cuba, attended a performance of a comic operetta titled *A Royal Rogue*.

Neither the show—nor the theater—are of much interest. But what happened before they got there—and just who this Mr. Formel was—indeed are.

Formel and Miss Gonzales had traversed up Broadway in a horse-drawn cab, when, as the *New York Times* noted:

At Thirty-fourth Street, one of the reins broke off at the bit, and the driver promptly complicated matters by falling off the box. The driver yelled, "Hi, there, whoa!" but instead of stopping, the horse broke into a run up Broadway. Faster he went, and his speed was accelerated by shouts from the sidewalks.

Mr. Formel took in the situation without delay; He instructed his companion not to move. Then he threw open the cab door, and, catching hold of the top, made a sudden spring and reached the driver's seat. Inside, Miss Gonzales sat still, too frightened to utter a sound. During these few seconds, the cab narrowly missed running into several other vehicles, and more well-meaning but misplaced yells only served to make the beast's course the more erratic. Mr. Formel had difficulty in keeping his seat. He looked for the reins, and then saw that one was broken. Gathering himself for a jump, he sprang forward and landed on the horse's back. The frightened animal let out another link of speed, and Mr. Formel working himself forward, grasped the bridle with one hand. With the other, he seized the horse by the nose and brought it to a standstill in front of the Normandie [Hotel at Broadway and West 38th Street]."

In February 1903, however, Formel went from hero to desperado when he blazed away in an incredible gun battle in the middle of the intersection of Broadway and West 28th Street, his opponent being Philip Black, a shady West 29th Street billiard parlor operator, whom Formel had accused of breaking into his 226 West 16th Street apartment and removing $500 in goods. Eight to ten shots were fired. Both men were hit. A passerby suffered a leg wound.

"Jules Formel," noted the *New York World*, "is known in the Tenderloin as 'Big Julius.' He is a fine looking, well-dressed man of twenty-eight years, and declared to the police . . . that he had no occupation.

"'I'm living off my money,' as he put it."

But Mr. Formel did have an occupation—and it was not "commission merchant." Like Arnold Rothstein, he was a gambler, and like A. R., he also operated at Saratoga Springs. Rothstein had his operation just outside of town—an elegant joint called The Brook. Formel operated a gambling house securely within that upstate gambling haven at 201 South Broadway.

In 1920, however, local authorities conducted one of their periodic crackdowns on illegal gambling. Among those arrested was Formel. His first trial resulted in a hung jury. So did his second. In both trials he was prosecuted by former state senator Edgar T. Brackett (father of Billy Wilder's screenwriting partner Charles Brackett) and defended by long-time Rothstein attorney William J. Fallon. The third time was the charm, however, and with Fallon (the master of the hung jury) not involved, the state finally convicted Formel, who served a year in Dannemora.

All the while, Formel's bitterness grew against Saratoga County district attorney Charles B. Andrus. (*See* **ISADORE RAPOPORT RESIDENCE 65 Central Park West.**) In 1926, Formel would allege that back in August 1919, he had spoken with Arnold Rothstein regarding Rothstein's difficulties with the law in Saratoga—specifically keeping The Brook safe from prying authorities. Yes, Rothstein had already greased a few palms, but Andrus, it seems, was not cooperating. Eventually, enough money crossed hands, and Arnold and The Brook now operated safely.

Formel's charges led to a state-ordered investigation. Arnold protested his innocence, writing to Andrus to deny all wrongdoing: "I never met you in my life, never heard your name before reading the above news item, consequently any acts that I have been accused of having perpetrated with you are false." Andrus, nonetheless, got the boot. Rothstein wasn't even called to the stand.

As for the Broadway Theatre, which Jules Formel attended back in January 1901, it had been rebuilt by James Bailey (The "Bailey" of "Barnum and Bailey") back in 1888. Converted to films and vaudeville in 1908, it was demolished in 1929.

As for the Hotel Normandie, where Formel's "horseplay" happily concluded, composer Pyotr Ilych Tchaikovsky had resided there in April–May 1891. It was razed in 1920.

Not to be confused with the more recent Hotel Normandie on West 45th Street.

4. HOTEL ALBANY 1446-1450 Broadway (134-138 West 41st Street)

Newsman Herbert Bayard Swope, the best man at Rothstein's August 1909 Saratoga Springs wedding, resided here in 1910, a year after having departed the *New York Herald* (located at Herald Square; the building was demolished in 1921) to join the staff of the *New York World* (downtown at 53-63 Park Row) and eventually become one of the nation's premier journalists, winning the very first Pulitzer Prize in 1917, becoming the first newsman to obtain a copy of the Covenant of the League of Nations, and finally emerging as the paper's executive editor in 1920. During the 1920s, he often whiled away his free time as part of the legendary Algonquin Round Table. (*See* **ALGONQUIN HOTEL 59 West 44th Street.**)

Swope departed *The World* in January 1929, forging a career as a "policy consultant." It is said he later coined the term the "Cold War."

Not quite buying into the Swope legend, however, was Stanley Walker, who wrote in his 1934 overview of New York's newspaper business *City Editor*:

> Swope is sometimes regarded, and not alone by Swope himself, as among the greatest of newspaper men. Even today he writes letters praising, with the air of mentor, the work of reporters, and he will tell a tired young editor, "My boy, you are the best bet in sight as a successor to me." What are the facts? He left the *World*, where he had been executive editor, just before the final death rattle had set in. . . . While Swope was there, he was in a position of tremendous authority. The imperious rattle of his heels upon entering the city room would strike terror into brave reporters; again, his bark over the telephone from the racetracks of Baltimore or Saratoga would change the make up of the front page. Swope years ago was a reporter of great vigor and enterprise; as an editor he was, when working at it, full of fire and fresh ideas. He made much money in speculations. He won the praise of Mrs. Arnold Rothstein for his talent for picking suitable names for racehorses.

Herbert Bayard Swope (Perhaps Shutting His Eyes to His Friend Arnold's Indiscretions) (AUTHOR'S COLLECTION)

But well before all that, Swope also shared a room somewhere in Times Square (exact address unfortunately unknown but somewhere above an Italian restaurant; perhaps it was above Mario's at 246 West 44th Street, later the site of Vincent Sardi's first restaurant) with the young John "The Great Profile" Barrymore. Swope, observed Barrymore's biographer John Kobler, "had a weakness for women and gambling, but, in contrast to most of the newspaper fraternity, he drank sparingly, wore spats and a Homburg, carried a cane and comported himself with such a patrician air that many doors closed to his rough-and-ready colleagues would open to him. His major spheres of interest were crime and politics."

Yes, definitely, quite the "patrician air."

"He demanded the deference customarily accorded to royalty," noted his biographer E. J. Kahn. "When he walked into a room, he expected all present, including his wife and children, to rise to their feet."

Crime and politics—a perfect match to get to know Arnold Rothstein.

As mentioned, Swope, like Rothstein, was obsessed with high-stakes gambling. Like Rothstein, who maintained Redstone Stables (*Redstone* being the translation of "Rothstein"), Swope maintained his own racing stable. And it was Swope who suggested the names of Rothstein's first six horses—Gladiator, Sporting Blood, Georgie, Wrecker, Devastation, and Sidereal.

Swope also distinguished himself as a member of the Algonquin Hotel's weekly Saturday night poker games dubbed the Thanatopsis ["a meditation on death"] Pleasure and Inside Straight Club, which included such luminaries as Irving Berlin, playwright George S. Kaufman, columnists Hcywood Broun and Franklin Pierce Adams, baking heir Raoul Fleischmann, and comedian Harpo Marx.

"Swope," remarked Marx, "was probably the best player there, but he only played at the Algonquin for fun. He did his serious gambling elsewhere. . . . Swope was not only a shrewd horseplayer but a State Racing Commissioner as well. So when he gave me a horse in the feature race [at Belmont] I made a bet of two thousand bucks . . . Swope's horse came in dead last. It was the last time I ever bet on the horses."

It is said that Swope might bet as much as $10,000 on a given Thanatopsis hand.

Swope eventually distanced himself from Rothstein—but not entirely. At the time of Rothstein's passing, as Swope biographer E. J. Kahn wrote, the newsman "had been heavily in debt to Rothstein, and the gambler had been quite lenient about repayment."

The Albany was sold and renamed the Hotel Jefferson in 1912.

5. NEDERLANDER THEATRE 208 West 41st Street (Between Seventh and Eighth Avenues) On April 21, 1930, this theater, then known as the National, debuted the opening of the drama *Room 349* (alternately titled *Bumped Off*), which purported to reveal the tale of Arnold Rothstein's fatal shooting on the night of November 4, 1928, in that room at the Park Central. (*See* **PARK CENTRAL HOTEL 200 West 56th Street**.) Cast as the dead man's mistress ("Babette Marshall") was his actual mistress, the showgirl Inez Norton.

"Miss Norton," wrote one critic, "is a very so-so actress, although a more than passingly attractive blonde type, quiet of manner and pleasant of voice." Silent film star Roy D'Arcy portrayed the thinly veiled "Harold Stromberg" in his only Broadway appearance.

The Real-Life (or Death) Room 349 (AUTHOR'S COLLECTION)

Assessed *Billboard*: "Except for a few moments in Act III there is nothing to recommend in this play. It is trite and exceedingly dull. Its dialog is of the variety ofttimes called mundane. Its characters are unreal, and altho the situations may, or may not, be realistic, they do not compose anything even approaching entertainment. . . . Room 349 presents a dull evening all around." It closed after fifteen performances.

Inez Norton (AUTHOR'S COLLECTION)

The Nederlander dates back to 1921 when it was built by an agent and theater owner named Walter C. Jordan. The Shuberts later took it over, and ran it until 1956, when showman Billy Rose bought it and with typical modesty renamed it the Billy Rose Theatre. It remained the Billy Rose until 1979 when, despite not being bought by anyone named Trafalgar, it became the Trafalgar. The following year it became the Nederlander after its new owner, David T. Nederlander. Notable productions have included the premiere of the Aaron Copland–scored ballet *Billy the Kid*, *The Little Foxes*, *Inherit the Wind*, and *Who's Afraid of Virginia Woolf?*.

6. **THE BANK OF AMERICA BUILDING 1451 Broadway (Between West 41st and West 42nd Streets)** Tammany Hall, as the most dominant (and clearly most corrupt) faction of Manhattan's Democratic Party, ruled city politics for decade after decade.

Here, from 1919 through 1931, were the offices of Tammany Hall's 17th Assembly District leader Nathan Burkan, who Rothstein estate executors

Helpful Hints for Wistful Warren

Who killed Rothstein? When Attorney William A. Hyman was preparing to defend the claim of Maurice Cantor that the murdered gambler's death-bed will was valid, he told reporters: "When Rothstein's safety deposit vaults are opened, there will be a lot of suicides. Go put that in your paper!"

The *DAILY NEWS* suggests that the police commissioner inquire: Why has District Attorney Banton delegated the State's interest in the examination of Rothstein's papers to Nathan Burkan, a lawyer in private practice?

Who did Hyman expect to choose death in preference to exposure when Rothstein's records were scrutinized?

The Daily News *pegged Burkan's appointment as highly suspicious.* (AUTHOR'S COLLECTION)

Maurice Cantor, William Wellman, and Samuel Brown engaged to help settle the estate's muddy affairs.

While Burkan was a loyal and powerful Tammanyite, he was also among the nation's foremost entertainment and copyright attorneys. At various times he represented Columbia Pictures; United Artists; Paramount; Metro-Goldwyn-Mayer; the Academy of Motion Picture Arts and Sciences; the Society of American Authors, Composers, and Publishers; Florenz Ziegfeld; Charlie Chaplin; Mae West; Al Jolson; and composer Victor Herbert.

Of Tammany Hall, Burkan once gushed:

New York City could not get along without Tammany Hall. You must have men who will take an interest in politics and, to put it briefly, keep it going. The very men of education and culture and refinement who are continually pounding Tammany think they have fulfilled their political obligation when they have voted and read the newspapers. If Tammany did not maintain its interest and provide the necessary political organization, who would?

Who would discover and push forward the young men of undoubted ability whose services are needful to the city and State and nation? Ninety per cent of the men whom Tammany has brought into public life have made good.

Who, if it were not for Tammany, would take care of the poor and unfortunate of the various districts in the city?

It turned out the purveyor of such sentiments was just the fellow Tammany and company needed to pore through the late Rothstein's papers to ensure nothing survived to embarrass anyone who needed embarrassing. Burkan did his job with his usual efficiency. Though, he failed to do it perfectly—and that slipup, involving a mysterious "loan" to Bronx magistrate Albert H. Vitale, would ultimately help unravel Tammany's once immense power.

7. **HOTEL METROPOLE South Side of West 42nd Street (Between Broadway and Seventh Avenue)** Before the Considine Brothers (William, John R., and George) owned West 43rd Street's Metropole Hotel (*see* **HOTEL METROPOLE 142-149 West 43rd Street**), they operated this establishment, once known as the Rossmere. It does not appear that these Considines (originally from Detroit) were related to "Big Tim" Sullivan's vaudeville partner John W.

(COURTESY OF COLUMBIA UNIVERSITY LIBRARIES)

Considine and his own brother Tom. (*See* **GEORGE F. CONSIDINE HOME 10 West 61st Street.**)

The old Metropole (this one, at West 42nd Street), as the *New York Times* noted in May 1912,

> was for years the rendezvous of those who followed the gaming tables, the races, and prizefights for a living. Nearly all the famous fighters were familiar figures in the lobby of Considine's place, and backers of the game were his close friends. It was told in those days that much of Considine's income went out again in the form of loans to friends who were in distress.

A huge number of high-stakes bets were placed here in connection with New York's 1903 Seth Low–George McClellan mayoral election, many by George Considine himself. Considine's wagers favored Tammany Democrat McClellan.

The property was sold to a burgeoning drugstore chain, the United Chemists Company, in 1909.

8. "BRIDGIE" WEBBER'S POOL HALL 102 West 42nd Street at Sixth Avenue

Arnold Rothstein and Beansie Rosenthal were hardly the only gamblers operating in the Times Square area or the so-called "Tenderloin" area to the south. Louis "Bridgie" Webber's nickname stemmed from his brief but memorable marriage to a two-hundred-pound prostitute named Bridget. This "pool hall," located here above a United Cigar Store outlet, also hosted his illegal poker games. It is now

Louis "Lefty Louie" Rosenberg and Harry "Gyp the Blood" Horowitz in custody, posing (involuntarily, of course) alongside their captors. (COURTESY OF THE LIBRARY OF CONGRESS)

Harry Vallon—A Man Who Definitely Did Not Look Innocent (of Anything) (COURTESY OF THE LIBRARY OF CONGRESS)

the much more respectable site of a Whole Foods.

In 1912, Lt. Charles Becker ordered three gamblers—Webber, Bald Jack Rose, and faro dealer Harry Vallon—to arrange for Beansie Rosenthal's murder. (*See* **HOTEL METROPOLE 142-149 West 43rd Street.**) They in turn engaged hoodlums from Harlem's Lenox Avenue Gang, Francesco Cirofici (Dago Frank), Harry Horowitz (Gyp the Blood), Louis Rosenberg (Lefty Louie), and Jacob Seidenshner (Whitey Lewis), to execute the deed (and Rosenthal).

Webber, Rose, and Vallon all testified against the murderers they hired and remarkably escaped prosecution. Becker and the others were all executed at Sing Sing.

As author Henry H. Klein noted:

Webber was a well-known east side gambler—short, slim and dapper, well-to-do and influential in Tammany politics. He and Rosenthal were political as well as business rivals. Herman was 'Big Tim' Sullivan's favorite and 'Bridgie' represented [the late Lower East Side alderman] 'Little Tim' [Sullivan]. 'Bridgie' had collected 'graft' for police officials for many years and had conducted 'stuss'[-game gambling] houses, poker houses, and even a 'hop joint' [an opium den] in Chinatown in his younger days. He had opened a gambling house on West 45th Street before Rosenthal came on the block; and he had a poker room on the northwest corner of Sixth Avenue and 42nd Street. He was also interested in a gambling house with [Abe, aka 'Jew'] Brown on 44th Street. Webber and Rosenthal were rivals in their gambling operations 'uptown' as well as on the lower east side.

In *The Great Gatsby*, F. Scott Fitzgerald wrote of the Metropole:

"The old Metropole," brooded Mr. Wolfsheim gloomily. "Filled with faces dead and gone. Filled with friends gone now forever. I can't forget so long as I live the night they shot Rosy [sic] Rosenthal there. . . . Then he went out on the sidewalk, and they shot him three times in his full belly and drove away."

"Four of them were electrocuted," I said, remembering.

"Five, with Becker."

A TAMMANY ADDENDUM: "Little Tim" Sullivan (Big Tim's cousin) was not only third ward alderman (his district was in the Lower East Side; his particular strength was in The Bowery) but also president of the Board of Aldermen.

In January 1908, upon hearing reports of such better restaurants as the Café Martin (southwest corner of West 26th Street and Fifth Avenue; formerly the site of Delmonico's) and also of Rector's allowing women to smoke inside their establishments, he sprang into action, sponsoring a local law banning the practice. It contained no penalties for the miscreant distaff smokers themselves but rather for establishment proprietors. It passed unanimously.

That same year, admirers honored "Little Tim" with a celebratory banquet at the Hotel Knickerbocker. In response, he penned the following explanation/defense of the patented Tammany way:

Show me the silk stocking who can quote Latin in his political speeches. Did he ever pay a widow's rent? Does the college graduate who talks politics to an audience in evening dress up at Carnegie Hall know what it means to bring a spoon to a christening—that it means more votes than all the quotations he knows from John Stuart Mill or Adam Smith? Did he ever think what bailing out a poor fruit peddler who has been run-in by some too officious policeman means? Does he know how many votes a ton of coal will bring in?

Organization to be effective, in representation as well as in action, must mean organization all year around. The Tammany man—if he's a good one—is doing business on the Fourth of July or Christmas Day just as same as he is on election day.

He knows everybody's troubles, and is expected to remedy them as far as he is able. If he can't, he goes to his district leader. There is one of these to every Assembly District in the city. These men are the great bulwark of Tammany Hall. Without them we should be helpless. They must be in court when a citizen is in trouble, ready with bail if the case demands it. They must feed the starving, clothe the naked, bury the paupers, and be good friends with everybody.

Little Tim died of Bright's disease the following year.

9. **ISAIAH LEEBOVE LAW OFFICE 11 West 42nd Street (Between Fifth and Sixth Avenues)** Leebove served not only as Arnold Rothstein's attorney but also for a full coterie of shady figures—gangsters Legs Diamond, Owney "The Killer" Madden, Salvatore Spitale, longtime Rothstein pal and assistant Sidney Stajer, gamblers Nick "the Greek" Dandolos, Nigger Nate Raymond ("a swarthy-complexioned, jet-black-haired man of 37, stockily built and casual of demeanor"), Jimmy Meehan, and con man Dapper Don Collins. Leebove relocated to Michigan in 1929, eventually emerging as a confidant of Democratic governor William Comstock. In May 1938, while sitting at table at a Clare, Michigan, barroom, Leebove was shot and killed by a former oil business partner.

10. **THE DOYLE BILLIARD ACADEMY 112 West 42nd Street (Between Sixth and Seventh Avenues)** Here, in 1914, stood the pool hall of famed billiard impresario and bookmaker Jack Doyle. Doyle had originally founded his billiard establishment in 1907 across Broadway from Times Square's New York Times building in partnership with baseball New York Giants manager John McGraw (*see* **LAMBS CLUB 130 West 44th Street**) and famed jockey Tod Sloan (they had met at Rector's), but by that May they departed Doyle's partnership. In 1910, Doyle himself departed the Longacre Building for 112 West 42nd Street.

In 1914, when Doyle received a number of bets on the hitherto woebegone Boston Braves, he mentioned the fact to Rothstein who (for his usual fee) agreed to accept Doyle's liabilities as layoff bets. For once, Rothstein's skill (and luck) departed him, and by the time Boston's upstart "Miracle Braves" had vanquished Connie Mack's favorite Philadelphia A's in that October's World Series sweep, Arnold had lost somewhere between $150,000 and $300,000 by today's standards.

In 1917, Doyle transferred his operation to 1456 Broadway.

11. KNICKERBOCKER HOTEL 142 West 42nd Street (1466 Broadway, at the southeast corner of West 42nd Street and Broadway)

In November 1910, Rothstein was operating his first gambling house, at 106 West 46th Street. His partner, Tammany politician Willie Shea, thought A. R. was skimming profits. One evening, Charles Gates, son of famed industrialist John Warne "Bet-a-Million" Gates, lost $40,000 at their house, and Shea walked away with the money. Rothstein confronted Shea at the Knickerbocker. Shea thought he was going to demand his money. Rothstein did nothing of the sort, telling Shea he could keep the cash if he dissolved their partnership. The drunken—and relieved—Shea agreed and signed the paper A. R. thrust under his hand. In the process, he signed away his share of Broadway's most promising gambling house.

After A. R. shut down his 46th Street gambling establishment, the Knickerbocker (550 rooms; 550 baths) also served as a venue for the Partridge Club, his high-stakes floating card and craps games.

The Knickerbocker also housed the offices of Rothstein attorney Bill Fallon, the most flamboyant and successful defense attorney on Broadway.

In 1910, Herbert Bayard Swope had tickets for that year's edition of Broadway's legendary series of reviews, the *Ziegfeld Follies*, and was to dine with his future wife, Pearl Honeyman "Maggie" Powell, at the Knickerbocker beforehand. Unfortunately, thanks to his participation at a concurrent crap game, Swope failed to arrive at the Knickerbocker until well after 11:00 p.m., missing dinner, missing the show, missing everything. When Swope did arrive, Maggie dumped the shredded remains of his theater tickets upon his head, before simply asking, "Shall we eat?"

Maggie, by the way, was a close friend of Arnold's former showgirl wife, Carolyn Green Rothstein. To those who criticized her for that, Maggie would respond that Carolyn was "more of a lady than most of the ladies I know."

———————

The twelve-story Knickerbocker was built in 1905. Caruso lived in a fourteen-room apartment on the ninth floor from 1908 until 1920 when it closed as a hotel. George M. Cohan also lived there. F. Scott Fitzgerald lived there briefly in 1920. Mary Pickford met Douglas Fairbanks there. The building later became the Newsweek Building. It is now condominiums. A remnant of its former history may be seen at the Times Square shuttle platform, where a locked door marked "Knickerbocker" still survives.

GANGSTERLAND

Restaurateur Vincent Sardi (*see* **SARDI'S RESTAURANT 234 West 44th Street**) once worked here as a captain of the hotel café and recalled serving such luminaries as Caruso, Gentleman Jim Corbett, composer Victor Herbert, the famed female impersonator Julian Eltinge, showmen Marcus Loew, Sam Harris, and Roxy Rothafel, future governor Al Smith, and Fiorello La Guardia, among others.

12. MAURICE F. CANTOR LAW OFFICE 152 West 42nd Street (Between Sixth and Seventh Avenues)

Future New York state assemblyman and Rothstein attorney Maurice Freeman Cantor conducted business here in September 1921 defending client Joseph Curry against charges of murdering patrolman Joseph A. Reuschle on a deserted stretch of Riverside Drive near West 169th Street. He had earlier shared a law practice with his younger sister Ethel Cantor, but by September she had returned to the family home in Buffalo.

Like Rothstein, Maurice (née Morris) was the son of a foreign-born dry goods merchant and the sibling of a brother with religious inclinations. Rothstein's brother Bertram (Harry) died young before becoming a rabbi. Cantor's brother Bernard had become a rabbi at Flushing, Queens' Free Synagogue before volunteering for relief work among the Jewish community in the Polish Ukraine where he was murdered by three Bolsheviks outside Lemberg (now Lviv) on July 8, 1920.

Cantor maintained offices here until becoming Rothstein's attorney (on retainer—"no less than $7,500 per year, plus expenses") and moving to Rothstein's headquarters at 45 West 57th Street in September 1927.

13. HAMMERSTEIN'S VICTORIA 201 West 42nd Street (Between Seventh and Eighth Avenues)

In 1899, a desperate Oscar Hammerstein I scraped together $8,000 to open Hammerstein's Victoria at West 42nd and Broadway. Its success paved the way for other theaters in Times Square.

Hammerstein's Victoria (AUTHOR'S COLLECTION)

The 950-seat Victoria presented an incongruous mix of class and vulgarity. It might offer a play by Tolstoy or a performance by Eleonora Duse. But it also presented "performances" by scandal-plagued Evelyn Nesbit, heavyweight champ Jack Johnson, or the atrocious Cherry Sisters; various jugglers; a man with a seven-foot-long beard; whistling monkeys; Siamese twins—and worse.

On the theater's rooftop, the Venetian Terrace Garden featured milk-maids, live barnyard animals, and the city's first singing waiters. "The ducks are even more blasé than last year," mused the *New York Dramatic Mirror*, "but the chickens are most condescending and communicative."

Monday matinees attracted smallish crowds, and they weren't there to see Blanche Walsh in Tolstoy's *Resurrection*. In the theater's basement, each Monday afternoon, bored stagehands and ushers organized a crap game. Soon toughs from the audience left the auditorium and joined the action, including gang members Monk Eastman, Whitey Lewis, and Dago Frank Cirofici, and aspiring young gamblers Herman "Beansie" Rosenthal—and Arnold Rothstein.

Hammerstein sold the Victoria to vaudeville magnate E. F. Albee in 1913. In 1915, however, the building was condemned and was replaced in April 1916 by a movie house—the Rialto ("a new palace of polite pleasure for the thousands")—operated by famed theatrical impresario Roxy Rothafel.

The WPA Guide to New York City later described the Rialto as a "small movie house and the only one with a separate entrance in the subway."

"Roxy outfitted his ushers with his usual pomp and circumstance," Broadway historian Ken Bloom noted. "Their uniforms were scarlet, the tunics featured gold piping and tassels. Every usher also carried a swagger stick whose mother-of-pearl tips lit up in the dark. To add to the splendor, the head usher carried a bugle. According to a press release, the ushers were all versed in first aid and knew how to use their swagger sticks as tourniquets."

Indeed, who needs a movie when you've got entertainment like that?

Nonetheless, in February 1930, the Rialto witnessed the New York premiere of Paramount's "all-talking" crime drama *Street of Chance* (it also appeared in a silent version), which *New York Times* critic Mordaunt Hall described as "a prototype of the late Arnold Rothstein," with William Powell starring as the Rothsteinesque businessman/gambler John D. Marsden, who "is seen staggering at the front door of a big hotel and is finally taken to a hospital in an ambulance." The film commences with Marsden winning a bet on passing license plate numbers (a known Rothstein ploy) before heading for an eating establishment bearing a more than passing acquaintance to the Rothstein haunt of Lindy's, and seeing his frustrated wife (the statuesque Kay Francis) sue for separation. Of course, that's soon followed by the usual Hollywood-style fact-free liberties.

The Rialto became the New Rialto in 1935 and the Cineplex Odeon Warner in 1987.

14. THE LYRIC THEATRE 213 West 42nd Street (Between Seventh and Eighth Avenues) Here on December 8, 1925, the Four Marx Brothers opened in their second Broadway show, *The Cocoanuts*. Shortly thereafter, Harpo Marx invented his trademark gag of frantically chasing a blonde across the stage. His idea was to grab a laugh and, further, catch younger brother Groucho flat-footed—not, of course, that there was much chance of the latter possibility. In any case, waiting

Legs Diamond (AUTHOR'S COLLECTION)

backstage, Harpo had cajoled "a blonde cutie from the chorus" to be the chorine in question.

"Luckily for me," Harpo recalled decades later, "my blonde's boy friend was not in the audience that afternoon. After the show, I found out I had picked the hottest girl in the company. Her boy friend was Jack 'Legs' Diamond ('lean and looking like an unusually vicious greyhound') and Legs wanted his bimbo stashed securely in the chorus, where she wouldn't 'get mixed up in no monkey business with them loony actors.' I made a quick switch of blondes before the evening show."

Diamond, explained Stanley Walker in his book *The Night Club Era*, "had caught the fancy of Arnold Rothstein, who was always on the alert for promising talent. Rothstein made Diamond his assistant bodyguard, no mean title. After big dice or card games, when some of the boys were afraid to go home with their winnings, Diamond would be assigned to escort them safely. It became the thing at Police Headquarters, when a gambler was found murdered with all his pockets empty, to ask, 'Did Legs take him home?'"

This was, as we shall see, only one of Mr. Diamond's pastimes.

Opened in October 1903 and originally designed to house The American School of Opera, the 1,350-seat Lyric converted to motion pictures in 1934. Closed in 1992, it was finally demolished in 1997, with only its 42nd Street and 43rd Street facades remaining.

15. NEW AMSTERDAM THEATRE 214 West 42nd Street (Between Seventh and Eighth Avenues) 1914's edition

of Florenz Ziegfeld's *Ziegfeld Follies* featured Rothstein attorney Bill Fallon's girlfriend Gertrude Vanderbilt (not to be confused with the far wealthier Gertrude Vanderbilt Whitney) in the chorus. Stars of its cast included Ed Wynn, Bert Williams, and the 4'10" Ann Pennington (famous for frenetically popularizing "The Black Bottom").

The following year's *Follies* included Rothstein's longtime mistress Bobbie Winthrop. Wynn, Williams, and Pennington continued in the cast, augmented by W. C. Fields, Flo Hart (a close friend of Winthrop's), Mae Murray, and the beautiful but ill-fated Olive Thomas (Mary Pickford's future sister-in-law). Thomas died in Paris in September 1920 after mistakenly ingesting mercury-bichloride—her husband's topical medication for syphilis.

1916's *Follies* included Fanny Brice, Williams, Pennington, and Fields— plus Brooklyn-born Marion Davies, whose presence so transfixed theater-goer William Randolph Hearst that . . . well, the rest is history. (*See* **THE CLARENDON 137 Riverside Drive.**)

In 1920, when Rothstein henchman Nicky Arnstein faced charges of hijacking literally millions in Liberty Bonds, A. R. met with Arnstein's wife, Fanny Brice, and with her attorney—Bill Fallon—at New Amsterdam's rooftop theater, the Danse de Follies, to arrange for Nicky's bail. Fallon's attitude nearly gummed up the deal, but Rothstein provided the cash, and Arnstein kept silent regarding A. R.'s fencing the bonds.

Brice, by the way, named her only son, William, after Fallon. Which leads us to an even more interesting tale. Previously, Arnstein had remained a fugitive from what passed for justice in Jazz Age New York. Eventually, though, he felt he had to square matters away and did so in the most spectacular manner possible—thanks to Arnold Rothstein.

"Rothstein liked his joke," explained a reviewer of Carolyn Rothstein's 1934 memoir, *Now I'll Tell*, "although he seldom smiled, for he had the inveterate gambler's poker face. He was responsible, however, for the prank which returned Nicky Arnstein to the police in 1920, according to his wife. Rothstein had announced that Nicky would give himself up, but he didn't say where. Thereupon, he had Nicky, who also loved a joke, motor down Fifth Avenue in an open car behind the imposing annual parade of the New York police department which had been seeking him for months. It was the joke of the metropolis, but one which the police did not relish."

1924's *Follies* featured showgirl Imogene "Bubbles" Wilson. Of Wilson, Broadway columnist Mark Hellinger would write, "Only two people in America would bring every reporter in New York to the docks to see them off. One is the President. The other is Imogene 'Bubbles' Wilson."

In other words, she was a dish.

But one of very poor judgment.

In August 1924, she exited a Broadway restaurant with her longtime paramour, the very-married blackface comedian Frank Tinney. As she did, *New York Daily News* photographer Nicholas Peterson snapped their photo, and the hard-drinking Tinney smashed Peterson's camera before proceeding to severely beat Peterson (as he had beaten "Bubbles" that previous May—and would again).

Peterson—no fan of broken cameras, personal beatings, or Frank Tinney—sued.

We don't usually note process servers in these pages but gladly identify who Peterson employed to serve legal papers on the nefarious Tinney: Arnold Rothstein's first cousin—George Ringler (née "Abe C. Ringel"), son of Rothstein's father's sister Sara Miriam Rothstein Ringel.

George Ringler, however, was much more than an ordinary process server.

"Ringler," noted an official history of the *New York Daily News*, "was a [*Daily News*] police reporter, had worked on other New York papers, knew policemen, city hall officeholders, judges, lawyers, and assorted characters on the shady side of the law. He was strictly a legman, passed on his reports to rewrite; working like a detective, he would be on several stories at the same time."

Also employed as a *Daily News* photographer, he eventually emerged as a right-hand man to future New York City mayor James J. "Gentleman Jimmy" Walker and thus also as a very personal Rothstein connection to New York's ruling Tammany machine. Walker eventually appointed Ringler as a confidential investigator for the city's board of health dealing with kosher food. "Walker," observed his biographer Gene Fowler (perhaps a tad too piously), "entrusted to Ringler many confidential matters, such as looking out for the welfare of numerous widows and children of Walker's old friends, all at Jim's own expense." Among those "many confidential matters" was responsibility for assisting showgirl mistress Betty Compton. (*See* **ALGONQUIN HOTEL 59 West 44th Street**.)

In August 1925, Mayor John F. "Red Mike" Hylan publicly charged that Rothstein had helped engineer Walker's primary against him—charges serious enough to trigger a public denial from Governor Alfred E. Smith, who derided Hylan's allegation that "a gambler nominated Walker."

Tammany chief George Olvany likewise denied "that my alleged poolroom king and big gambler adviser is Arnold Rothstein and that my B. M. T. [Brooklyn–Manhattan Transit Corporation] lawyer adviser is a man whom he calls Tom Chadbourne, I want to state that I do not know Arnold Rothstein or Tom Chadbourne, that I have never met either of them, that I have never

Frank Tinney (COURTESY OF THE NEW YORK PUBLIC LIBRARY)

had breakfast, lunch, dinner or supper with either of them and that I would not know either of them if I saw them on the street."

Ringler remained sufficiently close to Walker to accompany him to Governor Franklin Roosevelt's 1932 anti-corruption hearings in Albany.

It's speculated that Ringler, who enjoyed unusual connections to Chinatown's nefarious Hip Sing Society (its only "caucasian member"), may have been a useful bridge between cousin Arnold and Far Eastern drug dealers.

The 1,800-seat New Amsterdam opened in 1903 as the city's largest theater. In 1913, it became home to the already boffo *Ziegfeld Follies*, but its days as a live house couldn't survive the Depression, and like many other West 42nd Street theaters, it converted to movies. In the 1990s, the Disney Corporation acquired the property, reopening it as a live theater in May 1997.

NEW YORK'S LEADING THEATRES AND SUCCESSES

ZIEGFELD'S 2 OUTSTANDING SENSATIONS!!!
NEW AMSTERDAM THEATRE W. 42d St. POP. PRICE MATS. WED. & SAT.
BY ARTIFICIAL MEANS 15 DEGREES COOLER THAN ANY SPOT IN NEW YORK
A NATIONAL INSTITUTION—GREATEST OF ALL!
THE MOST IMITATED SHOW EVER CONCEIVED!!

ZIEGFELD FOLLIES
19th OF THE SERIES.   STAGED BY JULIAN MITCHELL.
GLORIFYING THE AMERICAN GIRL
458 SEATS RESERVED $1.00—SEATS AT BOX OFFICE

(clockwise from top) Ziegfeld Follies *Ad from 1924* (AUTHOR'S COLLECTION) *The New Amsterdam Theatre* (AUTHOR'S COLLECTION) *Mayor James J. "Gentleman Jimmy" Walker* (COURTESY OF THE LIBRARY OF CONGRESS) *Nicky Arnstein* (AUTHOR'S COLLECTION)

16.

APOLLO THEATER 223 West 42nd Street (Between Seventh and Eighth Avenues) When George White, producer of a series of successful Broadway reviews—*George White's Scandals*—learned that the severely cash-strapped Selwyn brothers, Archie and Edgar, were offering to lease their Apollo Theater for a three-year term at drastically reduced rates, White flew into action, calculating he could easily either use the theater for his own productions or sublease it to other producers. It was a no-lose situation—but he needed cash, a lot of it, to make it work and needed it quickly.

White knew Rothstein only as an occasional, but convivial, dinner companion. He now approached him for working capital. A. R. grasped the idea immediately and, as usual, had no problem profiting from the difficulties of his old friends the Selwyn brothers. Within a day, White had his cash, albeit accompanied by Rothstein's usual hefty interest rates. As White predicted, he had secured a tremendous deal, so lucrative the Selwyns tried breaking the lease. They failed.

———

The Apollo opened as a motion picture and vaudeville house, the Bryant, in 1910. The Selwyns (prominent ticket brokers, theatrical owners, and producers, and among the founders of Goldwyn Pictures) assumed

THEATRES	Booking Offices of	ATTRACTIONS
SELWYN THEATRE W. 42nd St., N. Y.	**THE**	The Guitry's
TIMES SQ. THEATRE W. 42nd St., N. Y.	**SELWYNS**	Jane Cowl
APOLLO THEATRE W. 42nd St., N. Y.		John Drew
		Mrs. Leslie Carter
SELWYN THEATRE Boston, Mass.	SELWYN THEATRE BLDG.	Richard Bennett
	229 WEST 42ND STREET	Ina Claire
SELWYN THEATRE Chicago	NEW YORK CITY	Florence Reed
		Barney Bernard
HANNA THEATRE Cleveland, Ohio	J. M. Welch, Manager	Alexander Carr

1921 Selwyns Organization Ad (AUTHOR'S COLLECTION)

management in 1920, renaming it the Apollo, though their new acquisition failed to host a hit production until W. C. Fields's *Poppy* in 1923. *George White's Scandals* ran there annually from 1924 through 1931. The theater's last legitimate show was the flop *Blackbirds of 1933* ("a floundering Negro review . . . a feeble imitation of itself").

From 1934 through 1937, the Minskys operated the Apollo as a burlesque house. "The Minskys," wrote Stanley Walker in 1933, "are, and were, a great family. There were four brothers, Abraham, Billy, Herbert, and Morton, and of the four, Billy, now dead, was the greatest. Once the first citizens of East Houston Street, they moved their burlesque shows to Broadway and carried on the tradition of heavy buttocks and heavier jokes."

Following the Minskys' brief tenure, the Apollo became a movie house, eventually closing in 1986. In 1998, the Apollo and the old Lyric Theatre (*see* **THE LYRIC THEATRE 213 West 42nd Street**) were thoroughly gutted and combined to become the new Ford Center for the Performing Arts. (Hot tip: if you crave a fascinating contemporary look at 1920s' burlesque, catch Helen Morgan and Fuller Mellish Jr. in 1929's early talkie *Applause*. It's truly startling how washed-out Morgan looked at barely twenty-nine.)

In November 1928, White sent flowers to Rothstein's funeral.

17. **SELWYN THEATER 229 West 42nd Street (Between Seventh and Eighth Avenues)** In 1918, Archie and Edgar Selwyn planned to build an 1,180-seat theater on West 42nd Street. Having known Carolyn Rothstein since her performing days, they approached her husband, Arnold, for a $50,000 loan. "Arnold lent it to me at once," Archie Selwyn recalled. "He didn't even want an I.O.U. All he wanted was six percent."

The ill-fated musical *Strike Me Pink* opened at the Selwyn on March 4, 1933—backed by former Rothstein associate Waxey Gordon (Irving Wexler—*see* **WAXEY GORDON'S RESIDENCE 590 West End Avenue**). In out-of-town tryouts, the production (originally dubbed

Forward March) featured such then-luminaries as Hugh Herbert, Ted Healey, and the veteran vaudeville team of Smith and Dale, but none of these stars actually appeared in its Broadway debut—though Jimmy Durante (*see* **CLUB DURANT 232 West 58th Street** *and* **ST. MALACHY'S CHURCH 239 West 49th Street**) and the sultry film star Lupe Vélez did.

The *New York Times* assessed the show as "fine" from a "vocal and musical standpoint," but it suffered from sketch comedy that wasn't "funny enough." *The New Yorker*'s Robert Benchley pronounced the second act "not so hot."

Of Waxey Gordon's participation in events, Craig Thompson and Allen Raymond in their 1940 book, *Gang Rule in New York*, reported:

> Of . . . these entertainments it is related that when it was in rehearsal, Waxey and some of his gangster cronies used to sit in the orchestra seats to watch the chorus put through its paces. Waxey noticed a particularly strapping wench in the chorus, tossing her legs with abandon.
>
> "Whose gal is that?" he asked the director.
>
> "She ain't nobody's girl," was the answer.
>
> In view of all the requests that had been made upon him by the gang to put their molls on the company payroll, Waxey was truly startled. "If she ain't nobody's girl," he said, "how'n hell did she get in the show?"
>
> Broadway showmen did not refer to him as Waxey, or Gordon, or any other such name. To them he was "Mr. W," and sometimes in very private places they called him simply, "The Louse."

(AUTHOR'S COLLECTION)

The Selwyn Theater's career as a legitimate house was short-lived (its most notable production was George

Kaufman and Edna Ferber's *The Royal Family*). By 1934, it converted to burlesque and motion pictures. In 2000, however, renamed as the American Airlines Theatre, it again functioned as a legitimate Broadway venue.

18. LIBERTY THEATRE 234 West 42nd Street (Between Seventh and Eighth Avenues) On Monday evening,

June 2, 1919, the first edition of George White's *Scandals* (the big rival to Flo Ziegfeld's *Follies*) opened at the Liberty—thanks to funding from Arnold Rothstein.

In 1925, the Liberty hosted Jerome Kern's *The City Chap* featuring George Raft (née Rauft) and Mayor Walker's mistress Betty Compton.

Built in 1904 by theatrical impresarios Klaw and Erlanger, the Liberty converted to a movie house in 1933. In the late 1990s, the Liberty and the Empire theaters combined into a new entertainment complex featuring a multiple-screen cineplex and Madame Tussaud's Wax Museum.

19. HACKETT THEATRE 254 West 42nd Street (Between Seventh and Eighth Avenues) Here,

Arnold Rothstein's future wife, showgirl Carolyn Green, was featured in *The Chorus Lady* starring Rose Stahl (after the show opened down at 67 West 35th Street's old Garrick Theater on Herald Square).

The Hackett opened in 1904 as the Lew M. Fields Theatre, was bought by Red Sox owner Harry Frazee in 1920, became a movie house in 1930, and was demolished in 1997 as part of 42nd Street's redevelopment.

In 1924, it was renamed Wallack's Theatre. There, in 1925, the show *Hell's Bells* featured two youngsters named Shirley Booth and Humphrey Bogart, plus pianist Oscar Levant in the orchestra. But the real excitement involved actor Eddie Garvis shooting fellow thespian Clifton Self—and nearly shooting Booth—in the second act (and the arm) with a pistol he did not know was loaded.

"During the play," Levant later recalled, "I prowled familiar haunts of Broadway, including a secret dice game run by the famous McManus brothers, professional gamblers, one of whom was later alleged to have

(above) *Carolyn Green Rothstein*
(right) *Rose Stahl* (AUTHOR'S
COLLECTION)

shot Arnold Rothstein. After these sorties I would rush back to the
theatre to finish my chores."

20. LOUIS MARTIN'S RESTAURANT West 43rd Street and Seventh Avenue
Florenz Ziegfeld produced not
merely legendary Broadway reviews—but also controversy. In June 1913,
he still carried a torch for his former *Follies* star (and ex-mistress) Lillian
Lorraine, occasionally a "steerer" of wealthy patrons to Arnold Rothstein's
West 46th Street gambling house.

Things were decidedly rocky between Lorraine and her spouse,
Frederick Gresheimer (aka "Freddie Gresham"). But, then again, their
story had always been, well, complicated. Married in March 1912, newspapers were soon reporting the existence of another Mrs. Gresheimer—
former showgirl Gertie McCauley Gresheimer. That problem eventually
resolved itself, and Lorraine and Gresheimer "remarried" in April 1913.

(above left) *Lillian Lorraine* (COURTESY OF THE LIBRARY OF CONGRESS)
(above right) *Florenz Ziegfeld in 1928* (AUTHOR'S COLLECTION)
(right) *Frederick Morris Gresheimer* (AUTHOR'S COLLECTION)

Which takes us to the evening of Saturday, June 28, 1913. Lorraine and Ziegfeld had dined at Louis Martin's and exited on to either Broadway or to Seventh Avenue (accounts vary), where they were spied by the jealous Gresheimer ("Say, don't you know this woman is my wife!"). He proceeded to beat the tar out of Ziegfeld either with his cane or with his strong right fist.

"After he hit me," Ziegfeld claimed to reporters, "Gresheimer jumped into a cab and drove away with Miss Lorraine, I had no chance to get at him and I have no idea what motivated his attack on me." Nursing his wounds at his Ansonia Hotel apartment (*see* **THE ANSONIA HOTEL**

West 73rd Street and Broadway), Ziegfeld at first refused to press charges.

By July, Lorraine had instituted annulment proceedings versus Gresheimer, charging he had misled her regarding not merely his former marital status but also his current finances and fortunes. "He had," she charged, "no other business than playing the races."

"It's difficult to describe the particular quality Lillian Lorraine had," mused Hearst columnist Adela Rogers St. Johns. "It wasn't just beauty. I've asked men who loved her and men who just saw her from across the footlights. I've sought a word myself, and the nearest I can come is the French 'Joie de vivre.'

"The love of life. But—there was something lacking, too. . . . She loved everybody—and nobody."

21. HOTEL CADILLAC Broadway at 157 West 43rd Street ■ (southeast corner) At a Hotel Cadillac (325 rooms, 150 baths) dinner party hosted by a mutual friend (Albert Saunders) in September 1908, A. R. met showgirl Carolyn Green, his eventual wife. The Cadillac was immediately south of the famed Broadway restaurant Rector's.

Carolyn Rothstein recalled:

As soon as Arnold Rothstein and I were introduced at the supper at [Belmont Park race track manager]Albert Saunders's, Arnold paid little attention to any one but me. He sat beside me and devoted himself to me while we ate broiled lobster, and every one except Arnold sipped champagne.

After the supper he drove me home in a hansom cab. And the next night he called for me at the theatre and took me to supper. After that he was in constant attendance.

Arnold, at that time, was a slim young man with a sensitive face, brown, laughing eyes, and a gentle manner. I cannot emphasize too much this gentleness of manner, which was one of his most alluring characteristics.

He was always extremely well tailored and presented a most dapper appearance, noticeable even on Broadway where it was the fashion to be well groomed.

Above everything else, from the moment he had been introduced, he had paid no attention to any one except me. That flattered me, his manner charmed me, his appearance pleased me. I was as much in love with him as he was with me.

Until 1910, the Cadillac was known as the Barnett House, which had opened on September 29, 1883. From 1910 through 1915, it was known as the Hotel Wallick. Eugene O'Neill was born there to successful actor James O'Neill on October 16, 1888 (a plaque marks that event). Complicating this history is the fact that the Cadillac and the Barnett had once been separate adjacent hostelries until they merged in 1902.

Demolished in 1940.

22. BENEVOLENT PROTECTIVE ORDER OF ELKS, LODGE NO. 1 108 West 43rd Street at Sixth Avenue

Where gambler Beansie Rosenthal first met Lt. Charles Becker. Erected in 1911. From that year's *New York Times*:

The building with its equipment cost $1,250,000, and has no mortgage, the money being subscribed for bonds held by the 3,000 members of the lodge. It is intended to be used as a big club.

The chief features of the Elks' home are a lodge room 87 feet by 93 feet, the walls rising to a height of 32 feet. There are two tiers of boxes, twenty-eight boxes in each, with a promenade encircling each tier for use when the room is used for balls or banquets. There is a foyer, lounging rooms, writing rooms, a handsome grill room and restaurant, billiard room, and spacious bowling alleys in the basement.

Above the lodge room there are 216 outside sleeping rooms, each with tiled bath. The charge for a room will be $1.50 a day, and there are twenty-four suites, which are rented at $3 a day. The entire roof is occupied by a solarium and roof garden.

Beansie Rosenthal recalled:

New York Lodge N°1. B.P.O.ELKS. West 43ᴿᴰ Street near Broadway

The first time I met Charles Becker, now a Lieutenant of Police in New York City, and who was holding the same office at the time of our first meeting, was at a ball given by the Order of Elks in Forty-third Street, near Sixth Avenue, and we had a very good evening, drank very freely and we became very good friends. Our next meeting was by appointment on New Year's Eve, 1912, at the Elks Club. Dinner was served for ten in our party, including Lieutenant Becker, Mrs. [Helen] Becker and Mrs. Rosenthal. . . .

We drank a lot of champagne that night, and later in the morning we were all pretty well under the weather. He put his arms around me and kissed me. He said, "Anything in the world for you, Herman. I'll get up at three o'clock in the morning to do you a favor. You can have anything I've got." And then he called over his three men, James White, Charles Foy and Charles Steinhart, and he introduced me to the three of them, saying, "This is my best pal and do anything he wants you to do."

According to the website nysonglines.com, the building was later the Hotel Diplomat, where radical activist Abbie Hoffman was busted with cocaine on August 28, 1973, leading to six years underground. The New York chapter of the Mattachine Society, a pioneering gay rights group, was founded here in December 1955. The New York Dolls had some of their first gigs in the hotel's Palm Room.

23. HOTEL METROPOLE 142-149 West 43rd Street (Between Broadway and Sixth Avenue) The

Metropole opened in May 1910, replacing the previously mentioned "Hotel Metropole" operating at Broadway and West 42nd Street. Run by Tammany boss state senator "Big Tim" Sullivan and brothers George F. Considine and William F. Considine, the Metropole featured not only prostitutes but gamblers. For a while, Rothstein, who was very close to Sullivan, ran the hotel's gambling concession. Nicky Arnstein and Bat Masterson once resided there—though, not together.

On Tuesday evening, July 16, 1912, gambler Herman "Beansie" Rosenthal, after meeting with Rothstein, arrived at the Metropole (70 rooms, 70 baths; men only) for a late dinner. Gambler Harry Vallon summoned him out onto the street ("Can you come outside for a minute, Herman?"). A gray Packard touring car drove by and the occupants (Dago Frank, Gyp the Blood, Lefty Louie, and Whitey Lewis) pumped Rosenthal full of bullets. He died almost instantly. Police Lt. Charles Becker, angered with Rosenthal over his plans to expose police corruption, went to the chair at Sing Sing for directing the assassination.

Of "Big Tim" Sullivan, there remained the greatest of ironies—this accomplice to the nation's first drive-by murder was also the author of a very contradictory piece of legislation. As M. R. Werner, a prodigious historian of Tammany Hall, observed:

While Sullivan was a State Senator, he sponsored two bills of importance to himself and to Tammany Hall. One was a bill making Columbus Day a legal holiday, and the other was the bill which still bears his name making the carrying of firearms without a license a penal offense. The first pleased Tammany's Italian constituency, and the other enabled the Senator and his associates to keep those same friends and their Jewish and Irish compatriots under control. Whenever a gangster who led repeaters [illegal voters], or an influential brothel keeper, grew obstreperous enough to prove inconvenient to the plans that were made in Tammany Hall, he could usually be found with a gun, or a gun could be planted upon his person, and he could be sent to the State prison under the Sullivan Law for a long enough time to keep him from being annoying. One of these men, "Big Jack" Zelig, found that the better part of discretion after the Sullivan Law was passed was to sew up all his pockets. He always travelled on his business expeditions thereafter with a henchman, who carried the gun and presented it, carefully wiped, at the proper

NEW METROPOLE HOTEL
43RD STREET AT BROADWAY NEW YORK CITY
GEO. F. CONSIDINE

(COURTESY OF COLUMBIA UNIVERSITY LIBRARIES)

time for the champion to do his work. The Sullivan Law prevented very little gunfire, because a person who wished to kill another did not trouble about the fact that he was also breaking another law. He wondered, if anything, how he was going to cover himself after the murder. But the Sullivan Law did prevent citizens from protecting themselves from thieves, and it probably made it more expensive for thieves and murderers to get guns in New York. But a five-cent ferry fare always carried them to the State of New Jersey. The Sullivan Law was, however, useful to Sullivan and to Tammany Hall, because it enabled them to control their gunmen friends when they [became] their enemies.

Showman George M. Cohan (check out his bronze statue at West 46th Street and Broadway) frequented both Metropoles. The scandal surrounding Rosenthal's murder soon hastened the New Metropole's bankruptcy, though, it soon reopened as the "Yates Hotel." In 1920, the property passed under the control of the T. Coleman du Pont chain of hotels. Du Pont later served as a United States senator from Delaware.

24. SHANLEY BUILDING 207 West 43rd Street (West Side of Broadway) Site of the most famous of Shanley's renowned "lobster palace" restaurants but, more significantly for this narrative, where "Big Tim" Sullivan maintained one of his several offices and where Lt. Charles Becker claimed to have first met "Big Tim" in 1912.

Beer baron Owney "The Killer" Madden maintained a suite of offices here to promote his boxing interests.

Opened in July 1910, the 1,600-seat Shanley's became a victim of changing times (i.e., Prohibition) and all versions of Shanley's finally closed in March 1923, but not before owner Tom Shanley once personally bounced a drunken F. Scott Fitzgerald (*see* **F. SCOTT FITZGERALD APARTMENT 38 West 59th Street**) from the joint.

"We are not playing cry baby," observed Shanley regarding his establishment's demise, "but we can't go on at a profit on soft drinks. We obey the law and lose money, and we can't afford that."

The New York Florists Club dines at Shanley's, March 1911. (AUTHOR'S COLLECTION)

Owned by the Astor family, the building was also known as the Putnam-Shanley Building in honor of it being the site of a September 15, 1776 meeting between George Washington and General Israel Putnam to plan the following day's strategy at Brooklyn's Battle of Long Island. (Spoiler alert: they lost.)

To celebrate 1918's Armistice (Spoiler alert: we won) at Shanley's Restaurant, William Randolph Hearst sprung for $50,000 of champagne for the house.

Now the site of the thirty-three-story art deco Paramount Building and the 708-seat Hard Rock Cafe.

A later edition of Shanley's functioned at 117 West 42nd Street (between Broadway and Sixth Avenue), near the former Knickerbocker Hotel. Prohibition agents raided it in December 1920, seizing $3,000 worth of "Scotch and rye, whisky, gin, white and red wines, Vermouth and a barrel or so of beer."

25. BOARDINGHOUSE 243 West 43rd Street (Between Seventh and Eighth Avenues)

Where Rothstein narcotics henchman George D. Uffner's lover Edna Wheaton boarded with her mother, Josephine Wheaton, and her older sister Marie in early 1920 after having relocated here from their home at upstate Ithaca, where the teenaged Edna sang in the local Tabernacle Baptist Church choir. Their plan: Edna would find fame and fortune vocalizing in the big city. (*See* **EDNA WHEATON APARTMENT 39 West 76th Street.**)

In 1921 Edna, her mother (and probably her sister Marie) moved to 307 West 100th Street (between West End Avenue and Riverside Drive). Edna entered a beauty contest co-sponsored by the *New York Daily News* and Paramount Pictures. The prize: being cast in the role of "Beauty" in Paramount's newest production, *Experience*, conveniently shooting across the East River at Paramount's Astoria studios.

Competing against six thousand entrants, she won.

(AUTHOR'S COLLECTION)

The American Film Institute summarized *Experience*'s moralistic, super-old-school allegorical plot as follows:

Youth [Richard Barthelmess] leaves his mother at the behest of Ambition and with Love and Hope goes to the city, where he encounters Pleasure [Lilyan Tashman] and asks Opportunity to wait; but she refuses and leaves him. At the Primrose Path (a cabaret), Pleasure introduces him to Beauty [Wheaton], Wealth, Fashion, and Temptation [Nita Naldi]. Youth's mother dies, and Love sends him a telegram, which is intercepted by Temptation; and when Love comes to the city, she is turned away from the Primrose Path. Chance directs Youth to a gambling house where he loses everything but the ring given him by Love, and he is haunted by Poverty and Delusion. With the exception of Temptation, all have forgotten him. He meets Vice and Habit and finally consents to go with Crime to rob Wealth's house. On the way he hears a church choir singing and decides to go home; with Experience he returns where Love and Hope await him. Ambition again seeks Youth, who with Love at his side starts a new life.

Unfortunately, however, few of the characters in this present volume ever paid the slightest attention to the advice *Experience* offered.

26. QUANG WAN Sixth Avenue North of West 43rd Street

Rothstein eventually became known as the father of the

modern drug trade. Rumors swirled of his own possible narcotics use, but as author and screenwriter Edward Dean Sullivan wrote in 1930:

> Those who knew Rothstein in his later years, when he was suspected of being a king pin in the narcotic traffic of the country, have denied with amused tolerance the suggestion that he was a drug addict. They intimate that he was too smart and careful of himself to take the slightest chance about it and that his abstinence from tobacco and alcohol was but an indication of his meticulous protection of his health.
>
> Yet even in the old Hesper Club days [on the Lower East Side] Rothstein was known at all of the larger hop joints of the East Side and he had a strange habit of being in the company of drug users then and in after years. Once in an East Side raid he was arrested in a drug round-up, but subsequently released and many years later he was taken in during a raid at the joint of Quong Wan, in Sixth Avenue, north of Forty-third Street. He was again released, asserting that he had merely delivered a message for a friend there.

27. THE FITZGERALD BUILDING 1482 Broadway ∎ (Between West 42nd and West 43rd Streets) Where Arnold Rothstein registered for conscription in September 1918.

In one of the more mysterious entries in the Rothstein saga we find that he then claimed his present occupation as "Fruit and Produce." His role in said business being "Member of firm," and the business being located at 39 Ninth Avenue.

A reasonable supposition would be that Arnold was somehow connected there to mobster Ciro "The Artichoke King" Terranova, later a resident of West 72nd Street's Rothstein-owned Fairfield Hotel. (*See* FAIRFIELD HOTEL 20-28 West 72nd Street.) The problem with said theory is that at that point in time, Terranova still remained in the plastering business on East 116th Street.

Terranova does, however, play a prominent role in the Rothstein narrative.

During 1929's mayoral election, Republican Fiorello La Guardia called attention to records of a $20,000 loan Rothstein provided to Bronx magistrate Albert H. Vitale, calling for a thorough cleansing of the city's notoriously corrupt judicial system, a system that Mayor James J. Walker biographer George Walsh explained thusly:

> Corruption was evident, not just in vice cases, but in all the courts. A gambling charge could be fixed, for instance, by bribing a clerk to fill out a form No. 0-14, which "informed" a lazy or venal magistrate that in the clerk's opinion the facts "did not present the basis for a legal complaint." In 1929, when there were 4,838 arrests for bookmaking, 4,677 were dismissed.

No one paid much attention to La Guardia's charges in 1929, however—or to La Guardia himself—and the jaunty incumbent Mayor

Walker coasted to a historic landslide (Walker: 60.70 percent; La Guardia 25.73 percent).

But then, on Saturday evening, December 7, 1929, the Bronx's Tepecano Democratic Club hosted a testimonial for none other than Judge Albert Vitale. Suddenly, seven gunmen burst in, relieving guests of their valuables. When Police Detective Arthur Johnson (one of three NYPD officers present) thought of resisting, Vitale urged caution, assuring him all would be made right—even though all three cops surrendered their firearms to the invaders. Vitale, however, knew what he was talking about. Within hours, Vitale had returned Johnson's gun to him. In fact, he would see that everyone's cash and valuables were expeditiously returned.

It was all *very* odd.

How could such bizarre events transpire? Well, the answer was this: also present were some Chicago-based gents who had executed Ciro Terranova–ordered hits on racketeers Frankie Yale (née Francesco Ioele) and Frankie Marlow (née Gandolfo Civito; *see* **LA TAVERNELLE RESTAURANT 252 West 52nd Street**)—and carried with them the actual physical "contract" for the murders.

Some mobsters evidently took the word *contract* a little too literally back then.

In any case, there was no honor among thieves, and Terranova refused to pay his murderous henchmen any more than the $5,000 he had already provided as a down payment. They, in turn, promised to make public the whole deal—and they had the documentary evidence to back up their claims. Somehow, they were unfazed by the fear of subsequent prosecution.

Hence, Terranova wanted the "contract" back—and this spectacular robbery was his spectacularly peculiar plan to retrieve it.

Vitale's subsequent behavior, however, betrayed his own all-too-obvious connection to the mob. Reformers demanded his head. They got it—plus a thorough investigation of the entire rotten magistrates system. Additional investigations of Tammany corruption followed, and, eventually, so did the resignation under fire of Mayor "Gentleman Jimmy" Walker, the end of Tammany dominance, and the election of the once-ignored Fiorello La Guardia.

Remarkably, Terranova was never charged with either Yale's or Marlow's murder.

Frankie Yale's July 1, 1928, murder was the first in New York to employ a Thompson submachine gun, long a weapon of choice among Chicago mobsters. Ballistics tests later established that the tommy gun used to slay Yale was also employed in February 1929's infamous St. Valentine's Day Massacre.

28. JARDIN DE PARIS 1514–1516 Broadway at West 44th Street

Before Fanny Brice took up with Nicky Arnstein, she had set her eye on another big, strapping, shady fellow, Chicago's Frederick Gresheimer. But before Fanny got much further with Fred, *Follies* star Lillian Lorraine (occasionally a steerer of rich suckers into Rothstein's West 46th Street gambling house) intervened.

Both Brice and Lorraine were then headlining here the 1911 edition of Flo Ziegfeld's *Follies*—and sparks flew.

The *New York Review* headlined:

LILLIAN LORRAINE AND FANNY BRICE
FIGHT ON ROOF STAGE.
PATRONS IN FRONT HEARD SIGNS
OF THE LIVELY SCRIMMAGES.

"When the scrimmage was ended," the *New York Review* explained, "Miss Lorraine's raiment was in rags, her face and her hair bore sundry marks of the conflict, and she had reached a state of hysteria which made it necessary for her to be carried bodily to her dressing room."

That's show biz, I guess.

IBDB.com says of the Jardin de Paris:

In 1895, Oscar Hammerstein opened an entertainment complex for which one fifty-cent ticket admitted you to two main auditoriums (Lyric, Music Hall), two small theatres (Concert Hall, Roof Garden), an Oriental cafe, bowling, and billiards. On June 29, 1898, the debt-laden Olympia was auctioned. The Roof Garden emerged as its own theatre. In 1907, Florenz Ziegfeld became manager, presenting the first five editions of his famous Follies format. Later, it was a movie theatre. It was razed in 1935.

(AUTHOR'S COLLECTION)

29. THE CANFIELD CASINO 5 West 44th Street (Between Fifth and Sixth Avenues) Even villains have heroes. And,

certainly, one of Rothstein's was Richard Canfield. For while the gambling path trod many, many roads, and while several traveled through the Lower East Side and to numerous cheap stuss parlors and saloons, Richard Canfield trod a path to high society, elegance—and *real* money and power. Originally from Rhode Island (with ancestral connections to *The Mayflower*), Canfield had established a series of elegant gambling houses catering to the nation's Gilded Age elite.

Previously, he had operated a gambling house on West 26th Street, but in mid-1898, he obtained a lease on this five-story 44th Street brownstone. Opulently outfitted at a cost of $500,000, it opened in March 1899 and proved to be an exceedingly fine investment, returning, as the *Brooklyn Daily Eagle* later noted, "an income of $1,000,000 a year during 1899, 1900 and 1901. This excluded probably similar expenditures that the Prince of

Gamblers blew for overhead, bird and bottle dinners for his guests, and 'presents' when the police and politicians called. The police-politico 'cut' was usual, 15 percent."

But "cut" or no "cut," reformers agitated for a crackdown, and on December 1, 1902, reform district attorney William Travers Jerome (first cousin once removed of Winston Churchill) finally raided the joint— though, with little effect.

"That the raid had been anticipated the police seem certain," pondered the *New York Times*. "The condition of the house indicated that such was the case, for nowhere in the entire establishment, from the basement to the fourth floor, on which are Mr. Canfield's private apartments, was there any sign of recent use.

"That the raid was anticipated . . . was also seemingly apparent, for the counsel for Canfield was in the house at the time the raid was made, although Mr. Canfield later said the lawyer had been dining late at Delmonico's, next door, and had 'just dropped in to see me.'"

While Jerome's raid, nonetheless, basically spelled *finis* to Richard Canfield's grand West 44th Street establishment, one may still catch a glimpse of his vanished splendor by visiting upstate New York to the horse racing mecca of Saratoga Springs. There, within downtown Congress Park lies another "Canfield Casino"—which, while no longer a casino, still remains an elegant meeting and event venue well worth a look.

30. ALGONQUIN HOTEL 59 West 44th Street (Between Fifth and Sixth Avenues) In the Roaring Twenties, the venerable Algonquin Hotel (209 rooms, 135 baths) featured a circle of wits known as the Algonquin Round Table: playwrights George S. Kaufman and Edna Ferber; newspapermen Franklin P. Adams, Heywood Broun, and Alexander Woollcott (a bystander at the Rosenthal murder; *see* **HOTEL METROPOLE 142-149 West 43rd Street**); comedian Harpo Marx (*see* **THE LYRIC THEATRE 213 West 42nd Street**); humorist Robert Benchley; *New Yorker* magazine founder Harold Ross; and the acerbic poetess Dorothy Parker. Among the Round Table's more affluent members was Herbert Bayard Swope (*see* **HOTEL ALBANY 1446-1450**

Broadway), editor of *The World*, then New York's most respected paper. Swope's past was not quite so respectable: he had been a close friend of Rothstein, and in August 1909 had served as best man at his Saratoga Springs wedding.

When James J. Walker's future mistress Betty Compton first arrived in New York from Montreal, she lodged at the Algonquin. Her next move was to present a letter of introduction to Rothstein associate Archie Selwyn (*see* **the APOLLO THEATER 223 West 42nd Street** *and* **THE SELWYN THEATER 229 West 42nd Street**), and from there she worked in vaudeville, in night clubs, and in a series of Broadway shows and reviews, including the *Ziegfeld Follies of 1924*.

The Algonquin opened in 1902, designed by architect Goldwin Starrett. William Faulkner wrote his Noble Prize acceptance speech at his Algonquin suite. Alan Jay Lerner and Frederick Lowe penned *My Fair Lady* at the hotel. James Thurber died there in 1961.

31. THE BELASCO THEATRE 111 West 44th Street (Between Broadway and Sixth Avenue) After depart

ing his Lower Manhattan offices, at 7:00 p.m. on the evening of Tuesday, August 6, 1929, Judge Joseph F. Crater purchased a ticket from his friend ticket broker Joseph Grainsky's Arrow Ticket Agency at 1539 Broadway (at West 45th Steet in the Astor Theatre) for that evening's performance of the recently opened comedy *Dancing Partners*. Why Crater did so is only one of the evening's smaller puzzlements, as he had already seen the show in previews at Atlantic City. Most accounts say he never attended this performance. (*See* **BILLY HAAS'S CHOPHOUSE 332 West 45th Street.**)

The 1,016-seat Belasco opened (as the Stuyvesant Theatre; renamed the Belasco in 1910) in October 1907. Atop the theater was the legendary David Belasco's ten-room apartment. In 1921, Bill Fallon's paramour Gertrude Vanderbilt replaced Ina Claire in the starring role in Belasco's hit *The Gold Diggers.*

Following Belasco's May 1931 death, the venue hosted the progressive Group Theatre. In the late 1940s and early 1950s it served as an NBC television studio. It reopened in 1953 as a legitimate house presenting Judy Holliday's memorable *The Solid Gold Cadillac.* Its subsequent hits have included *A Raisin in the Sun, Oh! Calcutta!,* and *Hedwig and the Angry Inch.*

32. THE HOTEL LANGWELL 123-129 West 44th Street (Between Broadway and Sixth Avenue) Here in 1923, a

former showgirl named Vivian Gordon (née Benita Franklin) was arrested by vice squad patrolman Andrew J. "The Lone Wolf" McLaughlin (an unpleasant man of suspicious finances) on charges of prostitution. She claimed a frame-up executed by McLaughlin at the behest of her former common-law husband. The motive: to secure custody of their daughter.

The charge, however, was not entirely far-fetched: as early as March 1915, the hotel was legally found to be a "disorderly house."

Convicted, Gordon received two years in the Bedford Reformatory. Whether guilty of this exact charge or not, the redheaded Gordon eventually (if not sooner) did enter into prostitution, with Arnold Rothstein later bankrolling her own bordello. In partnership with Legs Diamond, she entered into the much-seamier badger racket trade. (*See* **CLUB INTIME 205 West 54th Street.**)

Built as the thirteen-story Hotel Gerard in 1893 as an apartment hotel on the site of the Shaari Tephila Synagogue, the Gerard became the Langwell in 1920 and later the Hotel 1-2-3. It has now returned to being the Gerard.

Apartment hotels were all the craze at the time of the Gerard's construction and remained popular for decades. As the British periodical *Pall Mall* noted in 1903, actual residences were now no longer quite so desirable "when a perfectly appointed apartment, or suite of rooms in a hotel deluxe, may be engaged at any time, for a short or long period. Furthermore, the man who has 'made his pile' in Chicago, St. Louis, Denver or San Francisco, and consequently has plenty of money to spend, will surely visit with his family the financial and artistic centre of the country at least once a year, even if he cannot arrange to live there."

Aside from being quite the craze, these hotels were also an unintended (or, New York politics being what they were, perhaps an intended) consequence of 1899's new building code and 1901's Tenement House Law.

As hotel historian Stanley Turkel has explained: "Since apartment hotels were classified as hotels rather than tenements (i.e. regular apartment buildings) they were exempt from the stringent tenement house law and regulated only by the more flexible building code as applied to commercial buildings. As a consequence, apartment hotels could be less fireproof, taller, cover a larger portion of the lot and contain more units than apartment houses, giving builders a larger financial return."

———

Arnold Rothstein's close friend Sidney Stajer (*see* **HOTEL PRISAMENT 2120-2122 Broadway**), a key figure in his international drug smuggling operation, resided here in January 1932.

33. LAMBS CLUB 130 West 44th Street (Between Broadway and Sixth Avenue)

In August 1920, New York Giants manager, Rothstein pal, and onetime Rothstein pool hall partner John J. McGraw was drinking at the Lambs Club. There, he got into a brawl with actor William H. Boyd. "I didn't hit McGraw first," recalled

*New York Giants Owner Charles Stoneham
and New York Giants Manager John McGraw*
(AUTHOR'S COLLECTION)

Boyd. "It was an unfortunate affair, and I really don't want to discuss it. I did not bawl McGraw out, and the fact is, that he bawled me out. Some of the men standing nearby said to me, 'Don't hit him,' when they heard his language. I didn't want to hit him, but when McGraw rushed at me what else was I to do?"

McGraw rode home in a taxicab with another actor, John C. Slavin. Slavin ended up with a slightly fractured skull—and McGraw ("I never fight unless I am drunk") was charged with violation of the federal Volstead Act (Prohibition). It took Rothstein attorney Bill Fallon to extricate McGraw from federal charges. The Lambs, nonetheless, expelled McGraw, but he was reinstated in 1924.

Members of the Lambs Club in 1915 (COURTESY OF THE LIBRARY OF CONGRESS)

The establishment, a supper club for actors, was designed in 1904 by Stanford White. In 1975, it was sold to the Manhattan Church of the Nazarene. From 1978 through 2007 it hosted the Lamb's Theatre Company.

34. TEEPEE DEMOCRATIC CLUB 146 West 44th Street (Between Broadway and Sixth Avenue) Working with Bill Fallon's soon-to-be disbarred law partner Gene McGee in 1921, Rothstein unearthed a handy legal technicality to shield the various gambling establishments enjoying his protection. The law, it seems, provided that if a joint was unsuccessfully raided three times, it was then shielded from further raids for a full year. Thus, it was now *a good thing* to be raided—and better yet to stage such "raids" for the purpose of securing a year of blissful real-raid-free liberty.

Such was the case with the newly formed Teepee Democratic Club, an organization having little to do with politics or American Indians and much more to do with illegal gambling. In May and June 1925, police "raided" the club five times. They found nothing, and club officials petitioned the courts for protection. As City Corporation Counsel George Nicholson explained/complained:

> The police asked the President of the club why he had sent in complaints against his own club, and he did not deny that such was the case. The reason for such action is obvious. If he could entice the police into the premises on three occasions, with the result that no violation of the law was found, he would then have, in his opinion, sufficient evidence on which to secure an injunction against the police upon fraudulent charges of oppression. Having obtained such an injunction, the club could then be operated as a gambling house with impunity. . . .
>
> Most significant of all is that within five minutes after the police had left the premises on the three occasions the lights were extinguished and all the members departed, showing that they were simply there as a trap for the police, and not in good faith.

In 1931, with the lid blowing off Tammany corruption, the *New York Evening Post* listed the following establishments as having sought such protection:

> Vesta Club, Cree Club, Golden Democratic Club, Unity Bowling Club, Young Men's Democratic Club of the Thirty-first Assembly District, Elmore Club, Lenox Democratic Club, First Voters Democratic League, Bay View Athletic Club, Greenpoint People's Regular Democratic Organization, Merrick V. Nittoly Regular Democratic Organization, Welfare Democratic Club, Blue Ribbon Pleasure Club of South Brooklyn, Regular Democratic Club of Fifth Assembly, District, Queens.
>
> Native Chinese Social Club, Teepee Democratic Club, The Steamer Club, Park Athletic Club, Edward P. Scanlon Association, Highbridge Regular Democratic Club, Star Democratic Club, Yankee Doodle Boys. Inc., Lenox Colored Democratic Club, James A. Renwick Club.

35. VENDOME CLUB 156 West 44th Street (Between Broadway and Sixth Avenue)

Richard Canfield, Arnold Rothstein, Beansie Rosenthal, and "Bridgie" Webber weren't the only ones operating gambling houses in the Times Square area. Prior to 1912, former major league catcher and umpire "Honest John" Kelly had operated his own club at 141 West 41st Street, but following a particularly violent police raid, he relocated to this address, remaining in operation until 1922, when he leased the latter property to the "Active Republican Club." It was razed in 1925 and replaced by a thirteen-story apartment building.

It is said Kelly, also a prominent and respected boxing referee, earned his nickname when, umpiring in 1888, he spurned a $10,000 bribe to fix a crucial Providence-Boston National League game in favor of Boston.

"No man can say he was ever given anything but a square deal in any of my houses," said Kelly late in his life. "Another principle I've always had was not to give a cent to the cops. They kept me busy buying new front doors because I wouldn't work to fill their pockets."

In February 1926, the three-hundred-seat Mayfair Theatre opened at this location, and despite hosting Eugene O'Neill's *The Emperor Jones* and the American premiere of Sean O'Casey's *Juno and the Paycock*, it shuttered its doors by the following year and by March 1928 was to be ingloriously leased to a Chinese-American restaurant. That didn't work out, either, and by June 1929, Arnold Rothstein's former barber, "John the Barber" Reisler (*see* **JOHN J. "JOHN THE BARBER" REISLER BARBER SHOP 169 West 45th Street**), ballyhooed plans for a splendid new shop featuring "35 schooled barbers and 25 Follies Girls as Manicures." That December 1929, police raided its back room and seized 162 bottles of illegal liquor.

"Honest John" Kelly (Looking Pretty Much as You Might Expect a Fellow Named "Honest John" Kelly to Look) (AUTHOR'S COLLECTION)

The joint, it appeared, was solidly jinxed.

36. **HOTEL CLARIDGE** 160-62 West 44th Street (Between Sixth and Seventh Avenues) Headquarters of Rothstein associate and legendary organized crime figure Lucky Luciano in the 1920s. Site of Rothstein sponsored dice games. George Young Bauchle, Rothstein's high-society front man for his high stakes gambling club, the Partridge Club, found himself arrested in front of the Claridge in March 1915.

Prostitute Vivian Gordon (*see* **THE HOTEL LANGWELL 123-129 West 44th Street**) was involved in a fight here in 1927 and was brought to the local station house.

(CLOCKWISE FROM UPPER LEFT) *The Hotel Rector; Hotel Rector—Grand Entrance; The Hotel Claridge; Lobby of the Hotel Claridge* (COURTESY OF COLUMBIA UNIVERSITY LIBRARIES)

It was also where George Raft slipped heavyweight "Big Boy" Peterson a mickey in January 1930 to guarantee a Primo Carnera victory. (*See* **MADISON SQUARE GARDEN 825 Madison Avenue.**)

Originally built as Rector's Hotel by restaurateur Charles Rector. Opened in 1910. Renamed by its new owners following Rector's 1913 bankruptcy. Replaced by the National Motion Picture theater building.

37. THE SHUBERT THEATRE 225 West 44th Street (Between Seventh and Eighth Avenues) Here on July 5,

1927, there debuted the speakeasy-themed review *Padlocks of 1927*, featuring a distinctly appropriate cast that included Texas Guinan, George Raft, and the seriously alcoholic Lillian Roth. That August, Demaris Dore (witness to Rothstein bodyguard Fatty Walsh's 1929 murder) replaced Roth in the cast, while continuing to appear at the Club Frivolity "where she had achieved much popularity." (*See* **CLUB FRIVOLITY 1678 Broadway.**) Billy Rose supplied the show's lyrics.

The *New York Sun* wrote:

> Consider this new frolic merely as a revue and much of it will be found to be pretty shoddy stuff. Consider it as a stunt show, as a romp for Miss Guinan, and it becomes an interesting experiment. She ruled her theater as she rules her club. She shouted for "hands" and she got them. She took her regal position upon her chair and hurled clappers and paper balls. She yelled to this man and to that. She brought a Philadelphia patron to the stage, and gave the audience a glimpse of her mother and father. They were sedately tucked away in the center of the house, but took a bow when it was demanded.

Texas Guinan commenced each performance of Padlocks of 1927 *by riding a white horse down the aisle, but this Western-themed portrait actually dates from April 1922—when President and Mrs. Warren Harding entertained Guinan at the White House.* (COURTESY OF THE LIBRARY OF CONGRESS)

The familiar battle of the paper balls came at the finale of the first act, and those sturdy followers of Miss Guinan, who planted themselves in the front row last night, were peppered to their immense delight. They seemed to be having as great a time as when inside the club itself, paying fancy checks and having their hair mussed up.

In 1924, the theater hosted *Vogues of 1924*, starring Fred Allen but with future Mayor Jimmy Walker's mistress Betty Compton in the cast.

38. SARDI'S RESTAURANT 234 West 44th Street (Between Seventh and Eighth Avenues) We don't

know if Arnold Rothstein ever dined at Sardi's, but we do know it's one of Times Square's few surviving eateries from his era and, as such, is well worth a mention herein.

There is, nonetheless, a distinct Arnold Rothstein connection to said joint, and it involves its legendary hatcheck girl, Renée Carroll.

Carroll (née Rebecca Shapiro) was no ordinary hatcheck girl. In fact, she's probably the most successful hatcheck girl in history. Besides checking hats, she would famously critique scripts left off by producers and actors who welcomed her advice on what shows to involve themselves in—or not. Eventually, she perused more than five thousand of them. By 1933 she published a memoir, *In Your Hat*, and later wrote a gossip column. Jack Warner invited her to Hollywood as a screenwriter. In 1943, she appeared in the show *Bright Lights*—as a Sardi's hatcheck girl named "Renée Carroll."

But before all that, the redheaded Renée found herself at 2:00 a.m. one night at Texas Guinan's nightclub, when Arnold Rothstein blew in accompanied by "two other mob members who made a hobby of floating crap games and body-filling dum-dums."

Renée was seated alongside Guinan; Guinan's brother Tommy; "Feet" Edson, a member of Owney Madden's gang; Rothstein pal Jake Horwitz; and a friend of Renée who was dating Horwitz. Renée was there as a "beard" to disguise the fact her friend was Horwitz's "woman."

"Hello, Arnold!" Guinan shouted out. "Betcha three to two it rains before eleven this morning."

"You're a sucker for wet weather, Tex," Rothstein responded. "Aren't you even Boy Scout enough to know that rain before seven means clear before eleven? It's all over now."

"Is it a bet?"

"Don't be silly; I'm busy."

"Rothstein was looking at me," Renée recalled. "Suddenly he opened his Chesterfield overcoat and dug his hand deep down into his trouser pocket. He pulled out a roll of bills fat enough to choke Mrs. Astor's pet whoozis. He peeled the top bill off the pile and casually tossed it on the table in front of me.

"I couldn't quite get the idea. Especially when I noticed that it was a $1,000 note—and real. A thousand dollars to me then was as big as Eddie Cantor's heart. It still is, as a matter of fact. But it was the first time anyone had shoved the United States mint right smack in my face. I looked up at the most glamorous gambler Broadway ever knew. He looked intently at me for a moment and then smiled. "Could you go for one of these?' he almost whispered. 'Tell me when you're ready to leave.'"

Renée caught his drift. He wanted her to leave with him, with a mind toward emulating Eddie Cantor's trademark "Makin' Whoopee" (at least, that would be the polite term).

She wasn't interested. Her answer was a sneer. A. R. took the bill and put it back atop his big bankroll. She thought he'd been in this position at least a couple of times beforehand.

"Still no one said a word," Renée's narrative continued. "Rothstein turned to go and then changed his mind. He turned with a child-caught-in-the-pantry look on his face and took out a roll of bills again. He peeled off another one and walking over to where I sat, he said: 'Just to show you I'm a good sport, buy yourself some diamonds—Woolworth's.'

"And without my realizing just what he was doing, he stuck a crumpled greenback far down the front of my evening dress. Then he turned and stalked out of the place with his two guardian gorillas."

But the bill wasn't a thousand-dollar note. It was a measly one-dollar bill.

Sardi's Renée Carroll (AUTHOR'S COLLECTION)

"Somehow I liked Rothstein for doing that," Renée concluded her tale. "But I suppose the feeling wasn't very mutual because he passed me at least a dozen times in night clubs after that, and I might just as well have been a Federal spy on his trail for all the attention he paid me."

It was at Guinan's, by the way, that Renée discovered her vocation at hat checking.

Vincenzo "Vincent" Sardi, an Italian immigrant and formerly an employee at Rector's (*see* **RECTOR'S 48th Street at Broadway and Seventh Avenue**), the famed showbiz boardinghouse Bartholdi's Inn (169–77 West 45th Street, east of Broadway), and at the café within the Knickerbocker Hotel (*see* **KNICKERBOCKER HOTEL 142 West 42nd Street**), opened the joint on March 5, 1927, after having just operated "The Little Restaurant" in the basement of nearby 246 West 44th Street. Never noted for its cuisine, in its heyday, Sardi's, however, reigned as a star-studded center of the theater world and for many years hosted the announcement of the Tony Awards.

Sardi's is, perhaps, most famous for its extensive collection of its customers' caricatures, including the following luminaries found elsewhere within this narrative: Mayor Jimmy Walker, Flo Ziegfeld, Fanny Brice, Helen Morgan, Walter Winchell, Jack Dempsey, Dorothy Parker, Heywood Broun, Mark Hellinger, Alexander Woollcott, George S. Kaufman, Robert Benchley, Barbara Stanwyck, Bert Lahr, the Marx Brothers, Beatrice Lillie, Lillian Roth, Pat O'Brien, and Tom Bosley. John

Barrymore also dined there (or more accurately drank there), but may have been too liquored up to pose for a sketch.

39. THE BROADHURST THEATRE 235 West 44th Street ■ (Between Seventh and Eighth Avenues) Here, on
November 23, 1959, opened the smash musical *Fiorello!* based on the early career of famed New York City mayor Fiorello La Guardia. The show featured two very popular songs cynically focusing on machine politics—"A Little Tin Box" and "Politics and Poker." It's second act focused on La Guardia's failed 1929 mayoral bid versus incumbent "Gentleman Jimmy" Walker, a race in which the 5'2" La Guardia called attention to Rothstein's suspicious $20,000 loan to Bronx magistrate Albert H. Vitale—an issue earning little attention in 1929 but eventually detonating a series of events culminating in Tammany's 1933 downfall—and La Guardia's election as mayor.

In August 1929, La Guardia had also savaged the annual New York Police Department Report issued by Commissioner Grover Whalen and Whalen's omissions of the Rothstein and Frankie Marlow (*see* **LA TAVERNELLE RESTAURANT 252 West 52nd Street**) murders:

> The reason why Commissioner Whalen forgot the Rothstein case and the other murders of that kind is because he knows that Rothstein was the financier of Tammany Hall itself, and he doesn't dare bring that out. Mr. Whalen knows that Rothstein's web spread over every part of the Tammany political machine. He was afraid that if they solved that murder, it would give the opponents of Tammany Hall such a moral issue that Tammany would be driven from power forever.

Fiorello! starred Tom Bosley and ran for a healthy 795 performances.

A 1969 musical detailing Jimmy Walker's career, entitled *Jimmy* (unlike *Fiorello!* no exclamation point), fared less well at the Winter Garden

(1634 Broadway). Despite starring Frank Gorshin (as Walker) and Anita Gillette (as Betty Compton; *see* **Algonquin Hotel 59 West 44th Street**), *Jimmy* folded after only eighty-four performances. Perhaps it could have used that exclamation point.

———————

The 1,218-seat Broadhurst opened in 1917 as a Shubert property and has hosted such hits as *The Petrified Forest, Pal Joey, Auntie Mame, My Fair Lady, Cabaret, Grease, Les Misérables, and Mamma Mia!*. In 1928–29 (as Rothstein was being shot), it also hosted the boxing musical *Hold Everything!* featuring Bert Lahr (Rothstein's distant relative) and Mayor Walker's showgirl mistress, the British-born Betty Compton.

40. THE MAJESTIC THEATRE 245 West 44th Street (Between Seventh and Eighth Avenues)

In June and July 1930, the Majestic hosted a short-lived (fifty-five performances) edition of the Shubert Organization's review *Artists and Models* featuring the dancer Sally Ritz (aka Sally Lou Ritz or Sally Lou Ritzi), best known for being Judge Joseph F. Crater's dinner companion on the night of his August 1930 vanishing act, and Elaine Dawn, still another Crater acquaintance (she had accompanied him to the Club Abbey on August 4, 1930), Sally Lou Ritz's roommate, and also a dancer at the Club Abbey. It is said that Crater was "familiar" (whatever that meant) with at least a half dozen of the show's female cast members.

Unless you were hobnobbing with such cast members as Miss Ritz, however, it was hardly a great show. The anonymous (but clearly annoyed) critic for the *Times* damned it as "a dull show which attempts to make up in naughtiness and nudity what it lacks in pace and material . . . an unusually slow-moving and lackadaisical review." Not even an "undraped" glimpse into a ladies' locker room nor a female "dancing contortionist" could save it.

That aside, however, it's never been explained as to why Miss Ritz was having dinner with Crater when she should have been onstage or at least backstage, but, then again, nothing about the Crater case makes much sense.

In November 1929, *Billboard* reported the intriguing news that "SALLY RITZ, ballet dancer and niece of Beatrice Lillie, comedienne, is now a member of the *A Wonderful Night* ballet at the Majestic Theater. New York."

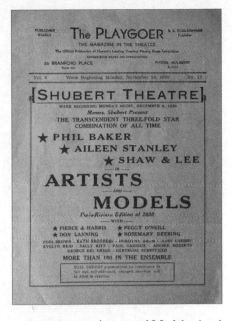

In December 1930, Artists and Models *played Newark—and scandal-tinged Sally Ritz rated billing.* (AUTHOR'S COLLECTION)

It's also known that Judge Crater attended the July 24, 1930, performance of *Artists and Models* at the Majestic Theatre in the company of one Mrs. Constance Braemer "Connie" Marcus, a "model in a 5th Ave. gown shop" and a longtime Crater acquaintance (as well as the recipient of many a Crater check). Mr. Marcus was indisposed while all this transpired, being incarcerated at Atlanta federal penitentiary for bankruptcy.

The 1,800-seat Majestic (among the largest theaters on Broadway) opened in March 1927 only to endure a series of flops under its original owners, the Chanin Brothers—even 1928's thirty-one-performance fiasco, *The Big Fight*, starring Jack Dempsey. The Shuberts gained control in 1929, and eventually the Majestic hosted such hits as *Carousel*, *South Pacific*, *The Music Man*, *Camelot*, *The Wiz*, and *The Phantom of the Opera*.

The original Barbra Streisand version of *Funny Girl* played here in 1966 after premiering in 1964 at the Winter Garden. Dramatis personae included Fanny Brice, Nicky Arnstein, and Flo Ziegfeld. Not included was Arnold Rothstein . . . so to hell with it.

41. HOTEL ASTOR 1511–1515 Broadway (Between West 44th and West 45th Streets)

In September 1919, two small-time operators, former major league pitcher "Sleepy Bill" Burns and former professional boxer Billy Maharg, had a plan to fix the upcoming World Series between the Chicago White Sox and the Cincinnati Reds. They needed large amounts of cash to bankroll their scheme and saw Arnold Rothstein as its logical supplier. They respectfully requested a meeting, and A. R. instructed the duo to meet with him at the Astor Hotel grill. There, at 8:30 p.m., most likely on September 27, 1919, Rothstein (with Val O'Farrell, one of the city's premier private detectives as a witness) exploded at the two, telling them he wanted no part of their idea.

O'Farrell later told a more than slightly different version of events, including New York Giants outfielder Benny Kauff. (*See* **BENNY KAUFF'S AUTOMOBILE ACCESSORIES BUSINESS 135 Columbus Avenue.**)

This is how O'Farrell's version went:

> Just before last year's world series, Rothstein asked me to meet him at the Hotel Astor one afternoon. He had an appointment with somebody and wanted me to be present. After waiting around a while three men came into the lobby. One of them I recognized as Orbie, a Long Island gambler, who is known as a friend of Abe Attell, the former featherweight champion. Benny Kauff was with him and there was another good-sized fellow who I was later told was Billy Burns, but of this I am not sure.

Orbie came over to Rothstein and in my presence asked him if he would listen to a World series proposition. Rothstein turned to me and said, "What do you know about that?" Then, pointing to Benny Kauff, he added: "I wouldn't listen to anything in which that man is concerned."

Orbie went over to Kauff and told him it was all off; that Rothstein wouldn't have anything to do with it because of his connection, and that it would have to be pulled off in another way. The man, unknown to me then, said a few words to Rothstein which I did not hear. The three then got together and walked out.

Rothstein turned to me and said, "Can you beat it? Trying to put over a deal like this with Benny Kauff in it. They are the kind of fellows that are killing baseball. I could never listen to any such proposition as that."

It was all a performance on A. R.'s part, carefully orchestrated to provide deniability in case anything went wrong regarding his own fix already in the works, through former world featherweight champion Abe "The Little Hebrew" Attell; Arnold's Saratoga Spring's gambling house partner Nat Evans (aka "Nate Evens"); and prominent Boston bookmaker Joseph "Sport" Sullivan.

Shortly thereafter, Abe Attell visited the Polo Grounds, home of manager John "The Little Napoleon" McGraw's New York Giants. There, he was informed by Giants first baseman "Prince Hal" Chase (a notorious fixer) that the upcoming Series was about to be thrown and warned not to bet on the White Sox. That news of the fix was leaking out disturbed Attell, and with Sport Sullivan in tow, he conferred with Rothstein at the Astor to warn him of his conversation with Chase.

Only now did Rothstein finally decide to work with Burns and Maharg, grasping the value of such a tangled web. "If nine guys go to bed with a girl," he later remarked about the situation with a smirk, "she'll have a tough time proving the tenth is the father."

Eventually, the fix was exposed, largely thanks to *New York Mail* sportswriter Hugh Fullerton, who wrote in part:

HOTEL ASTOR
TIMES SQUARE,
NEW YORK
Wm.C.MUSCHENHEIM.

(COURTESY OF THE NEW YORK HISTORICAL ASSOCIATION)

Hotel Astor Main Lobby (COURTESY OF COLUMBIA UNIVERSITY LIBRARIES)

There is in New York a gambler named Rothstein who is much feared and much accused. His name has been used in connection with almost every big thieving, crooked deal on the race track, and he is openly named in this baseball scandal. There has been no legal proof advanced against him beyond the fact that he is the only man in the entire crowd who had money enough to handle such a deal. At least $200,000 was used in actual cash, and no one concerned could command that much money excepting Rothstein, who is either the vilest crook or the most abused man in America.

Rothstein sits in the box with [Charles Stoneham,] the owner of the New York Giants. He has the entrée to the exclusive clubhouses on race tracks; he is prominent at fights.

(COURTESY OF COLUMBIA UNIVERSITY LIBRARIES)

Rothstein's suspected involvement led to his questioning by a Chicago grand jury (a tactic advised by Bill Fallon). Rothstein escaped unscathed (except, most likely, for outlays of cash to sandbag the wheels of justice). The episode also led to Rothstein informing the *New York Mail* on September 7, 1921: "From now on, I shall devote most of my attention to my racing stables and my real estate business. It is not pleasant to be, what some call, a 'social outcast.' For the sake of my family and my friends, I am glad that chapter of my life is over."

Not very likely.

In 1904, Lord William Waldorf Astor brought the city's biggest and grandest hotel close to Times Square—the opulent Astor (900 rooms, 600 baths)—at Broadway at West 44th Street. Its bar soon would be among Manhattan's most prominent homosexual gathering places. Replaced by One Astor Plaza in 1969.

(above left) *Herman "Beansie" Rosenthal* (above right) *"Big Tim" Sullivan* (AUTHOR'S COLLECTION)

42. HERMAN ROSENTHAL'S GAMBLING HOUSE 104 West 45th Street (Just West of Sixth Avenue, a rented

three-story brownstone) Herman "Beansie" Rosenthal and Rothstein were both protégés of Tammany's "Big Tim" Sullivan. "They're smart Jew boys," said Sullivan, "they're going places."

In November 1911, Sullivan, Rosenthal, and a brutal and corrupt NYPD named Lieutenant Charles Becker became partners in this gambling house. Soon, however, Sullivan began suffering from dementia, and the greedy and brutal Becker seized the opportunity to shake down Rosenthal for a bigger share of the take. Despite warnings from Rothstein, Rosenthal stubbornly wouldn't play ball, and approached Herbert Bayard Swope's *New York World* with the story. Swope directed Rosenthal to Republican District Attorney Charles Whitman, only further fueling Becker's rage. "I don't want him beat up," Becker ordered an associate. "I could do that myself. I could have a warrant for any gambling house that he frequents and make a raid on that place and beat him up for resisting arrest or anything else. No beating up will fix that fellow, a dog in the eyes of myself, you, and everybody else. Nothing for that man but taken off this earth. Have him murdered, cut his throat, dynamited, or anything."

Anything finally happened at the Hotel Metropole. (*See* **HOTEL METROPOLE 142-149 West 43rd Street.**)

Demolished.

43. **EL FEY CLUB 107 West 45th Street (West of Sixth Avenue, second floor)** During Prohibition, Rothstein bankrolled all aspects of the illegal liquor trade: rumrunning, bootlegging, speakeasies, political protection. One speakeasy he funded was racketeer Larry Fay's popular El Fey nightclub featuring hostess Mary Louise Cecilia "Texas" Guinan (a former silent films Western star—"The Female Two-Gun Bill Hart") and her catchphrases, "Hello, sucker!" and "Let's Give the Little Lady a Great Big Hand!" Ruby Keeler, Barbara Stanwyck (still known as Ruby Stevens), and George Raft (he started at $150 a week) all performed as dancers at El Fey.

"Hello, sucker!" was, however, not the phrase that most assumed it to be.

As Guinan's friend *New York Daily Mirror* editor Jack Lait later explained:

> As each show went on, Larry [Fay], would stand in the extreme rear, where it was dark and where he—always in plain blue serge suit, white silk shirt and black windsor tie—was inconspicuous. As Texas would mount her chair (that was how she worked) she would look across the long room at him. And, thinking of the [long-term] lease [Fay held on the joint], her [own lucrative] pay, the flop [of a Fay romance that caused Fay to hire Guinan rather than a paramour who jilted him and flew the coop to Florida], she would cast a glance right over the heads of the audience and call out—to him—"Hello, sucker!"
>
> Through some phenomenal human quirk, every other sucker in between thought it was addressed to him. And, as strangely, every man liked it. It became her trademark, long after Larry passed out of her picture . . . she still featured it—his only monument.

(clockwise from upper left) *Texas Guinan Amid a Distinctly Youthful-Looking Chorus Line; The El Fey Club; Larry Fay* (AUTHOR'S COLLECTION)

Guinan, it must be admitted (or, at least, according to Lait), was unusually solicitous of the virtue of her club's chorus girls. "Many a contented matron," Lait wrote in 1948, "perhaps now turning 40, may remember what a demon chaperone she was."

Yet not all such clubs were hardly all innocent merriment—no, not at all. As Loyola University's Lewis Erenberg observed: "Unscrupulous club operators operated 'clip joints' barely a step above whorehouses. These 'closed door' spots relied heavily on out-of-town buyers and cheating husbands seeking to blow off steam, as [Jimmy] Durante put it. Often run by low level criminals, they paid cab drivers and waiters at other clubs to steer unsuspecting customers to their spots. These club owners were also not above changing the sums on the checks of drunk patrons or using 'knock-out' drops to facilitate a robbery."

The El Fey Club was raided and closed in April 1925.

Formerly the home of the Friars Club (1908–1916). Demolished.

Fun Fact: Larry Fay *loved* swastikas. Before Adolf Hitler's National Socialists co-opted this ancient symbol, it was fairly popular and definitely non-controversial. Fay was particularly enamored of them, emblazoning not only his El Fey Club with swastikas (see photo on previous page) but also his sizable fleet of taxicabs.

44. BRIDGIE WEBBER'S FARO HOUSE 117 West 45th Street (Between Sixth and Seventh Avenues) In early 1911, "Bridgie" Webber, in cooperation with his partner "Jew" Brown, opened a faro house at this address, becoming the first members of the downtown "Hester Street" gambling crowd to operate a gambling house in the rising Times Square neighborhood.

45. JOHN J. "JOHN THE BARBER" REISLER BARBER SHOP 169 West 45th Street (Between Sixth and Seventh Avenues) Once, while Arnold Rothstein was receiving his usual shave and haircut here, the conversation turned to racing, and someone casually mentioned a specific race. Another party chimed in that it was just about to run—which was not true at all. It already ran. At this point. A. R. piped up, "Well, I'll bet you that such and such a horse wins." It did, and whispers flew that the Big Bankroll had again practiced sure-thing betting, arranging the whole scenario including having the actual results tipped to him by a prearranged signal, such as having an accomplice order a "close" shave.

Austrian-born "John the Barber" Reisler (née Jacob Reisler) was no ordinary tonsorial artiste. As he explained to the press in 1929: "I've been a theatrical manager, a fight manager, a shipbuilder, an oil promoter and now I'm a barber. Al Jolson and Georgie Cohan used to work for me at $25 a week. I managed Jack Dempsey in his early days. I started [actress] May Ward on the road to fame.

Not surprisingly, the newspapers enjoyed a field day with 1922's Reisler–Katz murder case.
(AUTHOR'S COLLECTION)

"When I went broke in the show business in 1907 I went to oil, made thousands, lost them and made more in shipbuilding . . . I've shaved the most important theatrical faces in New York."

Interesting enough. But hardly the most startling portions of his varied bio.

In 1912, Reisler had been a key (though inconsistent) witness in the Beansie Rosenthal murder case, first testifying that he had seen Bridgie Webber fleeing the scene of the shooting—before fearfully recanting his testimony. Manhattan district attorney Charles Whitman threatened him with perjury charges, and Reisler quickly recanted his recantation.

In March 1923, Reisler's son Morris (convicted of burglary in 1916) was sentenced to Sing Sing for twenty-years-to-life for the fatal July 1922 shooting of Morris's maternal aunt, twenty-eight-year-old Miss Bertha Katz, after Morris's mother (John the Barber's wife), the *distinctly* unattractive Mrs. Minnie Reisler, had accused her younger more comely sister of purloining her husband's affections (she phrased it "love piracy"). Miss Katz at one time served as a cashier at Reisler's West 45th Street shop.

"She was regarded as a pretty woman," noted the *Morning Telegraph* regarding Bertha, "unmistakably of the dark, Jewish type, clever and intelligent."

Forty-four-year-old Minnie Reisler ("I'm only sorry I didn't kill them both") consistently claimed credit for sister Bertha's slaying. In fact, however, it was a family affair, with Minnie; twenty-four-year-old Morris; Morris's nineteen-year-old brother, George (arrested in March 1928 for a Brooklyn burglary); and Minnie's twenty-six-year-old brother, Max, all involved in fatally gunning down Bertha.

For frosting on the cake, they did it in front of Bertha and Minnie's widowed mother, the seventy-three-year-old Mrs. Jennie Katz.

For the maraschino cherry atop the frosting, as Morris plugged Bertha, Minnie called out to him regarding her own mother: "Save one for the old witch."

Unsuccessfully assisting in representing Morris Reisler on murder charges was Charles Whitman's former Manhattan assistant district attorney, George Z. Medalie. Only a few months later, Medalie proved more successful in defending Rothstein in a trial regarding the failed Wall Street bucket shop of E. M. Fuller. Medalie later served as U.S. Attorney for the Southern District of New York and as a mentor to crime-busting Thomas E. Dewey.

Governor Franklin D. Roosevelt pardoned Morris in March 1930.

46. WILLIAM WOLGAST RESIDENCE 327 West 45th Street (Between Eighth and Ninth Avenues) Wolgast, thirty-nine, had the fatal misfortune to be working as a waiter at Leg Diamond's Hotsy Totsy Club on Saturday evening, July 13, 1929, when Diamond rubbed out fellow speakeasy owner William "Red" Cassidy. (*See* **THE HOTSY TOTSY CLUB 1721 Broadway**.)

Six days later, as the *Brooklyn Standard Union* reported, "police found Wolgast's bullet-riddled body on a lonely stretch of road known as Bordentown turnpike, between Cold Bridge and South Amboy, N. J., according to State police. The body was identified by means of fingerprints, which showed that Wolgast had been arrested in 1922 as a waiter who sold liquor. He had been killed by machine gun bullets. . . . The body was found . . . by workmen on their way to the plant of the Ceramics Products Corporation. It was three feet from the edge of the road and, from its position, apparently had been tossed there from an automobile. There were bullets in the arms, back, and head, and Wolgast had been dead for several hours."

"Police," reported the *New York Daily News*, "insisted the murder . . . had nothing to do with the Hotsy Totsy murders. They insisted Wolgast was merely a small-time beer runner killed by rivals."

Wolgast was lucky. At least his body was found. The bodies of three other potential witnesses—those of two other waiters and Hotsy Totsy Club manager Hymie Cohen—never were.

47. BILLY HAAS'S CHOPHOUSE 332 West 45th Street (Between Eighth and Ninth Avenues) On the night of Tuesday, August 6, 1930, New York State Supreme Court justice Joseph Force Crater, an alleged associate of Rothstein and Legs Diamond, dined here with his friend William Klein, an attorney with the Shubert Organization, the seventeen-year-old dancer Sally Ritz (née Ritzi), and Miss Ritz's parents, visiting from Youngstown, Ohio. Departing alone, Crater supposedly boarded a taxicab, never to be seen again. His disap-

Sally Ritz (left), *Elaine Dawn* (right), *and the "Honorable" Judge Joseph F. Crater* (bottom) (AUTHOR'S COLLECTION)

pearance remains the mystery of the twentieth century.

"If he is alive," mused a 1932 press account, "a secondary mystery is how a man with such unusual characteristics can remain undiscovered after his photograph and description have been spread so widely throughout virtually the entire civilized world.

"For Crater's appearance was such as would attract attention anywhere. Although he was six feet tall and weighed 185 pounds, his head was so small that he wore a size 6 1/8 hat. With all his bulk, he had a long, thin neck, and wore a size 14 collar."

Crater, an active Tammany Democrat, had served as Supreme Court justice (and future U.S. senator) Robert F. Wagner's secretary from 1920 through 1926 and also once as president of West Harlem's Cayuga Democratic Club at 131 West 122nd Street.

Crater was widely suspected of corruption, and it was the unveiling of such corruption in the New York City courts, the police department, and within Tammany Hall that eventually led to the fall of both Tammany and its high-living mayor, James J. "Gentleman Jimmy" Walker.

In 1930, federal agents raided the joint, arresting the Swiss-born Haas and three of his waiters. "The prisoners," noted one press account, "were taken to the W. 47th St. station and locked up on charges of sale and possession. . . . More than 150 persons were in Haas' restaurant. They were told to leave. None lost any time in complying."

Haas died in 1953.

48. HOTEL WENTWORTH 57 West 46th Street (Between Fifth and Sixth Avenues)

Lillian Lorraine resided here in 1922, and on December 27 of that year reported to police the theft three days earlier of the assorted contents of her jewel box, an ermine coat, plus a leopard skin coat. When her estranged husband, Fred Gresheimer, heard the news, he called to offer his assistance. "Oh, indeed you can. I've been wondering where you were. Just wait where you are for a moment." He did, and shortly thereafter was served with legal papers for the legal separation now desired by Lorraine.

The Wentworth began life as the Hotel Patterson, switching names in 1913. Late in life, silent film star Nita Naldi (co-star of Rudolph Valentino's *The Sheik*) lived there in very straightened circumstances, her rent payments being assisted by a motion picture relief fund.

Swindler George Graham Rice resided here in December 1908 when charged with fraud regarding Nevada mining stock.

The hotel is now the "Hotel at Times Square."

"The convenience of Broadway, with the exclusiveness of Fifth Avenue."

Hotel Patterson
58 West 47th Street.

A few desirable suites of 2 to 4 rooms with bath, extremely well appointed, to rent for the season. A well equipped hotel. Restaurant a la carte.

49. **HOTEL RICHMOND 70–72 West 46th Street (Between Fifth and Sixth Avenues)** Owned by Salvatore Spitale, an associate of Rothstein henchman Legs Diamond. Spitale and his partner Irving Bitz (a strong suspect in Diamond's December 1931 murder) were later designated as emissaries by a desperate Col. Charles Lindbergh to help solve the March 1932 kidnapping of Lindbergh's infant son. Bitz, long active in mob circles, disappeared on September 2, 1981—himself held for $150,000 ransom. Weeks later, his brutally beaten body washed up on the Staten Island shoreline.

───────────

Moderately successful Broadway, vaudeville, and motion picture actress Doris Sheerin (aka Mrs. Mary Elizabeth Dilson) was a longtime resident. She was, however, far more successful in cajoling the Rothstein-connected bucket shop operator "Dandy Phil" Kastel to part with a good portion of his ill-gotten gains from 1921's failure of his brokerage firm Dillon & Co. "The robber-dude," noted the *Daily News*, "treated her to every comfort a luxury-loving actress desires." (*See* **CHARLES A. STONEHAM APARTMENT 110 West 55th Street.**)

Sheerin, later a nightclub hostess, seemed to attract trouble. Or, at least, cars related to her did. In January 1923, she was involved in a Baltimore auto crash in which a male companion was killed.

At 3:09 p.m. on Saturday, June 17, 1928, while stopped at a Herald Square red light in Sheerin's gray-green Hudson Coupe, forty-five-year-old Chicago bootlegger and pickpocket Ed Carter (aka Edwin J. Jerge, E. Jack

Kayton, Harold Atwater, Edward Mack, among his many aliases) was shot six times when a blue sedan pulled alongside and a tall, heavyset man got out and opened fire. The twenty-nine-year-old Sheerin (who was to meet Carter later and West 51st Street and Broadway) was not aboard. A mysterious "woman in pink," who quickly melted into the crowd, was. Sheerin would not admit to knowing this mysterious passenger's identity. Carter died on the operating table a half hour later.

Doris Sheerin (COURTESY OF THE LIBRARY OF CONGRESS)

50. ARNOLD ROTHSTEIN'S GAMBLING HOUSE

108 West 46th Street, (Near Sixth Avenue) In 1909, Arnold Rothstein borrowed $2,000 from his new father-in-law, butcher Meyer Greenwald, to finally open his own gambling house in this three-story brownstone.

The house provided Rothstein with the opportunity to become Broadway's "Big Bankroll." He operated this establishment until the public outrage that followed Beansie Rosenthal's murder finally shuttered such houses.

Demolished.

Carolyn Rothstein recalled.

This house, my first home if it could be called that, was on the south side of the street, next to a garage which formerly had been a stable. The way I knew it had been a stable was this. One night I was sitting alone in the dining room when I heard a peculiar noise, a gnawing sound. I asked Thomas [Farley], our Negro houseman, what it was, and he said:

"Rats, Mrs. Rothstein. Rats always hang around a stable." We had exterminators of all kinds, ferrets and what not, constantly busy in that house, but it never was freed of the rats.

In this block were four or five music publishing concerns, sources of a great din. What air of respectability the street was able to show was offered by a church [The Episcopal Church of St. Mary the Virgin] *on the north side.*

The house when we took it was a brownstone front, three story and basement affair. The kitchen and dining room were on the ground floor. The first floor entered from the stoop, was taken up by two big rooms which had been designed as parlors, and the second floor held two bedrooms and a bath.

Our bedroom was in the rear room on the second floor. Because Arnold slept daytimes he always slept as far away from street noises as possible, and always had a big leather screen which stood against the windows to shut out light. . . .

I used to sit up in my bedroom and listen to the roulette wheel to learn whether the house was winning or losing. This was simple because if the house won, all that was necessary was for the croupier to rake in chips, but if the house lost, he had to take time to count out chips for the winners. Thus, when the house was winning the wheel spun with short stops, but if the house was losing the wheel spun with long stops.

Rothstein was still residing here (or at least claiming it as an address) when World War I rolled around, and he was required to register for conscription. (*See* **THE FITZGERALD BUILDING 1482 Broadway.**)

51. GLOBE THEATRE 205 West 46th Street (Between Broadway and Times Square)

GLOBE THEATRE 205 West 46th Street (Between Broadway and Times Square) Legs Diamond's girlfriend Kiki Roberts appeared here in the cast of Florenz Ziegfeld's two-act 1926 review *No Foolin'*, billed under her far less glamorous actual name of Marion Strasmick. Also appearing were humorist Arthur "Bugs" Baer; the popular blackface comedians Mack and Moran; columnist Mark Hellinger's future wife, Gladys Glad; and the young Paulette Goddard.

(above left) *Florenz Ziegfeld, Gladys Glad, and Mark Hellinger* (COURTESY OF UNIVERSITY OF MASSACHUSETTS AMHERST LIBRARIES SPECIAL COLLECTIONS AND UNIVERSITY ARCHIVES) (above right) *Kiki Roberts* (AUTHOR'S COLLECTION)

Diana Lanzetta, robbed by Jimmy Meehan at the Ansonia Hotel (*see* **THE ANSONIA HOTEL West 73rd Street and Broadway** *and* **JIMMY MEEHAN'S HOME 128 West 67th Street**) in 1937, was a *Ziegfeld* girl here in the *Ziegfeld Follies'* 1921 edition. As was Rothstein drug henchman George D. Uffner's lover, Edna Wheaton. (*See* **EDNA WHEATON APARTMENT 39 West 76th Street.**) Starring in the cast were the usual *Ziegfeld* suspects Fanny Brice and W. C. Fields.

Built in 1910, the 1,519-seat Globe converted to a movie theater in 1932 before being renamed the Lunt-Fontanne in 1958 and reverting to a legitimate theater.

52. **FULTON THEATRE 210 West 46th Street, Near Broadway** *Abie's Irish Rose,* a play chronicling the romance between the Jewish Abraham Levy and his Irish sweetheart, Rosemary Murphy, opened here on May 23, 1922, to lukewarm reviews and smallish audiences. Playwright Anne Nichols, however, retained faith in her creation. To keep the show alive until audiences built, she approached A. R. for $25,000. In return, she offered an interest in the show. Rothstein refused and held out for a standard Rothstein business loan—exorbitant interest plus forcing Nichols to take out several policies with his insurance agency. For once, the Great Brain outsmarted himself. *Abie's Irish Rose* survived to become Jazz Age Broadway's greatest hit, running a then-record 2,327 performances. Rothstein, who could have reaped a fortune, instead, netted a measly $3,000 on the deal.

Originally built in 1911 as a Parisian-style nightclub ("The Folies Bergere"), the Fulton was renamed the Helen Hayes Theater in 1955. Along with five other theaters, it was demolished in 1982 to make way for the Marriott Marquis Hotel.

In July 1922, *Abie's Irish Rose* transferred to 42nd Street's Republic Theatre where it ran until October 22, 1927. The Republic became a burlesque house in 1931 and, as the Victory Theater, converted to movies in May 1942.

(AUTHOR'S COLLECTION)

53. DINTY MOORE'S 216 West 46th Street West of Broadway

Where, in 1920, Abe Attell brazenly informed White Sox manager William "Kid" Gleason of fixing the 1919 World Series. Opened by James Moore on March 7, 1914. Like the Fulton Theatre, demolished for construction of the Marriott Hotel.

Kid Gleason: *So it was Arnold Rothstein who put up the dough for the fix.*
Abe Attell: *That was it, Kid. You know, Kid, I hated to do that to you, but I thought I was going to make a lot of money and I needed it, and then the big guy* [Rothstein] *double-crossed me, and I never got but a small part of what he promised."*

In 2016, *Playbill* magazine noted:

Over the years, [Dinty Moore's] was populated by everyone from Walter Winchell to Will Rogers to Audrey Hepburn to Frank Sinatra to Judy Garland. Bob Fosse and Gwen Verdon were said to have re-choreographed dances at the restaurant, away from the hubbub of the theatre. Florenz Ziegfeld was so depressed after the audience left the opening night of Show Boat *in silence, that he spent the night drowning his sorrows at Dinty Moore's—before returning to the New Amsterdam the next morning to discover lines around the block to buy tickets.*

Legend has it that George S. Kaufman was once kicked out of Dinty Moore's for ordering a hamburger without onions. James Moore was known for booting even the most notable of his patrons, and this time, he hollered, "I don't tell you how to write your g-ddamned plays, don't tell me how to serve my hamburgers!" In 1932, George S. Kaufman and Edna Ferber's play Dinner at Eight *opened around the corner at the Music Box, with a character uttering a passingly throw-away line: "I've only got a minute. I got a classy dinner date—I've got to meet a hamburger with onions, at Dinty Moore's."*

54. THE 46TH STREET THEATRE 226 West 46th Street (Between Broadway and Eighth Avenue) Here on

November 24, 1950, debuted the Broadway entertainment most associated with Arnold Rothstein and his world: Frank Loesser's brilliant musical *Guys and Dolls*, based upon Damon Runyon's tales of a begone Broadway. It's generally acknowledged that Runyon modeled the show's primary characters, Nathan Detroit and Sky Masterson, on Arnold Rothstein and Titanic Thompson, respectively. Unlike 1955's film version, *Guys and Dolls'* original Broadway production starred Sam Levene (not Frank Sinatra) as Detroit/Rothstein and Robert Alda (not Marlon Brando) as Masterson/Thompson. Both versions featured floating crap games, speakeasys, and a barely disguised Lindy's restaurant ("Mindy's").

Guys and Dolls' original 1950 production ran for an even 1,200 performances.

The 46th Street Theatre was built in 1925 by the Chanin brothers, Irwin and Henry, but was immediately leased to the Shubert Organization, who ended up purchasing it in 1931. Acquired by the Nederlanders in 1982, they renamed it the Richard Rodgers in 1990 (fending off an attempt to rename it after Ethel Merman).

The 1,319-seat theater has hosted such hits as *Anything Goes*, *Hellzapoppin'*, *Finian's Rainbow* (twice), *Damn Yankees*, *How to Succeed in Business Without Really Trying* (twice), *Chicago*, *In the Heights*, and *Hamilton*.

Original *Guys and Dolls* star Sam Levene boasts another Rothstein-style connection, this one in the iconic Robert Stack television series *The Untouchables*. Since even Chicago possessed only a finite cohort of gangsters, Eliot Ness/Robert Stack and the Untouchables would occasionally depart the Windy City to present rather fanciful versions of Prohibition-era New York, including episodes highlighting Legs Diamond, Dutch Schultz, Waxey Gordon, Ciro "The Artichoke King" Terranova (Rothstein's tenant at the Fairfield Hotel), and all-around racketeer Larry Fay. Despite looking nothing like the horse-faced, clean-shaven Fay, the mustachioed Levene got the job of portraying Fay.

He also portrayed the Rothstein-associated labor racketeer Louis Lepke Buchalter in David Susskind's 1961–62 CBS courtroom docudrama series *The Witness*.

Evidently, once a gangster always a gangster.

The Witness's pilot episode—one that never aired—profiled none other than Arnold Rothstein himself with Telly Savalas (!) in the title role. Savalas ended up starring in three other episodes, however, as Lucky Luciano, Al Capone, *and* Roger Touhy!

55. CAFÉ MADRID 1551 Broadway (Northwest Corner of West 47th Street)

Once, this was Churchill's, a popular eatery of the gaslight era. In the 1920s, it housed the Café Madrid, and Arnold Rothstein would meet there with one of his tenants at 28–30 West 57th Street (and then, supposedly, on East 17th Street; though the address may actually have been 5 East 19th Street), prominent stock swindler George Graham Rice. (*See* **HOTEL WENTWORTH 57 West 46th Street.**)

Rice (née Jacob Simon Herzig) pulled millions of dollars in scams. Like Rothstein, Rice came from respectable stock, his father being a Lower East Side furrier. Also akin to Rothstein, Rice was an inveterate gambler—though, in his case, a poor (or, at least, an unlucky) one. Twice to cover his losses, he stole—from his father—and twice ended up in Sing Sing.

After a 1911 conviction for stock fraud, Rice professed to go straight and in 1913 penned a tell-all confessional entitled *My Adventures with Your Money*. In April 1914, the supposedly repentant Rice opened his own brokerage—downtown at 27 William Street—probably with Rothstein's backing. Rothstein also eventually set Rice up with a new attorney: none other than William J. Fallon.

Of the Rothstein-Rice relationship, Rice biographer T. D. Thornton posited that "both men's business acumen was sound and authoritative. The two equated money with power, honesty with weakness, and found

The Café Madrid and Rector's (COURTESY OF COLUMBIA UNIVERSITY LIBRARIES)

'straight' people dull, even disdainful. Self-preservation was a highly honed instinct, based on the core belief that if someone was less intelligent than you, it was up to you to take advantage of the person. If you didn't, somebody else would."

Rice, a onetime racing form tip sheet publisher, now launched the *Iconoclast*, eventually the nation's largest circulation business newspaper. The *Iconoclast* initially provided investors with reasonable advice, but once Rice had established his paper's credibility, he employed its columns to steer readers into such fraudulent stocks as Columbian Emerald Co. and Idaho Copper. When a disgruntled subordinate finally exposed Rice's last round of machinations, he went into hiding but eventually served more jail time—this time at Atlanta. His cellmate: Al Capone.

The Café Madrid's site later housed one of the last remaining Howard Johnson's Restaurants (first floor) and the Gaiety Burlesque (second floor).

56. "CRIPPLE CREEK" West 47th Street, Broadway to Sixth Avenue "Cripple Creek" was the nickname for this

stretch of West 47th Street, noted as the hangout of unemployed musicians, but also once as a hotbed of fixed dice games.

As showbiz historians Abel Green and Joe Laurie Jr. wrote:

> In the heyday of the 1920s, when floating crap games got a big play in peripatetic gambling joints over a garage, in a mortuary, and places like that, there were a bunch of sharpshooters in the neighborhood of New York's Somerset Hotel [150 West 47th Street], hard by the Palace Theatre stage door on West 47th St., which got to be known as the Grouchbaggers. Acts coming off of an extended Pan, WVMA or Orpheum [vaudeville] route—even those playing the "death trail" houses for Ackerman & Harris, Gus Sun and the T. & D. Junior Orpheum time—invariably had their ready cash in the traditional actor's "grouchbag." This was a form of suspended money-belt worn underneath the man's shirt. . . .
>
> The 47th St. sharpies knew that, and many a tragedy occurred with educated dice when a glad-to-be-back vaudevillian indulged in the camaraderie so typical of the itinerant trouper. The dice cheaters knew their timing well; the *Variety* route lists always cued who was "due to come off the route," and naturally the first stop was in the Palace Theatre orbit. It was against these that [*Variety* publisher] Sime [Silverman] trained his guns, and only the threat of publication of names kayoed this mob.

57. THE COLUMBIA THEATRE 701 Seventh Avenue at the North-east Corner of West 47th Street

It was here in 1910 where Florenz Ziegfeld first discovered Fanny Brice. The theater was then part of the "Columbia Circuit" that presented "clean burlesque," very similar to vaudeville's family-friendly standards. It closed in 1927, but RKO re-opened it as a movie house, The Mayfair, in October 1930. It survived as a movie theater under a number of different names and owners until 1998. Its last tenant, before the building's demolition in 2015, was a Famous Dave's BBQ Restaurant.

On May 5, 1932, RKO's *State's Attorney* premiered here, starring John Barrymore as a vaguely Bill Fallon–type, brilliant-but-drunk mobster-defending attorney ("Tom Cardigan") in a rather implausible script penned by Fallon biographer Gene Fowler.

Movies approximately based on Fallon were momentarily all the rage. Besides Barrymore in *State's Attorney*, they included Edmund Lowe in that year's *Attorney for the Defense*, William Powell in 1930's *For the Defense*, and Warren William in 1932's *The Mouthpiece*, which premiered that April at the Winter Garden (1634 Broadway).

Columbia Burlesque Ad from December 1913
(AUTHOR'S COLLECTION)

The Mouthpiece was essentially remade twice: as 1940's *The Man Who Knew Too Much*, starring George Brent, and as 1955's *Illegal*, with Edward G. Robinson.

All of these guys (save Robinson), for some reason, had mustaches. Fallon did not.

Warren William (great in anything), by the way, would have been particularly great as Nicky Arnstein.

For its part, RKO remade *State's Attorney* in 1937 as *Criminal Lawyer*, starring the clean-shaven, fast-talking Lee Tracy as the Fallon character. Again, the film took stupefying liberties with Bill Fallon's actual story, but if anyone was made to portray Fallon, it would have been Tracy.

Tracy's *Criminal Lawyer*'s mob (and gambling house) patron, by the way, is, when shot, taken to Polyclinic Hospital, where he refuses to identify his assailant—a situation, of course, sounding more than a bit familiar. That, however, remains his sole resemblance to Rothstein.

Criminal Lawyer premiered at the Rialto Theatre (1141 Broadway at 42nd Street). (*See* **HAMMERSTEIN'S VICTORIA 201 West 42nd**

Street.) The *New York Times* assessed *Criminal Lawyer* as "the best job of its kind."

Lee Tracy pulls out all the patented Bill Fallon–style courtroom stops in 1937's Criminal Lawyer. (AUTHOR'S COLLECTION)

Abel Green and Joe Laurie Jr. noted of the theater:

> Sam S. Scribner was partial to Japanese ushers at his Columbia (burlesque) Theatre on Broadway and 47th Street (now the Mayfair); the Japs were Columbia University students.

58. **HOTEL ST. FRANCIS 124-26 West 47th Street (Between Sixth and Seventh Avenues)** On the night of May 16, 1917, gunmen burst into a floating card game hosted here by Rothstein. The game's thirty-odd participants included several well-heeled professionals, including Herbert Bayard Swope. A. R. employed the usual precautions but took one chance. In recent weeks gunmen had robbed several big games, relieving players of cash, jewelry, and sundry valuables.

One individual had attended a high percentage of them. Rothstein invited him to attend the night's festivities.

Four hours later, four masked men broke into the room. Arnold instantly knew who had betrayed him. He also quickly knew how to minimize losses, kicking his bankroll (somewhere between $20,000 and $60,000) under the carpet. All the while he maintained eye contact with his Judas.

Herbert Bayard Swope: *Rothstein always reacted faster than any other man I ever knew. This was as good an example of his reaction time as you could want. There were only a few seconds for him to figure out what was happening. He didn't need more than one or two. But hiding the roll was only part of what he had to do. He had to make certain the tipster didn't tell the holdup men where the bankroll was.*

His eyes were on that man from the moment the door swung open. He kept him under constant watch all the time the holdup was going on.

A. R. saved the bulk of his bankroll, but did lose $2,600 in cash, his gold pocket watch, plus a pearl stickpin.

While one intruder kept his weapon trained on his victims, his two partners collected their loot, becoming increasingly relaxed. One even removed his mask.

Swope entreated Rothstein to talk to the police, goading him with accusations that he was simply too afraid to bring the law into the case. Police arrested thirty-five-year-old small-time hoodlum named Eugene F. Price and twenty-eight-year-old drug addict Albert "Killer" Johnson. Johnson was the more dangerous of the pair, twice having been charged with murder. A. R. testified. Both criminals were convicted. As Killer Johnson's guilty verdict came in, he had to be restrained from attacking Arnold, threatening revenge if he ever got free. Two months later, Johnson escaped from Sing Sing.

A. R.'s friends advised him to skip town—or at least go into seclusion. Swope, worried that his gamesmanship might now lead to his friend's death—was among them. Arnold ignored him.

On more than one occasion, Johnson nearly nabbed Rothstein. One night he tailed A. R. to the dining room at Reisenweber's Hotel (50 rooms, 20 baths) at West 58th Street, on Columbus Circle. Johnson waited outside in a cab, sending word to Arnold that someone wanted to see him. A. R. didn't take the bait. He sent private detective Val O'Farrell (one-time boss of George McManus) outside to investigate. Johnson fled and shortly thereafter exited New York for the Midwest.

There, at Bedford, Ohio, in October 1921, Johnson tried robbing a particularly vulnerable-looking small town bank. He had not, however, counted on its unusual alarm system. Instead of merely alerting the local police, its bells clanged in dozens of local homes. The citizenry grabbed their rifles and shotguns and headed in the direction of their deposits. The scene must have resembled (i.e., inspired) the demise of bank robber Homer Van Meter (Harry Dean Stanton) in John Milius's 1973 biopic, *Dillinger*.

Arnold Rothstein never had to worry about the late Albert "Killer" Johnson again.

The St. Francis (110 rooms, 45 baths) later became the Hotel Stanley, and in November 1928, a federal grand jury questioned a Hotel Stanley resident and a former Rothstein love interest, Gertie Ward ("a raven-haired actress with big eyes"), regarding her late lover's involvement in the narcotics trade.

"[S]he denied knowing either Rothstein," reported the *New York Evening Post*, "or Miss Inez Norton, the former show girl who was made a beneficiary in the gambler's deathbed will."

At some point following this, the hotel's name reverted to the St. Francis.

Reisenweber's opened for business circa 1856 when the area was still farmland. By 1910, it had survived to become a massive entertainment and dining complex, employing a thousand persons, popularizing the emerging ballroom dancing craze, and hosting such entertainers as Sophie

Tucker and the Original Dixieland Jass Band, the first jazz band to really go mainstream and, in 1917, to record the first jazz phonograph records.

Prohibition eventually led to the establishment's demise, having been first raided in June 1920 after crack Prohibition agent Izzy Einstein (posing as a rabbi entertaining some friends from out of town) purchased six drinks at four dollars apiece.

Renamed the Paradise Restaurant, authorities finally padlocked the joint for a year in January 1923.

Later a Woolworth's department store. Demolished in the 1980s.

Reisenweber's Ad from 1924
(AUTHOR'S COLLECTION)

Reisenweber's
Multitudinous Waitstaff
(AUTHOR'S COLLECTION)

The Original Dixieland Jass Band (AUTHOR'S COLLECTION)

59. BILL FALLON'S BIRTHPLACE 134 West 47th Street ■ (Between Sixth and Seventh Avenues) Four-story

brownstone birthplace of Bill Fallon on January 23, 1886; demolished in 1904 to make way for the Hotel Portland (now the Portland Square Hotel); next door to the mission house of the Church of St. Mary the Virgin (Episcopal). Said Fallon of Rothstein: "Rothstein is a man who dwells in doorways. A mouse standing in a doorway, waiting for his cheese."

Fallon had begun his legal career respectably enough, as an assistant district attorney of Westchester County but claimed to have pangs of conscience regarding convicting presumably innocent defendants. He moved back to the city in 1918, exhibiting no such pangs regarding defending outrageously *guilty* defendants, often at Rothstein's behest, and including a whole raft of crooked Wall Street operators.

He specialized in hung juries (some send *bribed* juries) and in spectacular and outrageous courtroom stunts.

"I never manufactured any more situations than did the prosecution," he once defended himself. "If you mean a psychological effect, I think, off-hand, of the time I was defending a dumb fellow on a murder-charge, first degree. I got him a rosary and told him to wear it in his breast pocket, with a big handkerchief wrapped about it. He kicked, saying he was a Methodist; that a rosary was bad luck. I said: 'You do as I say, and when I lean over and point at you while you're on the stand, you start bawling and crying. Then pull out the handkerchief and let the rosary fall to the floor.' We had to rehearse the thing at least twenty times. I saw to it that several Catholics were on the jury. The day my client went on the stand, I worked him into a rather genuine cry. I pointed my finger, but

William J. Fallon (AUTHOR'S COLLECTION)

he didn't go through with the plan. I had to work on him some more, this time to lessen his grief to a point where he might respond to cues. Then I leaned over, cocked the old fore-finger and roared: 'Please don't cry. I know it is hard, but I must ask these questions. Use your handkerchief.' This roused the dumb cluck. He hauled out the kerchief and the rosary fell to the floor. I noticed that some of the jurymen almost jumped over the rail. Well, he was acquitted. I suppose the rosary didn't do him any harm."

60. **LYONS THEATRICAL AGENCY 245 West 47th Street**
Bertha Katz, paramour of "John the Barber" Reisler (*see*

JOHN J. "JOHN THE BARBER" REISLER BARBER SHOP **169 West 45th Street**), worked here at the time of her 1922 slaying. Coincidentally, the individual eventually convicted of her murder, her nephew Morris Reisler, operated a clothing store nearby at West 47th and Broadway.

61. THE PUBLICITY BUILDING 1572-76 Broadway (at West 47th Street; Between Broadway and Seventh Avenue) Another location where Owney Madden and his chums George "Frenchy" DeMange and "Big Bill" Duffy once maintained offices to oversee his boxing (and presumably other less legal) interests. His most renowned pugilist being the Italian-born heavyweight champion Primo Carnera.

The Publicity Building, noted George Raft's biographer Lewis Yablonsky, "also held the offices of many other enterprises, including vaudeville booking agents, lawyers, and boxing promoters. At almost any time of the day or night, fight managers, pugs, hoofers, out-of-work actors, and smalltime gangsters would mingle together in front of the building."

If you wanted to stage (or fix) a prizefight, the Publicity Building was the place to be. (*See* **MADISON SQUARE GARDEN 825 Eighth Avenue**.)

Noted for its blinking electric rooftop signage, often seen in motion picture montages of Times Square.

62. THE WARNER STRAND THEATRE 1579 Broadway (the Northwest Corner of 47th Street and Broadway) Here, in March 1929, premiered the speakeasy-themed film *Queen of the Night Clubs* starring Texas Guinan as "Texas Malone" and featuring George Raft as a dancer named "Gigola."

The *New York Evening Post*'s Creighton Peet simply despised it (and probably hated her as well). "As in real life," fumed Peet, "she is a sort of booming umpire in a hazy atmosphere of cheap gin, confetti and noise—the difference being that no real people could ever speak such stupid lines no matter how full of liquor they were."

GIVE THIS GIRL A GREAT BIG HAND

SEE New York in its NIGHT CLOTHES, all dressed up and READY for THRILLS! Make WHOOPEE with "The Whoopee Girl"—HAVE the TIME of your life! SEE and HEAR Texas Guinan in "Queen of the Night Clubs," a marvelous picture of "WINE, WOMEN and WRONG"! Your audience is sure to give THIS little girl a GREAT, BIG HAND! SEE and HEAR

TEXAS GUINAN in "QUEEN of the NIGHT CLUBS"

BOOK IT NOW and PLAY IT DAY AND DATE WITH BROADWAY!

STORY BY MURRAY ROTH AND ADDISON BURKHART

DIRECTED BY BRYAN FOY

(AUTHOR'S COLLECTION)

Built by the Mark brothers (*not* the Marx Brothers) in 1914, the 3,500-seat Strand is believed to have been the first large theater designed solely for motion pictures and soon featured Roxy Rothafel as its manager. Purchased by Warner Brothers in 1928. It finally closed in 1987, making way for the Morgan Stanley Building.

63. LEW FIELDS'S MANSFIELD THEATRE 256 West 47th Street (Between Broadway and Eighth Avenue) Here

on April 26, 1928, a teenaged dancer named Demaris "Hotsy Totsy" Dore opened in the Richard Rodgers–Lorenz Hart two-act musical, *Present Arms*. Also present onstage (in a last-minute move) was its choreographer: Busby Berkeley. Berkeley claimed to have "discovered" Dore (a former pal of Peaches Browning; *see* **FAIRFIELD HOTEL 20-28 West 72nd Street**) dancing at the Club Frivolity speakeasy (*see* **CLUB FRIVOLITY 1678 Broadway**) and recruited her for this show. Actually, the distinctly youthful Dore had already been working steadily since at least January 1926 where she appeared in *Ziegfeld's Palm Beach Nights* in Palm Beach.

In *Present Arms,* Dore led the chorus in a "jazzy" number titled "Crazy Elbows." The *Times's* Brooks Atkinson seemed unimpressed (perhaps, horrified) by her vocalizing in "the new guttural style."

"Miss Dore is eighteen years old and was born in Paris, a city in France," deadpanned the *Daily News.* "Her father, they tell us, was an entertainer in the Paris music-halls."

But far more significant to our tale than her genealogy was Miss Dore's location in the early morning hours of March 7, 1929—and who she was with: at a card game at Miami's luxury Biltmore Hotel with her boyfriend, former longtime Rothstein $100-per-week bodyguard Thomas "Fatty" (or "Fats") Walsh, who had departed Rothstein's employ five months prior to his Park Central demise, for, as, Walsh explained, he "was too cheap for me. That bird hung on to a dollar like nothing human. I figured I could make more money somewhere else, so I quit him."

Suspiciously, also registered at the Biltmore was Inez Norton. Some say Norton also attended the game in question. Suspiciously, also in town were Nigger Nate Raymond and yet another former Rothstein bodyguard, Tough Willie McCabe.

Walsh had been in Florida for four weeks, leaving New York, as his mother informed police, to recover from an "attack of grippe." She added that the cure had been going well, as her 220-pound son had recently written her that he had gained four pounds while down South.

Walsh ...

Norton ...

Raymond ...

McCabe ...

It was all like the national touring company of "Arnold Rothstein: This Is Your Life" (or, maybe death). As Walsh gambled at cards, however, on that fateful March 7, somehow, someone not only plugged Walsh's twenty-seven-year-old friend Arthur "Chick" Clark but also shot Walsh himself—shot him twice in the abdomen, shot him very, very dead. Dore readily admitted seeing the whole thing—and being nearly ventilated herself. "She is loaded with information," said New York City Police Commissioner Grover Whelan after grilling her full two solid hours. "She

Demaris Dore and Fuller Mellish Jr. in Present Arms (COURTESY OF THE NEW YORK PUBLIC LIBRARY)

has proved a mine of information about the Walsh case. She knew Rothstein and all his associates."

"She told [Whalen]," reported the *Times*, "of being frequently in the company of Rothstein . . . in various night clubs in the midtown section. She said that Rothstein had a financial interest in some of these clubs."

Yet Dore steadfastly refused to identify her boyfriend's murderer. "You'll get nothing out of me," she told police. "They'll kill me!"

"Chick" Clark wasn't talking either.

And so, Walsh's murder, like so many others, remained unsolved.

Police, however, provided this mysterious bit of information. They claimed that Walsh had already been marked for death back in New York. Walsh was to have been machine-gunned while exiting Rothstein's old 45–47 West 57th Street business headquarters. The reason: Walsh's incessant bragging that, "Say, I know all about who was out to get A. R." Police staked out the building, but no foul play ever transpired.

At the time of Rothstein's demise, Walsh resided at a five-room apartment at 250 West 99th Street (between Broadway and West End Avenue)—his apartment at the time of Rothstein's shooting. His mother still lived there at the time of her son's death, and his funeral was held in its living room. Demaris Dore said she would attend. She didn't. (*See* **LEW FIELDS'S MANSFIELD THEATRE 256 West 47th Street**.)

They buried Walsh at Woodlawn Cemetery.

64. 9TH PRECINCT HOUSE 345 West 47th Street (Between Eighth and Ninth Avenues) The word went

out from this police station house on the night of Rothstein's murder.

In 1928, Mae West was booked here on obscenity charges regarding the play *Sex*. Margaret Sanger was also brought here after her own November 13, 1921, arrest at Town Hall for discussing artificial birth control. Here, Legs Diamond surrendered to face charges relating to the Hotsy Totsy Club shooting. (*See* **THE HOTSY TOTSY CLUB 1721 Broadway.**) "John the Barber" Reisler (*see* **JOHN J. "JOHN THE BARBER" REISLER BARBER SHOP 169 West 45th Street**) was arraigned here following a December 1929 raid on his shop's latest location (156 West 44th Street) that uncovered 162 bottles of illegal liquor.

In 1912, Beansie Rosenthal's body was brought to the precinct's back room immediately following his murder. Bald Jack Rose later testified that Lt. Charles Becker then informed him: "It was a pleasing sight to me to see that squealing Jew lying there and if it had not been for the presence of [District Attorney Charles] Whitman I would have cut out his tongue and hung it on the Times Building as a warning to future squealers."

Featured in Otto Preminger's 1950 film noir *Where the Sidewalk Ends* and briefly in the 1935 Kay Francis weeper *Living on Velvet*, where a thoroughly soused (and unpleasant) George Brent is arraigned at its front desk.

The WPA *New York City Guide* wrote this concerning the place:

The ugly, yellow-brick EIGHTEENTH PRECINCT POLICE STATION . . . was put into service January 1, 1862, in good time to play a part in the draft riots of 1863. The district was not densely settled then, and most of the crimes were unspectacular; the single blotter entry for the first day recorded the return of a lost child to her parents. By the early 1900s, however, the gambling dives and gangsters of the West Side had made the station house one of the busiest in New York. Later, following occasional raids on theaters and night clubs, such names as Texas Guinan and Mae West [*see* **DALY'S THEATRE 22 West 63rd Street**] would appear among hundreds of underworld aliases on the blotter. Before the advent of the police radio car, reporters maintained headquarters in a basement across the street from the station. Among the newspapermen who worked this coveted "fly-beat" were David Graham Philips [himself murdered in 1911], Charles Somerville, Richard Harding Davis, and Louis Weitzenkorn.

The Old 9th Precinct House, circa 1939 (author's collection)

The building housed the 16th Precinct after 1929—but became the 18th Precinct in 1947. Demolished in 1969. Now a city playground, Ramon Aponte Park.

We have almost forgotten to properly record the exploits of the two greatest sleuths of the era: Prohibition Bureau agents Izzy Einstein (5'5", 225 pounds) and Moe Smith (5'7", 235 pounds), who in their five-year career pinched 4,933 suspects, achieved an astounding 95 percent conviction rate, and seized nearly 5 million bottles of illegal alcohol—all aided by their remarkable mastery of disguises and of foreign languages (Yiddish, Hungarian, Polish,

Moe Smith and Izzy Einstein, Post-Prohibition in 1935 (COURTESY OF THE
LIBRARY OF CONGRESS)

German, French, Italian, and Russian plus even a smattering of Chinese)—
but above all by their simply immense chutzpah.

That they weren't on the take didn't hurt either.

"Garages and warehouses were the places for the biggest hauls,"
Einstein revealed in his 1932 memoir, "[On December 6, 1922, in]
a decrepit flivver, I rode into a garage [the Indian Head Auto Truck
Service—Indian Head Storage Warehouse] at 611 West 46th Street asking
to have the engine given the once over. While they were tinkering with it,
I took a sniff around to confirm some rumors we had of this place. What
I smelt was plenty. Result: fifty thousand dollars' worth [of booze] seized.

"Three days later I scored practically the duplicate of it, at the warehouse of the Longacre Express and Van Company, across the street from
the West 47th Street police station. At this place [410 West 47th Street] I
applied in the guise of a victim of the [current] housing shortage . . . who
needed to store his furniture. I told 'em my wife had gone home to mama
because there wasn't any place for us to live. Result: another fifty thousand
worth [of hootch seized].

Crime expert author Herbert Asbury noted that Izzy and Moe "frequently scheduled their raids to suit the convenience of the reporters and the newspaper photographers, and soon learned that there was more room in the papers on Monday mornings than on any other . . . One Sunday, accompanied by a swarm of eager reporters, they established a record by making seventy-one raids in a little more than twelve hours."

Such publicity, however, engendered jealousy within the Bureau, triggering Izzy and Moe's shocking dismissal in November 1925.

In 1932, with the sun fast setting on Prohibition, Izzy dedicated his published memoirs "To The 4,932 Persons I Arrested. Hoping They Bear Me No Grudge For Having Done My Duty."

65. HAROLD ROSS RESIDENCE 412 West 47th Street (Between Ninth and Tenth Avenues) Alexander
Woollcott, a witness to Beansie Rosenthal's murder (*see* **HOTEL METROPOLE 142-149 West 43rd Street**), lived here in 1922 with fellow Algonquin Round Table member Harold Ross and with Ross's wife, Jane Grant. (*See* **ALGONQUIN HOTEL 59 West 44th Street.**)

66. JACK'S RESTAURANT West 47th Street at Sixth Avenue An early Rothstein haunt. Here he matched wits
not so much with gamblers, gangsters, and goons but with such intellects as newspapermen "Spanish" O'Brien, Frank Ward O'Malley, Ben De Casseres, and Bruno Lessing; songwriter Grant Clarke (he penned the words to Fanny Brice's "Second Hand Rose"), cartoonists Hype Igoe and "Tad" Dorgan; and all-around scamp Wilson Mizner. (*See* **HOTEL RAND 142-146 West 49th Street.**)

It was at Jack's on November 18, 1909, that Rothstein's associates goaded him into accepting a challenge to contest Philadelphia socialite sportsman Jack Conaway at John McGraw's "McGraw Billiard Academy" down at 35th and Sixth, reputedly the longest billiards match in history, thirty-two hours nonstop. Their idea was to cut the often-irksome Rothstein down to size, for as Arnold's early biographer Leo Katcher explained: "Because Rothstein was not a good mixer, because he had a supercilious twist to his lower lip, he irritated many people. They didn't like a man who appeared to be self-sufficient, whose attitude they felt was superior. Certainly Rothstein was given to being dogmatic. And he had a habit of referring to other people as 'chumps.' Presumably 'chump' was more offensive coming from Rothstein, if only because of his scornful manner, than Wilson's hearty greeting of 'Hello, sucker.'"

Mizner's ploy, however, fizzled in spectacular fashion. In fact, November 1909's epic Rothstein-Conaway contest elevated Arnold to Broadway's man of the hour. News of the match created a nationwide sensation. As the *Chicago Tribune* reported:

POOL GAME LAST 32 HOURS;

$4,000 STAKES IN CONTEST.

PHILADELPHIA AND NEW YORKER EAT

SANDWICHES, SOAK HEADS, AND STICK

TILL PROPRIETOR CALLS IT OFF.

New York, November. 25 – [Special] – Around Broadway they are talking about a pool game between two well-known young men which lasted about thirty-two hours. Probably breaking all records in point of time—in which the stakes were heavy, as much as $4,000 being involved.

When Jack Conaway, a broker of Philadelphia and noted whip, came over last week on one of his by monthly visits he played a game of pool with Arnold Rothstein, son of a wealthy business-man, but neither of them intended to make it a feat of endurance. When they met at dinner a game was suggested by mutual friends who knew the ability of each. It was decided to play a match. The two began around 8 o'clock in the evening. This was Thursday of last week.

The first game was for fifty points, and by lucky break, Conaway won it. The second, for 100 points, Rothstein took, although by a narrow margin. When 2 o'clock came Conaway was

Lt. Charles Becker (AUTHOR'S COLLECTION)

several hundred dollars [the] loser and wanted to continue. So interesting was the contest that they didn't stop for meals, snatching a bite at a sandwich now and then, and only stopping long enough to soak their heads in cold water. Finally, when 2 o'clock Saturday morning had passed, the proprietor of the place [McGraw] warned them that they would have to stop, and at 4 o'clock they put up their cues and entered automobiles which carried them to Turkish baths.

Conaway is by no means satisfied that the New York man is his master at the game and suggested a return match will be played in Philadelphia with a side bet of $5,000 on the outcome.

It was also here that Rothstein awaited news of Charles Becker's July 1915 execution.

Here, also, in September 1915, police nabbed Lillian Lorraine's ex-husband, Frederick Gresheimer, on fraud charges related to his soliciting $300 for the pro-German propaganda magazine *The Fatherland*. His victim: Boston Symphony conductor Carl Muck. (*See* **JARDIN DE PARIS 1514-1516 Broadway** *and* **LOUIS MARTIN'S RESTAURANT West 43rd Street and Seventh Avenue**.)

Raided by Prohibition agent Izzy Einstein in August 1921.

Jack's—unlike Rector's or Reisenweber's—was not exactly respectable. It was, assessed Donald Henderson Clarke, "anathema to many persons. In its prime no chap in the Social Register was apt to go into Jack's unless he had lost all his sense of values through too copious libations. It was not a place in which 'one should be seen.'"

Unlike many other Times Square establishments, Jack's never featured musicians, nor dancing. Irish-immigrant owner Jack Dunston closed the place on May 4, 1925. He died two years later.

67. RECTOR'S 48th Street at Broadway and Seventh Avenue

It was here, in December 1912, that George Young Bauchle (high-society front man for Rothstein's high-stakes floating chemin de fer sessions, the Partridge Club) casually bet Wilson Mizner, John Shaughnessy (a pit man at Rothstein's gambling house), and Nat Evans (Arnold's eventual partner in his Saratoga Springs gambling emporium, The Brook) $5,000 that they could not successfully board the next steamer bound for Europe. Thirty-five minutes later, all three were aboard the luxury liner SS *Mauritania* bound for Liverpool. A few days later, the trio wired Bauchle, "We counted on getting clothes from the purser and the barber, but we couldn't get things to fit us. Why, oh why, did you take advantage of our impulsiveness and our inexperience."

From London, Mizner later reported, "On board we succeeded in garnering pajamas and some shirts and other little things, but our clothes look as if we'd been marching for 36 dusty nights with troop X of the 3 a.m. Finnish rarebit consumers."

Rector's was among the many venues hosting Rothstein's aforementioned "Partridge Club." Well-heeled members included oil man Harry Sinclair (later of Teapot Dome scandal infamy), Broadway's Flo Ziegfeld and Lew Fields, newsman Herbert Bayard Swope, and stockbroker Charles A. Stoneham.

Earlier locations included the Fifth Avenue Hotel (200 Fifth Avenue, between West 22nd and West 23rd Streets), Delmonico's (Fifth Avenue at the northeast corner of East 44th Street), and the McKim, Mead and White–designed Hotel Imperial (the southwest corner of Broadway, occupying the full block between West 31st and West 32nd Streets; demolished in 1947).

"The Partridge Club," noted gambling historian Henry Chafetz, "which flourished before World War I in the Hotel Imperial, was ostensibly run by lawyer, sportsman, and man-about-town George Young Bauchle, but was actually just another of Rothstein's gambling houses. Supposedly select and private, for gentlemen only, the term 'gentlemen' was given a wide and loose interpretation. Anybody could gamble who planked down the thirty-dollar entrance fee, which entitled him also to an excellent champagne dinner. The district attorney tried but failed to establish the fact that it was nothing more than a high-class gambling joint."

In March 1918, when a grand jury quizzed the wise-cracking Mizner about his own adventures at the Partridge, he breezily admitted to some recent good fortune:

It so happened last week that I won 35,000 bucks from a rich German baker, at chemin de fer—but let me digress a moment while a new thought is fresh in my mind. That proves that I am not a professional gambler. If I were a professional, I should have to say. "It so happened that last week I win 35,000 bucks." Any professional who doesn't say "I win" when using the indicative mood, first person, past tense, loses his union card and is kicked into the amateur class.

The rest of his testimony included such varied impertinences as:

QUESTION: "How long have you played chemin de fer, Mr. Mizner?"
ANSWER: "Since infancy."
QUESTION: "How many played in the game you were in at the Ritz-Carlton?"
ANSWER: "Two Christians—and a number of others."

In July 1912, when Beansie Rosenthal was shot, a key to unraveling the case was the testimony of Charlie Gallagher, an unemployed cabaret singer on his way to the Metropole to find work. It was he who supplied the murder vehicle's license plate number ("NY-41313"). His last previous employment had been at Rector's.

———————

The mustachioed Charles Rector opened Rector's in September 1899 at a cost of $500,000. It is said that Mr. & Mrs. "Gentleman Jim" Corbett were Rector's first customers, passing through The Great White Way's very first set of revolving doors. "I found Broadway a quiet little lane of

(above left) *Rector's* (AUTHOR'S COLLECTION)
(above right) *Rector's Restaurant in Earlier Days* (COURTESY OF COLUMBIA UNIVERSITIES LIBRARY)

(COURTESY OF COLUMBIA UNIVERSITIES LIBRARY)

ham and eggs," Charles Rector bragged, "and left it a full-blown avenue of lobsters and champagne."

"Eight captains commanded 60 waiters in full evening dress with divided coattails and white vests," noted author Ken Bloom. "The maître d'hotel received a salary of $150 a month. In addition, he might make $30,000 in tips during the holiday season. The waiters were paid $25 from the captains and received almost $1,000 a month in tips. The coat room alone brought in $10,000 a year."

"For almost a quarter of a century," Charles's son George would later boast, "opera stars, explorers, actors, captains of industry, authors, adventurers, artists—all celebrated their successes with a night at Rector's. I doubt that Broadway really believed that Peary had discovered the North Pole or Dewey had defeated the Spanish fleet until both appeared in my restaurant."

It's said that all publicity is good publicity. This was, however, decidedly *not* the case with Rector's. In February 1909, the musical *The Girl from Rector's* opened at Weber's Music Hall (Broadway and West 39th Street). Its plot centered on a married lady from out of town who doubled as a blueblood's mistress in Manhattan—and convinced prim distaff onlookers that only the wrong sort of females dined therein. They avoided Rector's like the plague, and by 1913 it was bankrupt. By 1919 the famed restaurant finally closed.

68. PARK VIEW ATHLETIC CLUB 107 West 48th Street (Between Sixth and Seventh Avenues) Much like the previously mentioned Teepee Democratic Club (*see* **TEEPEE DEMOCRATIC CLUB 146 West 44th Street**), this Roaring Twenties gambling spot enjoyed protection from the law thanks to Rothstein's political connections.

"The Park View Athletic Club . . . ," noted author Henry Chafetz, "was a Rothstein business where trained personnel helped patrons build up their muscles. There were also private rooms where a man could strengthen his muscles by rattling and tossing dice and shuffling and dealing cards."

69. CHEZ FLORENCE 117 West 48th Street (Between Sixth and Seventh Avenues) Operated by Tommy Guinan,

Texas Guinan's brother. In 1930, *New York Sun* columnist Ward Morehouse praised the place as "the most interesting night club Manhattan ever had."

"Tommy Guinan," recalled columnist Whitney Bolton decades later, "was a colorful, sometimes whimsical and often alarming figure of those 20s and I, for one, delighted in knowing him. I never did know his sister, Texas Guinan, the nightclub empress, half as well. She was formidable. Tommy was engaging."

Site of the October 1928 brawl that cost Bessie Poole her life. (*See* **THE HOTEL DORSET 30 West 54th Street.**) In November 1926, actor Arnold Daly somehow "slipped on the floor" and fractured his skull.

Interesting, indeed.

Following the Bessie Poole incident, District Attorney Joab Banton issued the following warning: "Persons who patronize night clubs associate with criminals of the worst type. The night clubs are hangouts of criminals who watch for women with jewelry and men with money, follow them when they leave and rob them or else blackmail them."

Texas Guinan had operated two clubs on the Chez Florence's site prior to its existence. In January 1929, brother Tommy was convicted of operating a "public nuisance" here regarding federal liquor laws.

He wasn't alone in his woes. In June 1928, Feds had also raided such establishments as the Luigi's Restaurant (136 West Houston Street), La Frera, (692 Sixth Avenue), Club Frivolity (1678 Broadway), the Beaux Arts (80 West 40th Street), the Little Club (261 West 44th Street), J. T. Martin's Restaurant (263 West 44th Street), Larry Fay's the El Fey Club (107 West 45th Street), the U. S. I. Restaurant (108 West 45th Street), Dinty Moore's (216 West 46th Street), the Silver Slipper (201 West 48th Street), the Footlight Club (121 West 49th Street), the Furnace (180 West 49th Street), the Charm Club (37 West 51st Street), Sherman Billingley's Social Club (47 West 51st Street), Jimmy Durante's Club Dover (105 West 51st Street), the Knight Club (115 West 51st Street), the Rose Room Club (117 West 51st Street), the Marguery Rendezvous (121 West 51st Street), the Merry-Go-Round (123 West 51st Street), the Art Club (124 West 51st Street), the Greenwich Social Club (135 West 51st Street),

A 1926 ad for another of the Guinan family's many operations. Quirk and Texas Guinan (and probably Tommy Guinan) would all attend Valentino's funeral barely a month later. (AUTHOR'S COLLECTION)

The limber Nina Susov dancing for clearly admiring patrons of the raided Club Anatole. Among the club's better known hoofers were young Ruby Stevens, better known to history as "Barbara Stanwyck," and Mae Clarke (target of Jimmy Cagney's grapefruit in The Public Enemy*). Nina Susov went on to appear at the Winter Garden in 1926's* The Great Temptations, *a decidedly "daring" review featuring Jack Benny.* (COURTESY OF THE NEW YORK PUBLIC LIBRARY)

the Ferndale Club (139 West 51st Street), the Futuristic International Academy (104 West 52nd Street), the Don Royale (131 West 52nd Street), the Mimic (aka "the Benny Davis Club"—132 West 52nd Street), the Lauretta McDermott Club (135 West 52nd Street), the European Club (26 West 53rd Street), the Melody Club (114 West 54th Street), Helen Morgan's Summer Home (134 West 54th Street), songwriter Anatole Friedman's Club Anatole (145 West 54th Street), Harry Richman's Club Richman (157 West 57th Street), the Owl Club (161 West 59th Street), and last, but hardly least, Texas Guinan's Salon Royale (310 West 58th Street).

Bear in mind, this was just a *partial* list.

70. CLUB MORITZ 148 West 48th Street

(Between Sixth and Seventh Avenues) Another Texas Guinan-connected speakeasy. It followed the El Fey Club and preceded the 300 Club. Opened in December 1924. Raided in March 1925 and padlocked the following month.

Reported the *New York Sun*: "Charles Eno, counsel for the Club Moritz, issued a statement in which he said it had never been the intention of

Tonight at Eleven!
That popular
Terpsichorian team
Peppy De Albrew
The brilliant Brazilian
Sensation
And
Lovey Lee
The premiere
Musical comedy danseuse
And an indefinite
Lovemovent at the
The ovenustz
munen's music
covcome over

charge $2.00

[Phone your reservations to ZANI— Bryant 1678]

CLUB MORITZ
117 West 48th Street

the management to violate the law. If the law had been violated, he said, a waiter acting solely for his own benefit had been responsible."

Of course.

71. BILLY LAHIFF'S TAVERN 156-58 West 48th Street (Between Sixth and Seventh Avenues) A popular hangout in the 1920s, frequented by, among others, Damon Runyon. In the mid-1920s, when Bill Fallon was in hiding from jury tampering charges, Rothstein ran into Fallon's girlfriend, showgirl Gertrude Vanderbilt, at LaHiff's and offered to provide Fallon with bail money.

Opened in 1922 following LaHiff's ownership of another restaurant at 1573 Broadway (at West 68th Street). "It was accounted the finest chop house in the big town . . . ," recorded one observer, "and its enormous success was undoubtedly due to the personality of Billy LaHiff."

Observed Damon Runyon:

In that great valhalla where the good fellows go, they must have had a special chair way up front reserved for Billy LaHiff, gentleman of gentlemen, high class, and if ever a sweeter character walked in shoe leather, this writer has yet to know him. A small, dapper, good looking, smiling chap was Billy LaHiff, who parlayed a marvelous personality into a great business success, and who was never known to refuse a favor to a friend. He had no foes.

He helped literally an army of men and women over the rough spots in life during his time on the big white line. He was a quiet, unostentatious man in his manner of living, and his manner of giving, but he will be remembered long after many a more spectacular figure has long been forgotten.

Recalled 1920s dancer Barbara Stanwyck:

LaHiff and his waiter Jack Spooner were great friends to all kinds of people. Down and out fighters, chorus girls on their uppers, the broken and the bent of Broadway. LaHiff'd feed us and slip us a ten or a fifteen besides, just to be sure we'd be okay. He had his and was grateful for it. So grateful, that he had his heart and his hand and his pocketbook open for those who hadn't got theirs yet or who had had it and lost it.

LaHiff maintained rental apartments above his joint. Tenants included Runyon, Walter Winchell, humorist Arthur "Bugs" Baer, the Stork Club's future owner Sherman Billingsley (*see* **THE CASA BLANCA 33 West 56th Street**), vocalist and cabaret owner Harry Richman (he owned the Club Richman at 157 West 56th Street), and Mr. & Mrs. Ed Sullivan.

In early 1928, Rothstein's Cedar Point Realty Co. sold Woodmere, Long Island's 260-acre Cedar Point Golf Club to a syndicate headed by LaHiff. "The course and its clubhouse are valued at $740,000," noted a press account, "and it is understood that a price close to that has been paid for the property." Maurice Cantor represented Rothstein.

When LaHiff died in 1934, his son hired Toots Shor to run the joint.

LaHiff's closed in 1942. The site was later occupied by the Sam Ash Music Store.

72. THE SILVER SLIPPER 201 West 48th Street (Between Broadway and Eighth Avenue) A Frankie Marlow (*see* LA TAVERNELLE RESTAURANT 252 West 52nd Street) –operated speakeasy—in which Rothstein held a share. Marlow's girlfriend, Mary "Mickey of the Rendezvous" Seiden, appeared here. In February 1930, the *New York Sun* reported that Demaris Dore (witness to Fatty Walsh's March 6, 1929, murder) was "now running things at the Silver Slipper."

Dore had wasted little time mourning her lost paramour, serving as a "hostess" at Miami's Roman Pools gambling casino when the gambling halls (shuttered after Walsh's death) reopened that March 14. Within a week, she appeared in the vaudeville review *Broadway Night Life* playing at Brooklyn's Loew's Metropolitan (392 Fulton Street). That April 1, columnist Walter Winchell reported on her "'flash' act on the Loew circuit" and that she "gets a roof-lifting ovation when she appears."

A federal judge had padlocked the Silver Slipper for one year back on November 19, 1928.

Toiling as a chorus girl here was the much-married Patrice Amati del Grande Gidier, who wed Damon Runyon (the third of her four husbands) in July 1932. It was his second marriage.

73. CLUB LA VIE 204 West 48th Street (Between Broadway and Eighth Avenue) Longtime Owney Madden buddy "Big Bill" Duffy operated this club until August 1922 when mobster Frankie Marlow (*see* LA TAVERNELLE RESTAURANT 252 West 52nd Street) was shot dead there. It later reopened as the Parody Club, where Clayton, Jackson, and Durante commenced appearances in January 1927, and later as the Chez Folie featuring bandleader Ted "Is Everybody Happy?" Lewis as master of ceremonies. The top-hatted Lewis had once hosted his own clubs, the upscale Bal Tabarian, the Monmatre (1634 Broadway in the Winter Garden Building), and finally the Ted Lewis Club (808 Seventh Avenue at West 52nd Street—raided in August 1922)

74. HOTEL PRESIDENT 234 West 48th Street (Between Broadway and Eighth Avenue) In June 1930, Legs Diamond was arrested here for a Newark bank robbery.

The leniency exhibited to cheap hoodlums like Diamond only illustrates the corruption of New York City's court system. In 1931, author Emanuel H. Lavine (while missing the above incident) recounted the prerequisites Diamond mysteriously enjoyed:

> February 4, 1914 - Burglary in Brooklyn at the age of 17, sentenced to reformatory by Judge Norman S. Dike.

> May 12, 1916 - Assault and robbery, discharged by Magistrate McQuade.

> July 5, 1916 - Assault, acquitted in General Sessions.

> March 13, 1918 - Robbery, dismissed, grand jury refused to indict.

April 16, 1918 - Grand Larceny, dismissed by Judge Mulqueen, General Sessions.

March 24, 1919 - Arrested at Fort Jay [Governor's Island], charged with desertion from army and stealing while in service. Sentenced to five years in Leavenworth. Served year, got federal parole.

June 1, 1921 - Grand larceny, discharged by Magistrate Ten Eyck.

October 27, 1921 - Assault and robbery under alias of John Hart, discharged by Magistrate Brough.

November 18, 1921 - Burglary, discharged by Judge Francis X. Mancuso.

April 16, 1922 - Material witness under alias John Higgins, not held.

November 16, 1923 - Fugitive at Cliffside, N. J., turned over to New York police, no disposition.

November 28, 1923 - Robbery, discharged by Judge Olvany.

June 14, 1924 - Robbery, discharged by magistrate listed as "Magistrate Obermeyer."

January 7, 1925 - Carrying revolver, discharged by Judge Morris Koenig.

August 12, 1925 - Homicide, discharged by Magistrate Albert H. Vitale.

December 29, 1926 - Felonious assault, discharged by Magistrate Glatzmayer.

July 9, 1927 - Smuggling narcotics, at Mount Vernon, $15,000 bail, held for federal court trial, still pending.

October 15, 1927 - Homicide, discharged by Magistrate Andrew J. Macrery.

February 2, 1928 - Homicide, discharged by Magistrate Jos. E. Corrigan.

May 20, 1929 - Homicide, discharged by Magistrate Andrew J. Macrery.

March 10, 1930 - Homicide, discharged by Judge Max Levine.

August, 1930 - Deported by escorts from various European countries as international criminal and undesirable.

September 23, 1930 - Vagrant, arrested from liner *Hanover*, Philadelphia, discharged on promise to leave town.

Opened in 1928. Now the Gallivant Times Square.

75. DAPPER DON COLLINS RESIDENCE 242 West 48th Street (Between Broadway and Eighth Avenue)

Former Rothstein bootlegging associate (and Lillian Lorrain boyfriend) Arthur "Dapper Don" Collins lived here in February 1934 when federal authorities nabbed him for peddling counterfeit $100 bills in Times Square for $30. "The sprightly appearance that marked him in the older days was gone," remarked the New York Times. "His spats and cane and natty clothes were absent. He had put on some weight, but he was wearing a plain dark gray suit, a cheap hat, black shoes and a light brown coat."

But, *before* he hit the skids (and spent the remainder of his sorry life behind bars), he had his moments. He was, wrote *Daily Mirror* editor Jack Lait, "as well known on the Riviera and in Baden-Baden as he was in New York. In Paris a divorced wife of Otto Heyworth, Chicago millionaire, jumped out of a window in an attempt to kill herself because she couldn't hold Collins. He was named as the correspondent when Garnett Patton Inman, wife of an heir to the James B. Duke tobacco fortune, was sued.

"He was later involved in the shadows of the murder of Dot King (who was kept by the son-in-law of the Philadelphia Morgan partner, Edward T. Stotesbury) a crime with a blackmail background. After the murder of Arnold Rothstein, Collins was the constant companion of the blonde [Inez Norton] who had been the sweetheart of the gambler-racketeer."

76. RIVOLI THEATRE 1620 Broadway (Between West 49th and West 50th Streets) Arnold Rothstein dined

with his mistress, showgirl Inez Norton, on November 4, 1928, the night of his shooting. After he adjourned to Lindy's, she went to this ornate motion-picture palace, the 2,092-seat Rivoli, to view director Erich von Stroheim's silent classic *The Wedding March*, a film about the evils of marrying for money.

> Inez Norton: *Arnold was very gay—his normal, natural self—and very much in love. He didn't seem to have anything on his mind. He certainly didn't fear anything.*
>
> *We spoke of many subjects, but mostly of love; and he said that he hoped soon to be free to marry me. He said everything would be mine— his property and the money—but I cared only for him.*

Samuel "Roxy" Rothafel opened the Rivoli ("the stateliest of Broadway's big film palaces"), whose massive colonnade resembled the Greek Parthenon. The Rivoli, noted *The WPA Guide to New York City*, "revolutionized theater architecture when it opened in 1917 with a cooling system and balconies without posts."

"There is no building on Broadway," gushed Paramount's Adolph Zukor, "from the Battery to its northern end, that is more beautiful than the Rivoli."

The Rivoli's first offering was Douglas Fairbanks's silent film *A Modern Musketeer*, accompanied by a thirty-five-piece house orchestra standard operating procedure for Rothafel. "Roxy," noted author Ken Bloom, "presented a program that would become a standard feature at motion-picture palaces. It began with an overture by a symphony

The Rivoli Theatre in 1929 (AUTHOR'S COLLECTION)

orchestra, then the Rialto Male Quartet, a newsreel or educational fea-
turette, a number sung by [soprano] Gladys Rice with accompaniment
of Sepp Morscher on harp, William Feder on cello and Professor Firmin
Swinnen on organ. Finally, the motion picture would be presented."

In 1933, speakeasy queen Texas Guinan's funeral cortege passed by the
Rivoli. Inside, her film *Broadway Thru a Keyhole* (in which she appeared as
"Tex Kaley," a thinly veiled version of herself) still screened.

The Rivoli was twinned in 1984, closed in 1986, and after its owners
stripped it of its classic Greek Revival façade (supposedly to prevent
landmark status), it was demolished in July 1987 and replaced by the
twenty-five-story office building also known as 750 Seventh Avenue.

77. JACK DEMPSEY'S RESTAURANT 1619 Broadway (Between West 49th and West 50th Streets) In

September 1926, Gene Tunney challenged champion Jack "The Manassa
Mauler" Dempsey for the heavyweight title. Dempsey (coincidentally, later
Nate Raymond's best man) was the prohibitive favorite, but Rothstein bet
on Tunney, cleared $500,000, and because of certain pre-fight machina-
tions with Abe Attell and Philadelphia racketeer Max "Boo Boo" Hoff
soon caused many (including Dempsey) to question what happened.

Dempsey, once a despised roughhouser and World War I draft dodger,
eventually became a beloved elder statesman of sport, opening a popular

(AUTHOR'S COLLECTION)

restaurant in the Brill Building, just a few doors down from Lindy's. In 1974, the building's new owners argued with Dempsey about terms of the lease. The restaurant closed that October 6.

The Manassa Mauler died of a heart attack at age eighty-seven in New York City on May 31, 1983.

The Brill Building also once housed an outpost of the Reuben's Restaurant operation. (*See* **REUBEN'S RESTAURANT Broadway and West 73rd Street.**)

78. THE PUNCHEON GROTTO (AKA THE GROTTO, NO. 42, AND JACK AND CHARLIE'S) 42 West 49th Street (Between Fifth and Sixth Avenues)

Operated by former Greenwich Village speakeasy operators (and cousins) Jack Kriendler and Charlie Berns, until their property was condemned not by the police or the feds but to accommodate the planned Rockefeller Center. Undaunted, in 1930 they moved once more, this time to 21 West 52nd Street—becoming the famed "21 Club." Until it closed in 2020, patrons (including this patron) could visit its elaborate former speakeasy-style wine cellar. Banned from "21" in 1930, the *Daily Mirror*'s Walter Winchell retaliated by having the joint raided.

79. HOTEL PLYMOUTH 137-143 West 49th Street (Between Sixth and Seventh Avenues)

Artists and Models dancer Elaine Dawn (aka Elaine Orlay), one of Judge Crater's many female companions, lived here until he vanished when she suddenly decamped out into the Polyclinic Hospital (scene of Rothstein's death) for several weeks due to "rheumatism" on her knee.

The Plymouth, opened in September 1929, was torn down in the 1960s.

80. HOTEL RAND 142-146 West 49th Street (at Broadway)

Here stood the Hotel Rand, acquired in June 1907 by Rothstein's associate at Jack's Wilson Mizner.

The Rand, noted Mizner's biographer Richard O'Connor, "catered to crooks, whores, pimps, kept women and their keepers, and served as shore base for the cardsharps working the Atlantic liners . . . [it] is recalled as the most disorderly caravanserai in the history of Manhattan innkeeping, at least in the section north of the Bowery, and Wilson did nothing to upgrade its reputation. His No. 1 rule as Mine Host was to look with tolerance on his guests' foibles. As an occasional devotee of the opium pipe, then jocularly known as a Hong Kong Flute, he could not object to his patrons' indulgence in the poppy. Nor did he regard himself as a standard-bearer for conventional morality."

Mizer's house rules included:

"No opium-smoking in the elevators."

"Guests must carry out their own dead."

"No piano-playing before 5 p.m. as it may disturb the other guests."

"Guests jumping out of windows will try to land in the net placed around the third floor."

81. JOSEPH BERMAN RESIDENCE 213 West 49th Street (Between Broadway and Eighth Avenue) In 1932, Berman, a member of the Salvatore Spitale–Irving Bitz mob, resided here and faced trial regarding the gang's unloading of illegal liquor from the yacht Colonial at Gerritsen Beach, Brooklyn.

But the more interesting part of his story dates back to March 13, 1929, when Berman resided at 310 West 94th Street, and applied for a cabaret license for Legs Diamond's Hotsy Totsy Club. (*See* **THE HOTSY TOTSY CLUB 1721 Broadway**.) Police were skeptical, noting that the space had previously been occupied by another cabaret, where a whopping twelve law violations had already been reported.

Cabaret license forms contained a question regarding the general reputation of the application. Police captain Louis Dittman responded "Questionable" and predicted that "Violation of the prohibition laws will probably take place in this cabaret if license is granted."

"Commissioner [of Licenses William F.] Quigley," noted a press report following the Hotsy Totsy Club's July 1929 fatal shoot-up, "declined to explain why he granted a license to the cabaret, after being informed that violations would probably occur."

82. ST. MALACHY'S CHURCH 239 West 49th Street (Between Broadway and Eighth Avenue) Here, on

December 14, 1960, the sixty-seven-year-old Jimmy Durante (*see* **CLUB DURANT 232 West 58th Street**) married forty-one-year-old Margaret "Margie" Little, formerly a hatcheck girl at East 60th Street's Copacabana nightclub, a venue secretly owned by mobster Frank Costello. (*See* **MAJESTIC APARTMENTS 115 Central Park West.**)

Noted a press report: "Because of the Season of Advent in the Catholic Church, the wedding will be performed without a Mass and in the chapel of the church. . . . Jimmy, the [officiating] priest stated, is a devout Catholic and was instrumental in the conversion, recently, of Miss Little."

It was Durante's second marriage. His first was to Maud Jeanne Olson, a singer in his act, back on June 19, 1921, either here or at Holy Innocents Parish (128 West 37th Street). Accounts vary but point to a Holy Innocents nuptial because of the following detail: to marry in the Church, Jimmy required proof of his baptism. None could be found at his boyhood Lower East Side parish (St. James on Oliver Street, where the young Al Smith had also worshipped), thus Durante was "conditionally baptized" at Holy Innocents the day prior to his nuptials.

Twenty-one-year-old Joan Crawford (née Lucille Fay LeSueur) wed nineteen-year-old Douglas Fairbanks Jr. here in June 1929. Because it was a mixed marriage, they wed not in the church itself but in its rectory.

August 30, 1926, witnessed Rudolph Valentino's Solemn High Requiem Mass. Among the star-studded mourners was Texas Guinan, accompanied by one of her club dancers, seventeen-year-old Ruby Keeler. Shortly thereafter, Guinan hosted a séance in order to reach Valentino and question him regarding whether he had been poisoned. Also attending Miss Guinan's séance were her younger brother Tommy, Mae West, and

Jimmy Durante starred with Thelma Todd, Buster Keaton, and also Ruth Selwyn (wife of Edgar Selwyn) in 1932's Speak Easily, *which seemed to have nary a thing to do with speakeasies.* (AUTHOR'S COLLECTION)

gangster Owney "The Killer" Madden. Texas was herself buried from St. Malachy's in November 1933.

Two thousand mourners attended boxer James J. Corbett's services a few months earlier. America's favorite "mobster" Edward G. "Little Caesar" Robinson served as an usher. Other funerals included those for *Abie's Irish Rose* author Anne Nichols (a convert) in 1966 and September 1981 rites for actress Patsy Kelly, formerly the on-screen comedic partner of the far more beauteous and better remembered Thelma "The Ice Cream Blond" Todd, herself once married to reputed mobster Pasquale "Pat" DiCicco, an associate of Lucky Luciano. Todd, just twenty-nine, died in suspicious circumstances (of carbon monoxide poisoning in a Los Angeles garage) in December 1935.

Built in 1902 and still known as "The Actors Chapel." A unique (though bygone) parish feature was archdiocesan permission to offer a 4:00 a.m. (yes, that's indeed *a.m.*) Mass each Sunday to accommodate the theatrical profession. George M. Cohan provided its marble altar rail.

83. THE FORREST HOTEL 224 West 49th Street (Between Broadway and Eighth Avenue)

Mobster and gambler Charles "Chink" Sherman maintained a suite here at the time of his 1931 knifing and shooting at the Club Abbey. (*See* **CLUB INTIME 205 West 54th Street.**) Sherman (née Shapiro), a 130-pound Boston native, survived that bloody brawl at the Abbey. He did not survive a rub-out attempt in 1935, and his body was found outside a barn near Monticello in Sullivan County that November. Many believed the Dutch Schultz gang had done him in.

"He always was considered an enemy of Schultz," noted the *New York Sun*, "acting as an agent for other gang factions. He was a Broadway character, a gambler and racketeer, mentioned time and again in connection with the traffic in drugs and various rackets. He was at one time an associate of Arnold Rothstein . . . and he also was connected with various Owney Madden enterprises."

His criminal record ran like this:

- March 5, 1928, New York City, arrested as fugitive from Boston on a homicide charge. Dismissed.
- January 26, 1931, New York City, felonious assault. Dismissed.
- July 6, 1933, New York City, possession of four guns, opium, and an opium pipe. Discharged.
- August 31, 1933, New York City, felonious assault. Discharged.

Sherman's older brother Henry was a reputed hit man for Detroit's notorious Purple Gang. He committed suicide in the Bronx in October 1933.

———

Another, more infinitely remembered resident was Damon Runyon, who, following a 1928 separation from his wife Ellen Egan Runyon, occupied a three-room penthouse suite therein. Also residing there was a Silver Slipper (*see* **THE SILVER SLIPPER 201 West 48th Street**) chorus girl named Patrice Amati del Grande Gidier. She had so many names because she already had so many ex-husbands—two, to be exact.

Charles "Chink" Sherman (AUTHOR'S COLLECTION)

She would soon have a third. The tall, blonde Patrice and the widowed Damon were wed on July 7, 1932, with an inebriated Jimmy Walker performing the ceremony at 200 West 16th Street.

"The bride . . . ," noted the *Times*, "was one of the dancers in the original Texas Guinan troupe."

Observed the Hearst press:

The bride was a vision of blonde loveliness in frothy pink chiffon and lace.

Originally a Spanish dancer, Miss Gridier became a dramatic actress, appearing in minor roles in David Belasco's "Dancing Partner," and in Ethel Barrymore's "Kingdom of God." Her last stage appearance was in stock at Mount Vernon, N. Y., last winter.

She was born in Caldidas, Spain, and educated in the famous old convent at Huerta, in Yucatan. . . .

The importance of the occasion was marked by the fact that Mayor Walker, self-styled the "late mayor of New York," arrived not only on time, but 10 minutes early.

Runyon was forty-nine. His bride was twenty-five.

———

Built in 1925, the Forrest also served as home to Rothstein relation Bert Lahr, Jack Benny, Fred Allen, and to George Burns and Gracie Allen. Later renamed the Hotel Consulate, it became the Time Hotel in 1999. Originally named after nineteenth-century tragedian Edwin Forrest, the hotel was part of the complex that included a "Forrest Theatre," renamed in 1959 as the Eugene O'Neill.

84. THE EARL CARROLL THEATRE 759 Seventh Avenue (Between West 49th and West 50th Streets)

Florenz Ziegfeld and George White were hardly the only Roaring Twenties impresarios staging scantily clad Broadway reviews. So were John Murray Anderson and his *Greenwich Village Follies* and former songwriter Earl Carroll, who in 1922 opened this 1,206-seat theater to showcase his own even-racier series of *Vanities*.

Damon Runyon, in his fictional account of Arnold Rothstein's demise, "The Brain Goes Home," referenced Earl Carroll as well as a number of Arnold's girlfriends, including one he identified as "Cynthia Harris." Wrote Runyon: "Well, Mr. Earl Carroll feels sorry for Cynthia, so he puts her in the 'Vanities' and lets her walk around raw, and The Brain [Rothstein] sees her, and the next thing anybody knows she is riding in a big foreign automobile the size of a rum chaser [a Coast Guard Prohibition-enforcing boat]."

Which is all very interesting, but nowhere near as intriguing as what transpired at a private party here on February 22–23, 1926. With hundreds of guests in attendance, as his 4:00 a.m. *pièce de résistance*, Carroll unveiled a drunken seventeen-year-old showgirl named Joyce Hawley, bathing naked in a tub of champagne (or was it red wine? accounts differ)—from which men then lined up to drink from. It was all supposed to be hush-hush, but when the *New York Daily Mirror* published details, the Feds prosecuted Carroll for Volstead Act violations and for perjury. Carroll ended up serving four months in Atlanta Penitentiary. In 1924, Carroll had already served four days in The Tombs for displaying "lewd and immoral" posters at his theater. While he sojourned there, one of his former chorus girls (twenty-two-year-old Florence Allen), despondent over having lost her *Vanities* gig, attempted suicide by swallowing Lysol in a Midtown taxicab.

In 1927, *Zit's Weekly*, a vaudeville trade paper, became a tenant. In April 1923, police had raided publisher Carl F. Zittel's 300 Central Park West home, seizing an estimated $50,000 worth of liquor. In December 1930, jewel thieves relieved his wife, Martha, of $150,000 in jewels from their new 315 Riverside Drive apartment.

Florenz Ziegfeld acquired the six-story building in 1932. A few years later, Billy Rose converted it into his Casa Mañana nightclub. Demolished in 1990.

Earl Carroll and Friends, January 1925 (COURTESY OF THE LIBRARY OF CONGRESS)

85. THE ROXY THEATRE 153 West 50th Street (Between Sixth and Seventh Avenues)

In May 1934, the filmed version of Carolyn Green Rothstein's autobiography, *Now I'll Tell*, opened here, starring Spencer Tracy as gambler "Murray Golden" (Rothstein); Helen Twelvetrees as his long-suffering wife "Virginia Golden" (Carolyn); and the very blonde Alice Faye as "Virginia Warren" (a composite of Inez Norton and Arnold's longtime pre-Inez girlfriend Bobbie Winthrop). As with most Hollywood biopics, any proximity to an actual fact was pure happenstance, as the following synopsis all too readily indicates:

> A small-time gambler, Murray Golden, uses Blue Book names to gain prestige. He promises his wife, Virginia, who never associates with his activities, to quit when he has made $200,000. He fixes a fight, only to gain the enmity of Mossiter, a gang leader. A mix-up with [Virginia], who is subsequently killed in an auto accident, angers his wife, who leaves him. Golden finally loses his fortune to Mossiter. Pawning his wife's jewels, Golden buys an insurance policy and goes to meet his doom, leaving the insurance money to his wife.

Six-year-old Shirley Temple could be seen in a small part, as could Inez Norton, who was given a few lines to say at the film's version of Lindy's.

New York Times critic Mordaunt Hall wrote: "Although it is by no means an edifying narrative, it is a forceful and expertly fashioned film.

"As Golden, Spencer Tracy gives a vivid performance. It is, indeed, as thorough a characterization as has been seen on the screen."

"In a city where interest in Rothstein still ran high," observed Tracy biographer James Curtis, "*Now I'll Tell* filled the Roxy as no Tracy film had been able to do."

December 1931 witnessed the Roxy premiere of Fox Studios' romantic comedy *Good Sport* with Inez Norton in a minor uncredited role.

86. LINDY'S RESTAURANT 1626 Broadway On Sunday evening, November 5, 1928, Rothstein, as was his habit, entered Lindy's, a well-known Broadway restaurant described by *The WPA Guide to New York City* as " a contemporary landmark of black and red, set off by yellow [which] has acquired a national reputation through the Broadway columnists— . . . for the gossip and celebrities."

On the evening in question, Rothstein spoke with any number of fellow customers, including newsman Damon Runyon. At 10:12, cashier Abe Scher answered the phone. It was for Rothstein. Rothstein thereupon said he was going up to the Park Central Hotel to meet with George "Hump" McManus. McManus and Rothstein had issues—most significantly, the settling of Rothstein's huge losses at a September 1928 poker game at the apartment of fellow gambler Jimmy Meehan. (*See* **CONGRESS APARTMENTS 161 West 54th Street**.)

Outside Lindy's, Rothstein coincidentally ran into Meehan and handed him his revolver for safekeeping. Rothstein had decided to meet with McManus unarmed, as a sign of, if not good faith, at least a truce. Alone, having sent his chauffeur, Eugene Relman, to get more cash either from his home or office, he walked up Broadway in the cold and damp to his death. (*See* **PARK CENTRAL HOTEL 200 West 56th Street**.)

In August 1921, a short, bald German immigrant named Leo "Lindy" Lindemann along with his wife, Clara Gertner Lindemann, opened

Lindy's as a simple deli. Only after Al Jolson urged him to install seats did they convert Lindy's into a full-scale restaurant.

"Because [Arnold Rothstein] spent so much time in Lindy's, many people thought Rothstein owned the restaurant," noted Ed Weiner in *The Damon Runyon Story*. "Even the newspapers reported that Lindy's was the property of the slain gambler. Naturally, Leo Lindeman . . . was distressed at the printed misstatements and threatened to sue the papers for libel. He asked Damon [Runyon] for advice. For over a week, in every story he wrote on the murder, Runyon printed the names of the actual owners of the restaurant, and offered conclusive proof that Rothstein was in no way affiliated with Lindy's, except as a paying customer. Ironically, the so-called bad publicity the restaurant received as a result of the Rothstein shooting made Lindy's a Broadway institution with a national reputation."

"There was [also]," recalled *New York American* reporter Nat Ferber, "the night [Rothstein] and [stockbroker] Eddie Fuller stood on Broadway outside of Lindy's betting on the odd and even numbers of the license plates on cars turning into Broadway from the near-by side street. As much as $10,000 was wagered on a single number and Rothstein won, consistently. He won because he had the cars 'stacked' and by a system of signaling was able to produce the odd or even tag as desired."

———————

Leo Lindy argued with his business partner and in 1930 opened up a second Lindy's across Broadway. Both restaurants coexisted, until the original Lindy's—the one A. R. walked out of to his death—closed on July 27, 1957. Leo Lindy died less than two months later at age sixty-nine. His second restaurant shuttered its doors in September 1969.

> Abe Scher, Lindy's Cashier: *Mr. Rothstein comes in. Every night he comes here. Regular as clockwork, he comes here. Sunday night, Monday night, any night. Everybody knows that. Like always, there are some people waiting for him. They are waiting near his table, the same one where he is always sitting. . . . You got to understand. This place, it is like an office for him. People come in and they are leaving messages for him. All day and night, they are telephoning for him here. It ain't that*

*Mr. Lindy likes the idea, but what can he do? An important man like
Mr. Rothstein, you do not offend. So, like I am saying, he comes in and
he goes to his table. He is saying "hello" to people and they are saying
"hello" to him. Some fellows, they go to his table and they are talking
confidential to him. You know, they are talking into his ear. . . . Did he
give anyone money?. . . Who knows? Mr. Rothstein you see, but you do
not watch. . . . Does he have his little black book? Is there a time when
he is not having his little black book?*

Abe Attell: *I saw [Rothstein] once, outside of the old Lindy's restaurant
on Broadway, some years after the [Black Sox] scandal. Right out in front
of a crowd of people I told the rat what I thought of him.*

*"Rothstein," I finished up, boiling with anger. "You're going to die
with your shoes on!"*

He did.

Lindy's 1655 Broadway location was the site of another grisly mob outrage.
At 3:00 a.m. on the morning of April 5, 1956, newspaper columnist and
radio commentator Victor Riesel, a crusader versus labor union corruption, was exiting Lindy's, when racketeer Abraham "Leo" Telvi splashed
sulfuric acid in his face. Riesel was permanently scarred and blinded
but continued writing his syndicated column until 1990. Telvi, who had
greedily attempted to shake down the goons who had hired him, was soon
rubbed out downtown at 240 Center Street.

I once met Victor Riesel and looked into his sunglasses-shielded,
scarred face. When I think of Telvi's fate, what comes to mind is, "Good."

Another habitué of 1920's Lindy's was comedian Harpo Marx, who wrote
of the place:

> On the afternoon before the opening [of the Marx Brothers' first
> Broadway show, *I'll Say She Is,* which he thought would flop] I was sit-
> ting in Lindy's restaurant. It was sad to think that a month from now
> I'd be in Albany or Columbus or Baltimore. . . . [I had] a choice of two

Lindy's in 1928
(AUTHOR'S COLLECTION)

homes-away-from-home, Lindy's or Reuben's. I was back with my own people, who spoke my language, with my accent—cardplayers, horseplayers, bookies, song-pluggers, agents, actors out of work and actors playing the Palace, Al Jolson with his mob of fans, and Arnold Rothstein with his mob of runners and flunkies. The cheesecake was ambrosia. The talk was old, familiar music. A lot of yucks. A lot of action. Home Sweet Home.

87. **MADISON SQUARE GARDEN 825 Eighth Avenue ■ (Between West 49th and West 50th Streets)** Many a fight was fixed here, including one in January 1930 involving Owney Madden's prize pugilistic project Primo Carnera. With Carnera's glass jaw complicating his rise to the top of the heavyweight heap, various inducements or outright threats to opponents were necessary to guarantee his success. This night, his opponent, Eddie "Big Boy" Peterson, wouldn't listen to reason, so Madden dispatched his pal George Raft (a former pro fighter himself) to seal the deal. Raft eschewed violence, preferring to simply slip a proverbial mickey into Peterson's pre-fight champagne. He fell to Carnera in the first round.

Opened on November 8, 1925; closed in February 1968 (but not before hosting an infamous 1939 rally by the pro-Nazi German American bund—and Marilyn Monroe's memorably breathless 1962 birthday salute to John F. Kennedy) and demolished later that year. Despite the immense value of Manhattan real estate, its site remained vacant, utilized as a parking lot until 1989.

Two previous versions of the Garden existed downtown—both at Madison Square (of all places!). The second famously witnessed the 1906 shooting of its architect, Stanford White, by the deranged millionaire Harry K. Thaw and 1924's 103-ballot Democrat National Convention. The current Madison Square Garden essentially shares quarters with Penn Station and hosts the Knicks, the Rangers, various high-profile concerts, and the annual Westminster Kennel Club Dog Show.

88. POLYCLINIC HOSPITAL 335-361 West 50th Street (Between Eighth and Ninth Avenues) After being shot at the Park Central Hotel (*see* **PARK CENTRAL HOTEL 200 West 56th Street.**), Rothstein was brought here for surgery and blood transfusions. Appropriately, it was located just across 50th Street from the rear of Madison Square Garden. At 3:50 a.m., as Rothstein edged toward death, his attorney, New York State assemblyman Maurice Cantor, shoved a new version of his will under his feeble hand that substantially shifted assets away from his wife and family and to Cantor himself, Rothstein's associate William F. Wellman, and to Rothstein's mistress Inez Norton. Rothstein died there at 10:15 a.m. on Tuesday, November 6, 1928.

The Polyclinic's West 50th Street 334-bed facility opened in May 1912, replacing an earlier facility on East 34th Street. Rudolph Valentino died there on the eighth floor on August 23, 1926. Marilyn Monroe was hospitalized there twice—in December 1957 and in June 1961. On the latter occasion, Monroe underwent a two-hour-and-forty-five-minute, seven-doctor operation to remove her gallbladder. Her ex-husband Joe DiMaggio stood by to ensure her safety.

The 346-bed hospital shuttered its doors in 1977, was torn down, and is presently apartments.

Prominent among Rothstein's many nicknames—"The Big Bankroll," "The Man Uptown," "The Fixer," "Mr. Big," etc.—was the "The Brain."

Damon Runyon even based one of his characters on Rothstein, dubbing him "The Brain" and writing "Nobody knows how much dough The Brain has, except that he must have plenty because no matter how much dough is around, The Brain sooner or later gets hold of all of it."

But just how brainy was Arnold? Literally, that is. Well, the average male brain weighs 1,345 grams; the average female brain weighs 1,222 grams. When Dr. Charles Norris conducted Arnold Rothstein's autopsy, he found Rothstein's brain to be 1,400 grams.

The 1939 *WPA Guide to New York City* wrote of the place:

> Whenever a heavyweight boxer in Madison Square Garden . . . takes too many right-hands, or a circus trapeze performer misses his safety net, or a rodeo rider falls under the hoofs of a steer, the victim is carried across the street to POLYCLINIC HOSPITAL. . . . The 346-bed hospital serves the ordinary people of the neighborhood, for the most part, but because of its location it receives an unusual number of well-publicized patients. During the Prohibition era the bullet wounds of such notorious figures as Arnold Rothstein and Jack "Legs" Diamond were treated here.

Rothstein's Body Leaving the Polyclinic Hospital (AUTHOR'S COLLECTION)

89. ■ **MING TOY BOOTERY 1656 Broadway at West 51st Street (The Broadway Central Building)** In 1921, Abe Attell opened an opulent women's shoe store, the Ming Toy Bootery, across from Broadway's Roseland Ballroom. "Attell . . . ," reported *Boot and Shoe Recorder: The Magazine of Fashion Footwear*, "is now in the

business of selling the latest creations in novelty footwear to stage celebrities, near-celebrities and hope-to-be celebrities, in a new store that is
fitted up in Oriental splendor. The name which Mr. Attell has selected for
his shop has both an Oriental and stagey flavor—'The Ming Toy Bootery.'
The name, according to the old ring champion, came from the character
played by Fay Bainter in 'East Is West,' a popular Broadway production
of a couple of seasons ago."

The following May, a watchman felt a drop of something fall upon his
hand. It was gasoline, oozing from a five-gallon can, surrounded by some
oil-soaked newspapers, in the Ming Toy's stairway. Police summoned
Attell and his partner, E. M. Tausend, for questioning. Abe claimed old
enemies were attempting to "frame" him.

(above) *From the* Boot and Shoe Recorder *of October 1,*
1921 (right) *Abe Attell in His Championship Boxing Days*
(AUTHOR'S COLLECTION)

Abe Attell: *There is no reason I should set the store on fire. We are making money, and the business is in good financial condition.*

The Ming Toy entered receivership that July.

90. THE CLUB MAURICE 209 West 51st Street (Between Broadway and Eighth Avenue) The nightclub operated

in part by still another of Lillian Lorraine's paramours, one Charles C. Wagner (aka "Billy Lloyd"). But the Club Maurice also served as the place of employment for watchman Garbino Caseri who discovered the fire, the gasoline, and the oil-soaked newspapers at the aforementioned Ming Toy Bootery—since the Club Maurice was located in the basement below Abe Attell's bootery. Moreover, it was only a mere five days after said fire that private detectives tailed Charles Wagner/"Billy Lloyd" and Miss Lorraine from Club Maurice to her apartment. (*See* **LILLIAN LORRAINE RESIDENCE 120 West 71st Street.**) It was definitely a helluva eventful week at 209 West 51st Street.

91. EARLY ROTHSTEIN APARTMENT West 51st Street (address unknown) Bachelor Rothstein shared quarters

here with fellow gambler Felix Duffy prior to his marriage to Carolyn Green. The place doubled as headquarters for his betting operations.

Carolyn Rothstein: *At the time I met him, but unknown to me, Arnold was operating what might be termed a pool room, and living modestly in an apartment, in West Fifty-first Street, with Felix Duffy. They had a room with two or three telephones, and handled bets.*

I did know that Arnold played poker and bet on horse races, but that seemed to be the usual thing with all the men with whom I came in contact. Arnold never seemed to have much money in those days. He sent me flowers on one or two occasions, but not more than that, had funds enough to take me to dinner, and drive me home in hansom cabs. He never made me any presents.

As a matter of fact, I noticed none except pleasant qualities about Arnold. He was devoted to me exclusively. I never had gone out to supper after the theatre alone until I met him, and after I met him, it seemed natural and wonderful that we should be together as much as possible.

92. MARK HELLINGER THEATRE 237 West 51st Street (Between Broadway and Eighth Avenue) Here, on

December 26, 1988, the musical *Legs Diamond* opened, featuring veteran Broadway performer Joe Silver in the role of Rothstein. Peter Allen wrote the show's words and music and starred as Legs Diamond. The show closed after just sixty-four performances.

New York Herald Tribune City Editor Stanley Walker, in his seminal work, *The Nightclub Era*, wrote of Diamond that he was:

> a frail, tubercular little rat, cunning and cruel. He liked to burn men's feet with matches. He would pour bullets into the bodies of men who lay helpless and dying on the floor. Once he tied a blindfolded man to a tree, put the man's index fingers into the barrels of a shotgun, and went into conference with him on a matter of business.
>
> The police dismissed him as "a cheap little package thief." The master minds of the underworld, particularly the powers who fancied themselves "right-guys" and frowned on the torture chamber and assassination, disapproved of Diamond's philosophy of life. He was dangerous and senseless. And yet, the truth is that for a time Diamond was feared above all other New York gunmen; more, for a time he was powerful, and if he had had more executive ability he would have gone far.

———————

The Mark Hellinger opened as the "Warner Bros. Hollywood Theatre," a motion picture venue, in April 1930. Renamed after Broadway columnist Hellinger and converted to a legitimate house in January 1949, it witnessed its greatest success with Lerner and Loewe's *My Fair Lady* and later with

Rodgers and Hammerstein's *The Sound of Music*, though, the latter show did not premiere there.

Converted to the Times Square Church in February 1989, its ornate interior remains landmarked and untouched. It's worth sticking your head inside when the doors are opened.

93. DAVE'S BLUE ROOM 791 Seventh Avenue, above 51st Street

Rothstein protégé Lucky Luciano's hangout in the 1930s—in its time a real celebrity-laden venue with such stars as Frank Sinatra, Edward G. Robinson, Eddie Cantor, George Raft, Milton Berle, and Lillian Roth counted among its regular patrons. It closed in the 1940s. Luciano stopped dining there, however, much earlier thanks to his 1936 conviction on prostitution charges. His girlfriend, the beautiful but a bit plump White Russian refugee Galina "Gay" Orlova, hosted a Blue Room news conference to complain about her lover's prosecution by Thomas E. Dewey—and to attest to his besmirched character. "I don't believe any

Obviously Not *a Class Picture: Lucky Luciano (along with Meyer Lansky) in the center of this Chicago lineup in 1930.* (AUTHOR'S COLLECTION)

of those charges. . . . He was nice," she protested, "but he didn't give me anything too wonderful!"

Queried on another occasion about a previous suitor, the elderly stockbroker Theus Munds, Orlova cracked, "Oh, Theus is O.K. But all he's got is money. Lucky, he's sinister!"

And, come to think of it, so in his own way was Thomas E. Dewey, who had Orlova deported.

94. THE ALBANY APARTMENTS 1651 Broadway (aka 224 West 52nd Street and 215 West 51st Street) Fanny

Brice's residence (along with her Hungarian-born mother, Rose Stern Borach) commencing in 1910 when she first starred in the *Ziegfeld Follies*. "The rooms were large (30' x 30')," wrote Fanny's biographer Herbert Goldman, "and consisted of two bedrooms, a living room, a maid's room, and a kitchen. Rosie and Fanny lived alone, Fan's social life being confined to girlfriends and an occasional drink with a stage-door Johnny."

It was here, however, that Brice first took up residence with Nicky Arnstein, then still inconveniently married to his first wife, Carrie Greenthal Arnstein. In 1914, Brice and Arnstein moved out to lodgings on West 58th Street, across from the Plaza Hotel. Rose Borach headed uptown to 520 West 139th Street where she lived with her son Philip.

95. ROTHSTEIN RESIDENCE 1672 Broadway at West 52nd Street Rothstein moved here in 1913 after closing his West

46th Street gambling house. (*See* **ARNOLD ROTHSTEIN'S GAMBLING HOUSE 108 West 46th Street**.) "The main quarters comprised eight rooms and two baths," wrote Rothstein biographer Leo Katcher, "with separate quarters for a maid and a butler. The rent was high for the time—$2,400 a year." Carolyn Rothstein provided this as her address in July 1914. Now the site of the high-rise Earle Building.

96. EIGHT BALL RESTAURANT (aka Abe Attell Steak and Chophouse) 1667 Broadway (at West 52nd Street) Abe

Attell operated a restaurant and bar here for several years. By January 1951, Abe's chophouse was out of business, but authorities, nonetheless, raided the location's subsequent tenant, The Spotlight Café, arresting three men (including four-hundred-pound Sidney "Fats" Brown) on charges of running a $100,000-per-week college basketball betting operation.

Demolished.

97. AUTO ACCIDENT Broadway (Between West 52nd and West 53rd Streets) Here, at 5:00 a.m. on October 5, 1943,

Abe Attell was hit by a passing automobile. According to a press account, he "suffered a compound fracture of the right leg, shock, lacerations of the forehead, and possible concussion."

Another account revealed these details:

> Police said the car which hit Attell was abandoned by the driver [Sam Bortz]. He fled into a nearby subway entrance but later returned and surrendered to police. They said when he was told who his victim was, he exclaimed: "That's my old rival! I've boxed him many times."

98. FRANK BARRETT CARMAN APARTMENT 64 West 52nd Street (Between Fifth and Sixth Avenues) On

the night of December 31, 1922, three men chloroformed and robbed Irene Schoellkopf, the forty-five-year-old wife of wealthy Buffalo industrialist C. P. Hugo Schoellkopf as she departed a poker party thrown by thirty-seven-year-old vaudevillian Frank Barrett Carman ("Vaudeville's Premier Hoop Roller and Juggler"—and, for that matter, a mean baton-twirler!). Carman and Irene would wed in 1928.

Irene Schoellkopf's assailants dragged her to an apartment on the floor below and stripped her of $285,000 in jewels, including one 201-pearl necklace, a 99-pearl necklace, and two eight-carat diamond rings.

Among Irene Schoellkopf's three assailants was Eugene "Red" Moran (alias "John Rice"), who had previously teamed with Legs and Eddie Diamond in protecting A. R.'s bootleg scotch shipments while they snaked their way across Long Island toward Manhattan. Moran and company had fenced their Schoellkopf haul through Times Square jeweler John W. "The Phantom Fence" Mahan—netting, however, just $35,000 for their immense haul. Mahan in turn fenced his loot through Rothstein. When police caught up with Mahan and the Moran trio, Mahan negotiated a deal with them: no arrest for him if he returned the loot. He finally returned all but $40,000 of the haul, and in the bargain, no one dared finger Rothstein.

Earlier in 1922, Rothstein, fearing kidnapping, engaged Moran, Legs Diamond, and Thomas "Fats" Walsh as bodyguards. Moran received $1,000 per week. The *New York Times* later reported that, "Shortly after the trinity went to work, Moran and Walsh were badly beaten. As the result of the beating the Diamond brothers [Legs and Eddie] and Moran and

Murderers' Row: Eddie and Legs Diamond, Fatty Walsh, Lucky Luciano (AUTHOR'S COLLECTION)

Walsh quarreled. Walsh and Moran gave up their post, but the Diamonds continued." At least for a while. Eventually, the Diamonds and Rothstein parted acrimoniously.

All of which was interesting enough. But also very interesting was this: also attending Frank Carman's soiree was former stockbroker Alberto Santos Guimares and his girlfriend, showgirl Dot King. We will meet them again on West 57th Street. (*See* **DOT KING APARTMENT 144 West 57th Street.**)

99. LA TAVERNELLE RESTAURANT 252 West 52nd Street (Between Broadway and Eighth Avenue) Here, at this speakeasy on Monday evening, June 24, 1929, mobster Frankie Marlow (*see* **THE FITZGERALD BUILDING 1482 Broadway**) received a mysterious phone call while dining with five others, including the joint's owner, Ignatius Coppa, former middleweight champion Johnny Wilson, a pickpocket named "Boston Louie" Lewis, and nineteen-year-old dancer Mary "Mickey of the Rendezvous" Seiden who had formerly performed at Marlow's Silver Slipper (201 West 48th Street) and Rendezvous (St. Nicholas Avenue) night clubs. Marlow then handed Seiden (née Betty Farley) his Hotel Victoria (145 51st Street at Seventh Avenue) room key, saying, "I'll see you in the room in two hours. I've got a date." Seiden, by the way, was pregnant.

Outside, two men awaited Marlow. As "Mickey of the Rendezvous" waved goodbye, he joined the pair in getting into a blue sedan. Within an hour, he was found in a clump of bushes outside Flushing Cemetery in Queens (Forty-Fifth Avenue, near 166th Street). Three .38 caliber bullets had been fired at close range into Marlow's temple, jaw, and neck. He died before the ambulance arrived.

Press reports described Marlow, a former Al Capone ally, as a "prize fighters' manager, night club owner, and racketeer . . . a child of the Ghetto, who for more than a score of years had had a finger in every enterprise of Broadway's underworld." Another report termed him "an intimate friend of Rothstein."

"Boston Louie" Lewis soon found himself represented by attorney J. Arthur Adler who had recently represented torch singer Helen Morgan on federal liquor charges relating to her own cabaret, "Helen Morgan's Summer Home" (134 West 54nd Street).

Police also hauled in speakeasy owner Larry Fay for questioning. It was to Fay that Marlow had sold his former holdings in the Rendezvous. Fay claimed to have been in Atlantic City all weekend and quickly went free.

100. EDWARD DEVLIN FUNERAL PARLOR

408 West 52nd Street (Between Ninth and Tenth Avenues) "Fatty" Walsh's body was brought here from Miami following his March 1929 murder. To avoid publicity, he made the trip under the name "Hennessy."

Thomas "Fatty" Walsh, Probably Not a Jolly Fat Man (AUTHOR'S COLLECTION)

101. CLUB FRIVOLITY 1678 Broadway (Between West 52nd and West 53rd Streets)

Fatty Walsh's girlfriend Demaris "Hotsy Totsy" Dore danced here before her run with the *Padlocks of 1927* (*see* **THE SHUBERT THEATRE 225 West 44th Street**) and was noticed by Busby Berkeley. (*See* **LEW FIELDS'S MANSFIELD THEATRE 256 West 47th Street.**)

While appearing at the Frivolity in January 1928, Dore was sued by her former booking agent, David Schornstein, for $528 for booking fees not paid by her during the course of her engagements in Chicago.

Dore was a former friend of the notorious Peaches Browning, though that ceased when Dore stood ready to testify in favor of Peaches's estranged husband, "Daddy" Browning. (*See* **FAIRFIELD HOTEL 20-28 West 72nd Street.**) "Last night," the *Daily News* observed, "it was reported that [Peaches] didn't have a single tear to shed for Demaris's misfortune and wouldn't feel a bit sorry if her former friend lost every string of costume beads she has."

In March 1929, columnist Walter Winchell reported:

> You've probably read in the newspapers that Demaris Dore is better known along the Main Artery as "Hotsy Totsy," a tag given her because of her stage style and pep, zip and torrid warbling. . . . She has "walked out" of more shows and cafe revues than perhaps any other local entertainer, because she is difficult to handle, although her longest stay was at the Frivolity Club before it was Mabel Willebrandted [i.e., raided], where she enticed handsome trade. She is a clever lass, and should have clicked in a big way long ago. . . .
>
> In fewer words, she can get into more jams than a Broadway paragrapher.

A federal judge had padlocked the Frivolity for one year on November 19, 1928.

102. MIKE BEST SHOOTING West 53rd Street (Mid-Block Between Broadway and Seventh Avenue) Mike Best (née William Besnoff or Bestoff), an associate of George McManus (*see* **POLLY ADLER'S BROTHEL 303 West 92nd Street**), was at one time considered second only to Rothstein among Manhattan gamblers. With Rothstein and Owney Madden, he owned pieces of Harlem's famed Cotton Club (644 Lenox Avenue at West 142nd Street). But by 1937, Best had been reduced to hosting floating crap games in Manhattan's nondescript Yorkville neighborhood. On Monday evening, March 8, 1937, he was shot here over a decade-old $4,000 gambling debt. His assailant, Joseph Pledge (née Emetio Polizio), was immediately arrested and booked at the 47th Street Station. Best was rushed to Polyclinic Hospital (*see* **POLYCLINIC HOSPITAL 335-361 West 50th Street**), where he was operated on and recovered. Best, however, refused

to testify (even fleeing to Hot Springs to avoid the witness chair) against Pledge, who ended up serving a mere ten months at Rikers Island for Sullivan Act violations.

103. WEST SIDE PRISON 317 West 53rd Street (Between Eighth and Ninth Avenues) Where

District Attorney Whitman held Bald Jack Rose, Bridgie Webber, and Harry Vallon prior to placing Charles Becker on trial. Immediately adjacent to the West Side Magistrates Court (314 West 54th Street). The website correctionhistory.org says of the West Side Prison, one of several city "district" prisons, that it held "38 cells and a large holding 'cage.' Male inmates stayed overnight, some remaining months and years. Women inmates didn't remain overnight. The fortress-like structure featured back-to-back cells, each a small stone cavern with no shelving and hardly enough space for a single inmate. But its 38 cells sometimes held 157."

Closed in mid-1949.

104. ZIEGFELD THEATRE 1341 Sixth Avenue at West 54th Street Here, on the theater's opening night,

February 2, 1927, Legs Diamond's girlfriend Kiki Roberts (aka Marion Strasmick) appeared in the chorus of *Rio Rita. Rio Rita* went on to a successful run before being bumped that December for the immortal Jerome Kern–Oscar Hammerstein II musical *Show Boat*.

Heading for the Ziegfeld to attend *Rio Rita* (it had been arranged for him to watch from backstage while it remained at the Ziegfeld) was the still largely unknown Charles Lindbergh, who suddenly received news of sudden clear weather across the Atlantic. He skipped the performance and spent a sleepless night at Long Island's Garden City Hotel before heading for Paris—and history.

On his return from Paris, however, he finally *did* see the play.

Show Boat opened on December 27, 1927, starring torch singer Helen Morgan. Three nights later, federal agents raided (and smashed up) her Chez Morgan speakeasy. (*See* **THE 300 CLUB 151 West 54th Street.**)

The 1,638-seat Ziegfeld was built with the financial assistance of William Randolph Hearst. Converted to motion pictures in 1933 and later to an NBC television studio. It reverted to a legitimate house in 1963. Demolished in 1966.

The Ziegfeld Theatre in 1931 (AUTHOR'S COLLECTION)

105. HOTEL DORSET 30 West 54th Street (Between Fifth and Sixth Avenues)

Lillian Lorraine resided here in 1928 after her hospitalization at Park West Hospital (168–170 West 76th Street) for a ruptured appendix. A woman of too many assignations, her recent boyfriend was then "Dapper Don" Collins, an infamous confidence man—described by the tabloid *New York Graphic* as "an international crook, heartbreaker and shadowy figure in the underworld." Back in 1921, Collins had secured Arnold Rothstein's backing in a scheme to secure a sizable cache of whiskey (850 cases, 1,200 cases 1,600 cases, or 2,000 cases—accounts vary) for just $75 each and to resell each case stateside for a whopping $250.

Staying with Lorraine at the Dorset was her close friend showgirl Bessie Poole—W. C. Fields's longtime girlfriend and the mother of his illegitimate son.

Like Fields, Poole was a very heavy drinker, most likely an alcoholic. On Saturday evening, October 6, 1928, shortly after Lorraine's return from Park West Hospital, she and Poole dined at Dinty Moore's (*see* **DINTY MOORE'S 216 West 46th Street**) with two very married business executives before returning to the Dorset, where yet another Lorraine paramour, multimillionaire Coca-Cola executive Joseph Whitehead (married, of course), awaited them. Lorraine, still feeling the effects of her recent illness, opted to remain in for the evening. The others beelined for West 48th Street's Chez Florence (*see* **CHEZ FLORENCE 117 West 48th Street**), where a melee broke out. Most likely, the club's owner, Tommy Guinan (Texas Guinan's brother), slugged the thirty-three-year-old Poole, broke her nose, and, as she was in no great shape to begin with, she died from her injuries. Her attending physician suggested foul play but soon completely reversed himself, assigning her death to alcoholism and heart disease. *You reversed yourself back then if you knew what was good for you.*

In her will, Poole left a diamond ring to Fields. He denied knowing her.

106. HOTEL WARWICK 65 West 54th Street (At Sixth Avenue) Carolyn Rothstein provided this as her address when she returned from Europe in December 1927.

By now, Carolyn had requested to separate from Arnold, a move he mightily resisted, as his longtime Black valet Tom Farley testified in New York State Supreme Court in January 1930: "He asked me to plead with Mrs. Rothstein and try and get her to come back to him. I saw her and then told him, 'Mr. Rothstein. I talked with her two hours, and she will not yield.' He answered, 'I am a ruined man. I really love Carolyn.'"

William Randolph Hearst built the thirty-six-story Warwick in 1926 at a cost of $5 million. Counted among its more prominent guests were Meyer Lansky, James Dean, Elizabeth Taylor, Elvis Presley, the Beatles, and Cary Grant (a twenty-seventh-floor resident, who stayed there for twelve years). Among its less prominent guests was this work's author, whose laptop was totally fried by a short in the joint's electrical system.

New York's
Most Dis-
tinguished
Residential
Hotel

An address *sans reproche*. Home
comforts of rare luxury. Fault-
less hotel service. Furnished, or un-
furnished, 1 to 4 room suites. Serving pantries; electric refrigeration.
Occupancy now—or as of Oct. 1st.
Select Transient Accommodation

The **Warwick**

A RESIDENTIAL HOTEL
65 West 54th Street
Direction; Mr. A. F. Miller

(AUTHOR'S COLLECTION)

In June 1927, Hearst honored Charles Lindbergh (just returned from Paris) at a dinner here. Among their guests were Mayor James J. Walker and Charlie Chaplin.

Owney Madden associate "Frenchy" DeMange died here (quite peacefully in bed) on September 18, 1939. He was reputedly worth somewhere between $2,000,000 and $5,000,000.

107. BUDA GODMAN APARTMENT

161 West 54th Street (At Seventh Avenue) Indicted jewel thief, twenty-two-year-old Samuel "Sammy the Hook" Entratta (aka Sam Ippolito), fearing prison, put a bullet through his brain here June 14, 1932.

On January 21, 1932, Entratta and two other armed men, the Indelacato brothers, thirty-two-year old Joseph (an Elizabeth Street undertaker) and twenty-seven year old Anthony (a longshoreman), all posing as bootleggers, had relieved millionaire hairnet manufacturer Harry C. Glemby of $305,000 in jewels at his 22 East 67th Street home. Their plan was to fence the loot through longtime crook, opium addict, and former Charles A. Stoneham mistress, the forty-three-year-old Buda Godman. It was not a good plan, for when Godman and an accomplice met with Seattle jewel fence "Abraham Rothstein" on the corner of Broadway and West 63rd Street on April 13, "Rothstein" turned out to be an undercover police department clerk, Abraham Gralla.

Yet there was even more to the story. When cops raided Buda's apartment, they discovered two identical cretonne bags, one containing the stolen jewelry, the other filled with broken glass. Buda planned on making love to the diminutive "Rothstein" (i.e. Gralla) and then to switch bags on him and then peddle her stash again to another fence.

Godman, who had escaped punishment years ago for her part in an Ansonia Hotel (*see* **THE ANSONIA HOTEL West 73rd Street and Broadway**) badger game, was no longer so lucky, earning a four-to-eight-year sentence at upstate Auburn Penitentiary. A pre-sentencing report revealed her to be the longtime mistress of New York Giants owner Charles A. Stoneham. (*See* **CHARLES A.**

Buda Godman (AUTHOR'S COLLECTION)

STONEHAM APARTMENT 110 West 55th Street.) At one point, she alleged that she had planned to peddle the Glemby gems to Stoneham. Despite all that, Stoneham (seemingly loyal to everyone save his wife) vowed he would still provide her support.

As for the Indelicato brothers, Joe earned a ten-to-twenty-year sentence in Attica; Anthony beat the rap—though not for long. In January 1933, police discovered his bullet-riddled body in a Patterson, New Jersey, field.

At some point, someone tried poisoning Joe Indelicato. It didn't work.

108. FIFTY-FIFTY CLUB 119-121 West 54th Street (Between Sixth and Seventh Avenues) A particularly upscale speakeasy ("the last word in exclusiveness") whose clientele included Jack Dempsey, Jack Pickford and his wife Olive Thomas, Jack's restaurant owner Jack Dunston, and lightweight champion Benny "The Ghetto Wizard" Leonard.

Here, Lillian Lorraine suffered the January 31, 1921, tumble that shattered her spine and hamstrung the remainder of her stage career. As one press report contended: "Trying to negotiate the steep and narrow stairs her heel caught, and with no one to stay her flight she pitched headlong to the bottom of the stairs, where she was picked up unconscious and rushed to the hospital. There an X-ray examination disclosed the fracture of two vertebrae in her backbone near the neck."

Here, also, George Uffner's girlfriend Edna Wheaton again captured beaty contest honors, this triumph being the grandly named "Award of the Apple of Paris" in a competition judged by famed magazine cover illustrator Harrison Fisher.

Located on West 54th Street's "Garage Row" on the third floor of one of those garages. Raided and closed by axe-wielding police in June 1922.

Fame Is Fleeting Department: Edna Wheaton receives the Apple of Paris. (AUTHOR'S COLLECTION)

109. THE 300 CLUB 151 West 54th Street (Between Sixth and Seventh Avenues) A speakeasy operated by Texas Guinan—and previously as the "Helen Morgan Club," run by *Show Boat* star Helen Morgan.

Morgan's biographer Gilbert Maxwell speculated that, perhaps, the 300 Club was partly owned by Rothstein—and for that reason escaped raiding by federal agents, causing them to instead raid Morgan's nearby new speakeasy Chez Morgan (143–45 West 54th Street).

As Maxwell recorded, on the evening of December 30, 1927:

The place was packed, the eight-piece orchestra was swinging, and Helen Morgan, wearing black velvet and her strand of matchless pearls, had already finished her first show. While Miss Morgan and her companions rode down to the West Thirtieth Street precinct, the FBI's dry agents wrecked the Chez Morgan bar, smashed glassware,

shredded lace curtains and tapes-
tries, destroyed electrical fixtures
and tore out the plumbing in the
men's and women's lounges.

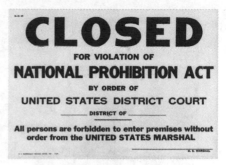

CLOSED

FOR VIOLATION OF

NATIONAL PROHIBITION ACT

BY ORDER OF

UNITED STATES DISTRICT COURT

——— DISTRICT OF ———

All persons are forbidden to enter premises without
order from the UNITED STATES MARSHAL

(AUTHOR'S COLLECTION)

In February 1928, a federal judge
dropped all charges against Morgan
and ordered her furnishings ($50,000
worth) returned. That March, she
opened a new club, Helen Morgan's
Summer Home, in the basement of
a 134 West 54th Street brownstone. Arrested again on June 29—she won
acquittal in April 1929.

At some point, Texas Guinan opened a new speakeasy here, the Club
Argonaut. There, in 1932, that all-around psychopath Vincent "Mad Dog"
Coll (a deadly rival of Dutch Schultz) kidnapped "Big Frenchy" DeMange
(possibly the club's owner) to collect a $35,000 (some say $50,000) ransom
from Frenchy's bosom pal Owney "The Killer" Madden.

Madden quickly paid Coll. Coll soon paid with his life when Madden
ordered him machine-gunned while at a phone booth in the "London
Chemists" drugstore (314 West 23rd Street).

110. CONGRESS APARTMENTS 161 West 54th Street
(at Seventh Avenue) From September 8 through 10,
1928, small-time Broadway gambler and sometime Rothstein bodyguard
Jimmy Meehan (née Raffaele Marino) hosted a big-time card game here
at Apartment 32. The game's participants: Arnold Rothstein; San Francisco
gamblers "Nigger Nate" Raymond and Joe Bernstein ("a quiet mild mannered
chap . . . from the Pacific Coast"); Alvin "Titanic" Thompson (Damon
Runyon's model for "Sky Masterson"); and New York gamblers George
"Hump" McManus, Martin "Red" Bowe ("florid and partly bald"), and
brothers Sam and Meyer Boston (née the Solomon brothers).

"Meyer Boston," observed one press report, "who is a little fellow, hardly
more than five feet tall, with eyebrows so arched that he wears perpetually a

A Rendering of September 1928's Infamous Poker Game (AUTHOR'S
COLLECTION)

surprised expression, said he won $3,000 in the stud poker game, a feature
of which was side betting for large sums on the highest cards."

Rothstein was the big loser, over $300,000 in all. He suspected cheating
and refused to pay, a very foolish—and fatal—decision, as it turned out.

As Titanic Thompson later revealed to poker authority John Scarne:

Before that game of high spades began that night—Rothstein
took me [Thompson] aside and suggested that we play partners,
and I agreed. However, later in the evening, when Raymond and
Bernstein entered the game, I decided to end the partnership in
order to work with Raymond and Bernstein. We knew each other
real well, having participated in many swindles together. We had
worked together in many Poker games in Texas and California.
We knew all the Poker cheating methods such as signaling and
playing the best hand, fixing the high spades, using strippers
and marked cards. Raymond and Bernstein were two of the best
Poker cheaters and connivers, and I thought we might do a little
business together that night. Sure, we cheated Rothstein out of

the $319,000 in markers, and if it wasn't for that drunk McManus shooting Rothstein, we might have collected our money.

Concluded Scarne:

After reading the court records of the McManus trial and all the front-page testimony carried by *The New York Times* concerning the game and the Rothstein shooting, plus my conversations with four of the principals who were involved, I'm of the firm opinion that George McManus, Titanic Thompson, Nigger Nate Raymond and Joe Bernstein as a team had set out to fleece Arnold Rothstein at poker with marked cards and stripper decks.

Titanic Thompson (AUTHOR'S COLLECTION)

Said the *Brooklyn Daily Eagle*:

It is a positive fact that Rothstein believed he was the victim of "readers" in that game. Just how he could have been fooled is something which puzzles the detectives. Rothstein is looked upon here as the most astute gambler in the city. But he told friends that "readers were pulled" on him and he said he would not pay a cent of the money he owed. These "floater" games are usually run with I O U's. Too much money is too dangerous in the hotels.

Briefly residing at the Congress in early 1925 was up-and-coming pianist Oscar Levant, having moved into the apartment of his oldest brother, Harry (a longtime Broadway orchestra leader); Harry's wife, Pearl; and their daughter, Doris. Not surprisingly, it didn't work out.

The Congress Apartments lay just two blocks south of the Park Central. The fifteen-story brick apartment house, its once-gleaming marble lobby still remarkably intact, is almost untouched save for nine decades of grime. A decade or so ago, its mezzanine housed a talent agency for go-go girls, a far cry from the site's previous use, Grace Reformed Dutch Church.

Nigger Nate Raymond (AUTHOR'S COLLECTION)

111. POLLY ADLER'S BROTHEL 201 West 54th Street (aka 842-844 Seventh Avenue)

Rothstein was among the many of the celebrity madam's high-profile clients, and this address served as her primary establishment for a number of years. There were, however, numerous other locations including 303 West 92nd Street (at West End Avenue), 57 West 58th Street, the Abbottsford Apartments at 411 West End Avenue (at West 80th Street), 115 West 73rd Street, on West 69th Street and Columbus Avenue, at West 77th Street and Amsterdam Avenue, on West 83rd Street, and at the Hoffman Arms at 640 Madison Avenue (at East 59th Street).

A regular—and significant—customer was George McManus. In her memoirs, *A House Is Not a Home*, the diminutive, Russian-born Adler recounted her connection to McManus and to the Rothstein murder case. It went like this: In 1926, McManus and a bunch of his friends, including Legs Diamond's younger brother Eddie, and prominent gambling syndicate head Mike Best (*see* **MIKE BEST SHOOTING West 53rd Street**) arrived at Adler's bordello, in a particularly nasty state. "All were very drunk," she recalled, "and McManus was drunker than all of them." McManus was particularly ugly and dangerous, waving his pistol in her face. But when she asked McManus to check his pistol with her, he did. Later one of McManus's cronies fired a shot through the whorehouse's French doors.

When McManus was held for the [Rothstein] murder I got a phone call from one of the [McManus] gang, who asked if the District Attorney had sent for me. It seemed that one of my girls had talked about that night at the apartment and had said it was George who fired the shot through the French doors. If the D.A. could prove that George went around shooting up places just for his own amusement, it would certainly strengthen the case against him, and my informant had heard I was going to be questioned. Since I was the only one who could back up George's statement that he had turned over his gun to me before the shooting occurred, this placed me in a rather ticklish spot. I assured the caller that my girls would do no more talking. Luckily, I was never called and George was acquitted without my having to testify.

There may—or may not—be a further Polly Adler connection to Arnold Rothstein's demise. Registered down the hall in Room 330 from George McManus's Park Central Room 349 was a twenty-three-year-old blonde "freelance model" from Chicago, Mrs. Ruth Keyes. Mrs. Keyes was most likely *not* a "freelance model." More likely she was a prostitute of some sort, and in the hours leading up to the Rothstein shooting she cavorted with McManus and friends in Room 349 ("It was really a suite and quite an expensive one too"), drinking and laughing and doing whatever "freelance models" do under such circumstances. "Jack [the name McManus called himself]," Keyes told a reporter back in Chicago, "was the life of the party. . . . He did solo dances and sang."

Ruth Keyes, Evidently Enjoying the Publicity and Looking Not a Bit Blond (AUTHOR'S COLLECTION)

A recent author that I won't name hinted rather broadly (and not necessarily convincingly) that Mrs. Keyes worked for

Polly Adler. That may *or may not* be the case. While many a prostitute *did* work for her, many did not. In the absence of proof, we remain skeptical.

Yet another interesting theory regarding the Adler establishment involves the maddeningly mysterious Judge Crater. The story is that Crater (obviously the libidinous sort) ended up visiting Adler's on the night of August 6, 1930, keeled over, and to avoid embarrassment to Miss Adler and her associates, was ingloriously dumped in the Hudson.

An alternate theory (one of several) holds that driving the taxi that Crater supposedly entered was Legs Diamond henchman Frank Burns, brother of NYPD officer Charles Burns. Diamond, the story goes, was upset with Crater and wanted some sense beaten into him. Under this theory, Crater was driven to Coney Island, but just a tad too much sense was applied. Crater died and was buried under the boardwalk.

You pays yer money . . . and takes yer choice.

112. CLUB INTIME 205 West 54th Street (Between Seventh Avenue and Broadway) Located in the basement of the Hotel Harding, the Club Intime was yet another mob-controlled, Texas Guinan–hosted speakeasy—this time operated by Owney "The Killer" Madden.

It was here in the early hours of March 4, 1929, that Guinan hosted a séance whose fifty-or-so participants included such hot-shots as writers Heywood Broun, Alexander Woollcott, and Nunnally Johnson; actresses Ethel Barrymore and Fanny Ward; composer Samuel L. M. Barlow II and his second wife, the lecturer and famed beauty Ernesta Beaux; Guinan's own stockbroker, the playboy Freddie Ziegler and his wife; and the Zieglers' twenty-three-year-old friend, the Austrian-born wife of a "fabulously wealthy Paris banker," Margot Colin.

In charge of the evening's proceedings was the famed (but eventually debunked) Neapolitan-born medium Nino Pecoraro. As Pecoraro commenced, Margot Colin turned to Ziegler and nervously remarked, "Here, keep this for me. Rothstein is the first ghost."

With that, Margot handed Ziegler her $10,000 three-inch-wide sunburst brooch. At its core was an eight-carat diamond, surrounded by 380 "minor brilliants." Ziegler placed it inside his vest pocket, as Guinan interjected, "You wouldn't trim us, would you, Arnold? Tell us about yourself."

"Something that looked like smoke started to arise between Tex and the medium," the *Daily News* later reported. "It took on shape . . . and those who knew Rothstein clutched their jewelry, and grew rigid. . . . But Freddie Ziegler had felt a plucking at his coat, and the ghost disappeared."

"Rothstein" wasn't the only one vanishing. The Zieglers and Mme. Colin also soon departed, not even sticking around to hear the spirit of the late Rudolph Valentino strum upon his guitar (or was it his banjo? who could tell?). Such ghostly musical interludes were a hallmark of Pecoraro's act.

Soon Ziegler and Colin discovered a more ominous disappearance: Colin's brooch was gone! And some fingers pointed to none other than the specter of Arnold Rothstein!

(above left) *Ernesta Beaux (Mrs. Samuel Barlow)* (above right) *Margot Colin ("Hello! Is that you, Mr. Rothstein?")* (AUTHOR'S COLLECTION)

(right) *Artist's Rendering of 1931's Club Abbey Brawl: Mavis King, Dutch Schultz, Chink Sherman* (below) *Dutch Schultz Wanted Poster (1934)*
(AUTHOR'S COLLECTION)

"Tell them they don't need to worry," chortled Hump McManus from his cell in The Tombs. "If it's gone, Arny's got it!"

A pretty good yarn—which eventually grew even better. The half-French Margot Colin was, in fact, not *the* spouse of a "fabulously wealthy Paris banker." Actually, she was an ex-typist and the estranged second wife of former lightweight prizefighter Herbert Van Blarcom (ring name: Johnny Burt). Blarcom had been looking for his missing "Margie" without any great success until spying her visage in all the tabloid headlines, leading him to find her improperly ensconced with a "prosperous appearing man" at her $20,000-per-year 14 East 60th Street apartment. He sued her for divorce. She did not contest it.

The Intime was replaced by the Club Abbey, whose own ending was punctuated by a December 1931 brawl involving denizens of the Dutch Schultz and Waxey Gordon mobs. Slashed by Schultz in the melee was Gordon's key lieutenant Charles "Chink" Sherman, whose life was believed to have been saved thanks to the quick thinking of cigarette girl Mavis King, a Hotel Harding resident, who switched off the lights and hailed a cab to rush Sherman off to a private room at Polyclinic Hospital, there to be treated for twelve stab wounds from a penknife plus three bullet wounds.

According to Polly Adler biographer Debby Applegate, the Club Abbey also served as a hangout of Legs Diamond and the redheaded prostitute Vivian Gordon. Gordon (whose foray into operating her own bordello had originally been bankrolled by Rothstein) and Diamond became partners in a lucrative badger game operation. "Vivian and Jack [Legs]," a friend of Gordon's told the *New York Daily News*, "had been taking the boys right and left. They were the envy of every racket mob on Broadway."

The 5'4", fortyish Gordon eventually came to a very Beansie Rosenthal–like ending. After testifying to investigator Irving Ben Cooper against vice squad patrolman Andrew J. McLaughlin, on February 26, 1931, her body was found along a roadside in the Bronx's Van Cortlandt Park. Cause of death: strangulation. Missing were her mink coat, her watch, and pocketbook, though robbery may not have been the actual motive. In life, Gordon had worked many angles and accumulated even more enemies.

"Like Legs, Vivian was reckless and greedy," notes Debby Applegate. "She was a heavy user of cocaine and sleeping aids like Veronal and Alinol and was an exceedingly ugly belligerent drunk. If she suspected that one of her feminine accomplices was keeping more than her share of the loot, Vivian would set her up to be arrested by one of her pals on the vice squad."

A week following Vivian's demise, her distraught sixteen-year-old daughter, Benita, committed suicide.

Another habitué of the Club Abbey was the mysterious Judge Crater, who visited (with dancer Elaine Dawn, roommate of his girlfriend Sally Ritz) there just two nights previous to his fabled disappearance. A few nights earlier, he visited in the company of an attorney named Kaplan. It remains a possibility that he revisited the Abbey after dining at Billy Haas's. "I'm sure he is dead," his fellow Supreme Court justice Louis Valente is recorded as saying. "We traced him to Club Abbey but then we lost his trail. I believe, like many of his friends, that he flashed a large roll of bills and was taken for a ride."

Yet, still another interesting aspect of the Club Abbey . . .

Vaudeville had long featured a surprisingly substantial number of female (and, to a lesser extent, male) impersonators, most notably the wildly popular Julian Eltinge, for whom the Eltinge Theatre was named in 1912 and which in part survives as the lobby of the AMC Empire 25 (236 West 42nd Street) movie theater.

By the early 1930s, vaudeville, of course, was on its last legs, but various clubs and speakeasies now witnessed a rebirth of such acts, in what was known as the "Pansy Craze," among the prime examples of which was the wild success of the Club Abbey's openly effeminate, lisping master of ceremonies, Gene Malin (née Victor Eugene James Malinovsky, aka Jean Malin and Imogene Wilson). Though usually a drag performer, Malin did not appear in drag at the Abbey, but rather in a more conventional tuxedo, flamboyantly introducing other drag performers.

"I never cared for Malin," wrote *Daily News* columnist Ed Sullivan, "or the type of entertainment which he represented, but there is no doubt that he earned considerable success on the Dawn Patrol. He was the wittiest and least offensive of his curious brigade."

It is said that the aforementioned December 1931 Dutch Schultz–Waxey Gordon tussle at the Abbey led to a police crackdown on the city's various "Pansy" clubs.

Despite Malin's open homosexuality, in January 1931, he married former showgirl Louise Helman, later convicted of operating a string of Manhattan brothels. Drowned following a Venice, California, auto accident in August 1933, he was buried out of Brooklyn's St. Mary's Queen of the Angels Church.

––––––––––

At 10:30 p.m. on the evening of October 5, 1928, two goons from Legs and Eddie Diamond's gang popped out from behind a parked car to eliminate rival mobster Tony Marlow, standing outside the Hotel Harding, casually smoking a cigarette.

"Marlow," explained one press report, "imported to New York the Chicago custom of making and selling unripe, vicious beer. He induced Bronx garage men and the like to make the brew in the backs of their buildings. He peddled it cheaper than the New Jersey gangs, who, at least, made drinkable, authoritative brew. Marlow cut in heavily with his cheap beer and damaged the Jersey business."

Damaging anyone's business in *this* business was dangerous business. Damaging Legs Diamond's business was invariably *fatal*. Marlow's assailants felled him with a single shot then pumped four more slugs into him as he lay wounded on the pavement. He died the next day, but not before swearing revenge upon his assailants. "I'll take care of them myself when I get well." Literally hundreds of persons witnessed Marlow's slaying, as thousands of theatergoers were exiting the nearby Winter Garden, the Capitol, the Roxy, and the Fifty-First Street theaters.

Marlow's assassination triggered the subsequent November's Joey Noe–Louis Weinberg Wild West–style shoot-out. (*See* **CHATEAU MADRID 234 West 54th Street**.) In May 1929, police finally held Legs Diamond for questioning regarding Marlow's death. Nothing, as usual, stuck.

Replacing the Club Abbey was *yet another* speakeasy, the Triangle Club. Police and federal Prohibition agents raided it on January 14, 1932. Unlike the usually visualized frantic, axe-wielding "raid" scene so often seen in movies, in this case, as the *Brooklyn Eagle* reported, "Patrons were asked to finish their meals and leave." Just five days before that raid, *Daily News* Broadway columnist Sidney Skolsky placed this item (in mock telegraphic form) in his column:

LILLIAN LORRAINE

TRIANGLE CLUB, WEST 54TH ST CITY

SUCCESSS TO YOU WHEN YOU START WORKING AT THE TRIANGLE CLUB AND RETURN TO THE BROADWAY SCENE STOP SOME OF THOSE OLD "FOLLIES" STAGE DOOR JOHNNIES OUGHT TO DROP AROUND AND SEE YOU

More recently the building's basement has hosted an elegant little bar called "Flute."

113. CHATEAU MADRID 234 West 54th Street Outside

this speakeasy at 7:00 a.m. on October 16, 1928, Dutch Schultz associate Joe Noe engaged in Jazz Age New York's most spectacular shoot-out.

Noe (a Bronx special deputy sheriff!) was, according to the *New York Times*, "the alleged head of a local gang running beer into New York for a Newark syndicate and competing for the trade of the Broadway speakeasies with the Diamond brothers' gang."

At 10:30 p.m., October 5, Noe henchman Tony Marlow had been executed near here as part of the Noe–Diamond turf war. (*See* **CLUB INTIME 205 West 54th Street**.) Outraged, the twenty-five-year-old Noe challenged Marlow's killers to meet him there to settle the score. Noe arrived first. Then, three Diamond men pulled up, including thirty-four-year-old ex-convict Louis Weinberg. Weinberg and Noe faced off in a pistol-blazing, Western gun fight–style, and Noe went down. But Weinberg's bulletproof steel vest failed to protect him when Noe's gunsels opened fire from a nearby rooftop, and a slug ripped into his jugular. Some sources say Dutch Schultz was among his assailants. A few hours later, police found Weinberg's bullet-riddled body in his gang's bullet-riddled Cadillac in a 604 East 13th Street garage.

"At the hospital," the United Press syndicate reported, "$960 was found in [Noe's] pockets. This was given to an orderly for safekeeping, and the orderly disappeared, giving the police another problem to solve."

Noe lingered until late November before perishing at Bellevue, as the *Times* delicately phrased it, "from infection from two bullet wounds and a light attack of pneumonia."

Some later theorized that Rothstein was actually shot in retaliation for Noe's murder.

———

Singer and entertainer Joe E. Lewis (the victim of a vicious 1927 mob attack in Chicago; Sam Giancana was a participant) later bought the establishment and installed an impressive list of guest masters of ceremony that included Al Jolson, George Jessel, Jack Benny, and Joe Frisco. Schultz was a regular patron and became a friend. Once, after having toured Times Square, Schultz headed for St. Patrick's Cathedral. "Here's where I leave you," protested the Jewish Lewis. To which the equally Jewish Schultz replied, "I'm as kosher as you are, but I'm a Catholic too. I ain't passin' up nothin'. In our business we need all the good luck we can get."

114. THE HOTSY TOTSY CLUB 1721 Broadway (Between West 54th and West 55th Street, second Floor) In July 1929, at his Broadway nightclub, the Hotsy Totsy Club, former Rothstein bodyguard Legs Diamond and his associate Charles Entratta (aka "Charles Green") engaged in an argument with fellow gangster (and speakeasy owner) William "Red" Cassidy, age

thirty-six, stinking drunk, and not about to reach thirty-seven. The topic: the talents of their fellow patron, welterweight pugilist Ruby "The Jewel of the Ghetto" Goldstein. Cassidy ended up shot dead. As was bystander (and ex-convict) Simon Walker. A waiter, a bartender, and Cassidy's younger brother Peter were wounded.

Said Police Commissioner Grover Whalen:

> Diamond jumped across the little bar, dropped Red Cassidy with one bullet, then emptied his revolver into his victim's body, while his [business] partner Hymie Cohen kept the piano playing to drown out the shots.

Through witness intimidation (a polite word for outright murder), Diamond once more escaped justice. (*See* **WILLIAM WOLGAST RESIDENCE 327 West 45th Street.**)

Legs Diamond's Hotsy Totsy Club (Note the Small Sign for It to the Left of the First Lamppost) (AUTHOR'S COLLECTION)

It was also at the Hotsy Totsy Club, back in 1927, that Diamond made the acquaintance of girlfriend Kiki Roberts (Marion Strasmick), a chorus girl at the joint.

Another less-famous Diamond paramour was *Ziegfeld Follies* acrobatic dancer Grace LaRue (later Grace LaRue Graham—not to be confused with an earlier and more famous actress, Grace La Rue). Decades later, Grace recalled this visit to the club:

> I remember one night when some of us girls were sitting in on a backroom meeting at Jack's Hotsy Totsy Club and Al

Mr. & Mrs. Charles Entratta (AUTHOR'S COLLECTION)

Capone, in from Chicago, was there too. Just to be friendly and make conversation I asked him how he had gotten the scar on the side of his face. Boy, did I ever get hustled out of there in a hurry! You can guess why Jack Diamond never took me to another one of those meetings.

115. CHARLES A. STONEHAM APARTMENT 110 West 55th Street (Between Sixth and Seventh Avenues)

Here, from 1918 through 1929, bucket shop operator and New York Giants owner Charles A. Stoneham resided with his ultra-shady mistress, Buda Godman, a former badger game artist and counterfeiter. (*See* **ANSONIA HOTEL West 73rd Street and Broadway**.) Many a time, Buda, a great beauty in her younger days, was thought to be "Mrs. Charles A. Stoneham," though the authentic "Mrs. Charles A. Stoneham" resided in New Jersey.

In 1907, the Chicago-born brunette had wed songwriter Tell Taylor, author of 1910's "Down by the Old Mill Stream" and a partner with Jimmy Walker in a Tin Pan Alley music publishing firm. But the Taylor-Godman union soon fizzled, for, as Taylor eventually confessed to reporters, "I married Buda when we both were drunk, and I found out she was quite incapable of loyalty to anybody."

Buda met the rather-lumpy (but highly lascivious) Stoneham at Havana, where Stoneham enjoyed interests in the local racetrack and casino. At first, he ensconced her at a Manhattan hotel suite before shacking up with her on 55th Street. Such long-term domesticity, however, failed to reform her, for as the *Daily News* would later report:

> During Stoneham's absences . . . the 55th St. apartment was frequented by "suspicious looking men." Neighbors complained that opium was being used there, and on one occasion three opium pipes were found in the apartment.

There was, however, a remarkable surprise coda to Stoneham's infidelities. Following his January 1936 passing, yet another "Mrs. Charles A. Stoneham" emerged when his former mistress Margaret Leonard (aka Bernice Leonard) brought suit against his estate to ensure support for their two children, eleven-year-old Jane Elizabeth Stoneham and fifteen-year-old Russell Charles Stoneham. Leonard, a former showgirl, had long resided with Stoneham in their eight-room home at 141 Kensico Road, Greenburgh, Westchester County.

Stoneham's connections to Rothstein were threefold: high-stake gambler, New York Giants owner, and bucket shop operator.

GAMBLER

Stoneham not only participated in Rothstein's high-stakes Partridge Club; he was a prominent habitué of A. R.'s luxurious Saratoga Springs gambling house, The Brook.

One night, Stoneham was laid up and was unable to visit The Brook. So, instead, he phoned in his bets on the spin of Rothstein's roulette wheel—eventually losing $70,000.

On another evening in August 1920, Subway Sam Rosoff was $400,000 to the good, threatening to break the bank at The Brook. Rothstein phoned Stoneham who rushed $300,000 to A. R. from his nearby private safe. (*See* **SUBWAY SAM ROSOFF HOME 179 West 113th Street.**)

NEW YORK GIANTS OWNER

In 1918, when the New York Giants baseball team went on the block, speculation on its new ownership centered on either candy manufacturer George Loft or Broadway's George M. Cohan. But, instead, a new ownership triumvirate emerged victorious: Stoneham (1,166 shares), longtime Giants manager John J. McGraw (70 shares), and New York City magistrate Francis X. McQuade (70 shares). McQuade had long lobbied to allow Sunday baseball in the city, and when it finally arrived in May 1919, he threw out the ceremonial first pitch at the Polo Grounds.

Rothstein had brokered the deal. Some said he may have even bankrolled it.

McQuade, coincidentally, was the judge who helped make Rothstein's 1919 cop-shooting charges vanish. (*See* **SITE OF FLOATING CRAP GAME 301 West 57th Street.**) McQuade later sued Stoneham for using New York Giants funds as loans to his personal enterprises. Under fire for corruption charges, McQuade resigned from the bench in December 1930.

In 1921, with the Black Sox Scandal engulfing baseball (and Rothstein), Stoneham, nonetheless, hosted Rothstein in his private Polo Grounds box, earning a reprimand from Major League Baseball Commissioner Kenesaw Mountain Landis.

Not altogether surprisingly, the Giants suffered from an unusual number of gambling related scandals involving such personnel as first baseman Hal Chase, pitchers Heinie Zimmerman, Jean Dubuc, and "Shufflin' Phil" Douglas, infielder Jimmy O'Connell, and coach "Cozy" Dolan. Faced with criticism from Commissioner Landis, Dolan threatened to sue. His attorney: Bill Fallon.

It was, however, on Wall Street where Stoneham, a protégé of George Graham Rice, and Rothstein really intersected.

Stoneham's brokerage firm, Charles A. Stoneham & Co., operated not only in New York but in numerous locations nationwide—including Chicago, Cleveland, Milwaukee, and Hartford. Unfortunately, it was also a bucket shop—the kind of firm that neglected to actually purchase the stocks ordered by customers in the hopes that said stocks would sooner or later decline in value, then desperate customers would "sell," and the bucket shop would pocket the difference. If stocks, however, increased in value, the bucket shop could easily be ruined—and so might its investors.

Rothstein was not only Stoneham's shield from prosecution for all his shady dealings but also a secret partner in many of his operations. For example, the two were secret partners in the E. P. Dier and Company bucket shop, whose January 1922 failure cost investors $4 million.

When Stoneham closed his own firm in 1921, he referred his clients not only to E. P. Dier but to other shady firms such as the recently formed Dillon & Co., controlled by yet another Rothstein crony, "Dandy Phil" Kastel. Dillon & Co.'s quick collapse cost investors $300,000, with Kastel pocketing $150,000 of the firm's assets. Rothstein had assisted in securing the debonair Kastel's seat on the Consolidated Exchange. In return, Dillon & Co. "loaned" Rothstein $407,000, a sum he never repaid. Authorities eventually convicted Kastel of mail fraud and grand larceny. He later became a close partner in Frank Costello's lucrative New Orleans gambling operations. It is said Rothstein introduced the two. (*See* **MAJESTIC APARTMENTS 115 Central Park West.**)

Authorities indicted Stoneham on August 31, 1923, for denying his secret partnership in another bankrupt firm, E. M. Fuller & Co., which between August 1, 1916, and September 30, 1921, had transferred a total of $336,768 to Rothstein—and which ultimately cost investors $5 million.

Several other indictments followed. Stoneham beat the rap each time.

Hearst's *New York American* eventually exposed eighty-one of these bucket shops, 30 percent of which (including Dillon & Co.) were defended by Bill Fallon.

116. THE CASA BLANCA (formerly The Club Napoleon) 33 West 56th Street (Between Fifth and Sixth Avenues)

A speakeasy connected to (but not owned by) Larry Fay as his luck—and finances—turned sour. Following his announcement of pay cuts for Casa Blanca employees, a highly drunken Casa Blanca doorman named Edward Maloney shot Fay four times at close range at eight thirty on Friday evening, January 1, 1932. Fay was dead by the time the ambulance arrived. In Fay's pockets, according to the *New York Times*, was a mere "three thin dimes."

The *Times* also reported that "the police search of the premises proved somewhat embarrassing for Fay's business associates. Detectives came upon about 300 bottles that they insisted contained alcohol and ordered them transported to the West Forty-seventh Street station. Two patrol cars were used for the moving operation."

The Casa Blanca's predecessor, the Club Napoleon, was operated by Tommy Guinan (*see* **CHEZ FLORENCE 117 West 48th Street**) and future Stork Club (132 West 58th Street and later 3 East 53rd Street) owner Sherman Billingsley.

Paramount's 1932 film *Night After Night* starring George Raft and Mae West was inspired by Club Napoleon events. West's character "Maudie Triplett") was modeled upon Texas Guinan. It was West's first film.

117. HOTEL WELLINGTON 871 Seventh Avenue (Between West 55th and West 56th Streets)

Larry Fay lived here in 1930. He listed his occupation as "manufacturer taxicabs."

Built in 1905, the twenty-seven-story hotel eventually served as a homeless shelter during the COVID-19 pandemic. Its closing was announced in late 2021.

HOTEL WELLINGTON, SEVENTH AVENUE AND FIFTY-FIFTH STREET, NEW YORK

(COURTESY OF COLUMBIA UNIVERSITY LIBRARIES)

118. BACK STAGE CLUB (aka "the Stage Door") 110 West 56th Street (Between Sixth and Seventh Avenues)

In the fall of 1924, showman and all-around hustler Billy Rose (née William Samuel Rosenberg) opened his first speakeasy on the second floor above a garage. "He had the joint rigged out like the backstage of a theater," recalled one of Arnold Rothstein's bodyguards, "Big Max" Arronsen. "You stepped into the place over some footlights. Rose always had this theater bug in him, and he thought this would appeal to the showbiz crowd."

Joe Frisco served as his master of ceremonies; torch singer Helen Morgan as his house vocalist. Here Morgan perfected her trademark style of singing while draped up on a piano—a style many alleged was caused by her being too drunk to stand up.

It was also here that the 4'11" Billy Rose met 5'6" Fanny Brice, when she visited the joint in 1926 to hear Morgan—and also to check out Rose, whose songwriting skills she admired, particularly his line "in the middle of a moment, you and I forgot what no meant."

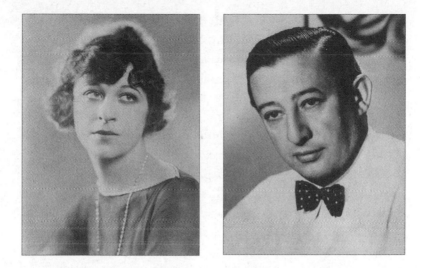

(above left) *Fanny Brice in 1920* (above right) *Billy Rose circa 1948* (AUTHOR'S COLLECTION)

They said "yes" (i.e., tied the knot) in 1929. They untied it in 1938.

Meanwhile, as "Big Max" Arronsen also recalled decades later, "Arnold Rothstein was looking over the place. He decided it was a money-maker and he wanted to be cut in. Rothstein arranged for the club to get raided. Arnold was the law. He told the cops what to do, what not to do, and he paid them off. Billy didn't keep much liquor on hand and he had a signal set up in case there was a raid. For two or three nights in a row the club was raided."

Only then did Rothstein dispatch "Big Max" to Rose to demand (in exchange for a paltry $1,000) a 25 percent partnership in the very lucrative club. Rose refused. Police again raided his operation, smashing every bottle of booze in the joint. Rose finally got the message. Arronsen got his 25 percent—but not *all* of it.

"Billy split with me," Arronsen recalled decades later. "I paid off Rothstein. Arnold paid off the cops on the beat, a desk sergeant, and people at City Hall. I don't think Billy ever knew I was working for Rothstein and splitting my take with him. Rothstein came into Billy's place regularly. They were pals and Billy never knew."

119. PARK CENTRAL HOTEL 200 West 56th Street, Actually Fronting on Seventh Avenue

Opened on June 12, 1927, the Park Central was an early favorite of gamblers and gangsters. Rothstein himself maintained a suite there, as did George McManus's younger brother Frank in Room 252 and McManus's bagman, Hyman "Gillie" Biller, in Room 1463. (*See* **THE BLOSSOM HEATH INN 50 West 77th Street** *and* **HYMAN BILLER HOME 315 West 99th Street.**) Nate Raymond resided in Room 763.

On Friday, November 4, 1928, "George A. Richards, Newark, N.J." registered without benefit of luggage. "Richards" paid $12 cash for a day's rent for Room 349, a two-room suite, paying again each morning thereafter.

The *Brooklyn Eagle* wrote on November 6, 1928:

Who was "George Richards"? The hotel waiters and bellboys describe him. A rather large man, with peculiarly broad and heavy shoulders that made him look a little like a hunchback. Dark of face and smooth faced. Always well dressed. Talks with a rather quiet voice.

And that description is also the description, so Marty Owens and Paddy Flood, two able Broadway [police] detectives say, of one George McManus, called "Hump" because of his shoulders. McManus has not been seen in his usual haunts since last Friday afternoon. "Richards" took the room that after noon.

On Sunday night, McManus placed a call to Lindy's, summoning Rothstein to a meeting to discuss the $319,000 owed Nate Raymond from Rothstein's ill-fated September session at Jimmy Meehan's. (*See* **CONGRESS APARTMENTS 161 West 54th Street.**)

Arriving alone at Room 349, Rothstein still refused payment. McManus pulled out a gun, shot him, grabbed Rothstein's chesterfield overcoat by mistake, and fled—leaving his own monogrammed (and nearly identical) coat in the closet as evidence.

Poker authority John Scarne recorded a conversation he once had with Joe Bernstein, one of the participants in Rothstein's ill-fated poker

The Arabian Room, The Park Central Hotel (COURTESY OF COLUMBIA
UNIVERSITY LIBRARIES)

game. Scarne had begun by asking Bernstein if that game was indeed
fixed. Bernstein responded:

> Scarne, I won't answer that question, but I'll tell you—what
> happened the night Rothstein was shot. As you already know,
> McManus had brought Titanic Thompson, Nigger Nate
> Raymond and me to Meehan's game that night. So, when he
> heard Rothstein wasn't going to honor his $319,000 in markers,
> Nigger Nate told McManus he was responsible for the marker
> collection. When Rothstein told McManus he wasn't going to
> honor the markers because he said he was cheated, McManus
> became worried and he began to drink. He drank a lot. He tele-
> phoned Lindy's that fatal night and asked Rothstein to meet him
> at the Park Central Hotel, where he had rented a suite. When
> Rothstein arrived, McManus was drunk, and he had a gun which
> I guess he hoped would frighten Rothstein into paying off at
> least part of the markers. He pointed the gun at Rothstein, who
> was sitting down. Rothstein pushed the gun away and acciden-
> tally it went off. McManus panicked and threw the gun out the
> window and ran from the room, forgetting that his overcoat was

left in the room. It was an accident, no doubt about it, but it screwed me out of seventy grand.

Like the Kennedy assassination, Rothstein's slaying has produced any number of theories. As author Leo E. McGivena recalled:

Jack Lait, then editor of the *Mirror*, claimed to have found the solution: that Rothstein was shot by a drunken ex-pugilist who had been trying to get a loan from one of the characters in Room 394 [sic], who claimed that he couldn't make it until Rothstein paid him. The stalling had been going on for days. Lait said the frustrated fighter bumped unto Rothstein in the service entrance, recognized him, and shot him in a rage.

An interesting idea, but one unraveling far too quickly in consideration of the murder weapon—tossed out a third-floor window and badly damaged from its downward flight—a condition at odds with Lait's theory.

In 1933, Mildred Sitamore, wife of Rothstein-associated jewel thief Harry Sitamore, unveiled this additional possibility:

So far as the underworld was concerned, there was no mystery about the Rothstein murder. None at least if the stories I heard were true. Rothstein, the underworld believes, went to his death at the hands of a frightened boy—a boy who was only a sort of poor relation to crime, not even a criminal in his own right, but just a collector for his father, who was a politician, dealing in crime protection on the side.

The underworld version of the killing is that the youth entered the room in the fashionable hotel on Seventh Avenue where Rothstein, McManus and others were betting thousands of dollars on the turn of a card [sic], and dunned Rothstein for a few hundred dollars which the racketeer owed him. The story is that he became enraged at the inopportune call made by the youth.

Rothstein was betting thousands of dollars. He had no time to be annoyed by a demand for a few hundred.

The racketeer lashed out verbally at the youth. Frightened, the boy drew a gun, and with trembling hands pointed it at Rothstein. The action was so unexpected that no one in the room had time to interfere. Rothstein, no coward, whatever else he was, started to rise from his chair, his face twisted with anger. The boy's trembling fingers squeezed too hard on the trigger of the gun, and Broadway's crime czar sank back to the table, a bullet in his stomach.

One of Rothstein's henchmen, released from his surprise by the bark of a gun, jumped halfway across the poker table, grabbed the still hot gun from the youth's hand and hurled it from him. The gun crashed through a screen in an open window and fell onto the street, seven stories [sic] below, where it was found, by a taxi driver. George McManus, who was charged with the murder later, had nothing to do with it.

That is the story, as I have heard it.

Her story, of course, contains a number of certainly patent inaccuracies, but *does* provide a somewhat more compelling reason as to why the city's political establishment took such a compelling interest in *not* solving the crime.

So, why did it protect George McManus? Many were the theories (many involving his connection to Tammany boss Jimmy Hines), but here's an additional reasonable possibility: What exactly was Hump doing holed up in said $12-a-day Room 349 for three solid days besides drinking heavily? Most logically, he was conducting a very high-stakes gambling session, this time not with his fellow gambling professionals but with very prestigious and powerful individuals who obviously did not relish McManus revealing their names and habits if push came to shove. Hence, no one would have really pursued what transpired on that Friday and Saturday. Moreover, just about all the fingerprints that should have been found in that room, somehow, were wiped conveniently clean.

ITALIAN ROOM — THE PARK CENTRAL, NEW YORK

The Italian Room, The Park Central Hotel (COURTESY OF COLUMBIA UNIVERSITY LIBRARIES)

There also remains the crucial question of the murder weapon—a Colt .38 caliber revolver—which at one point before the murder lay in the possession of the NYPD's detective bureau before simply vanishing from it. That Hump McManus's older brother Stephen toiled as a New York City police detective certainly indicates that it was wielded that evening not by any mysterious and perhaps mythical "frightened boy" but rather by a member of said McManus clan.

Some have suggested that the event was a mob rub-out. It obviously wasn't. Why not? Because in such planned rub-outs, the rubber-outers (if there is such a word) do not fire a single measly shot into their victim and then let him just casually wander away to be hospitalized—or, worse, to possibly testify against them. No, this shooting was either an accident or an act of momentary rage followed by the absolute panic of men not used at all to committing murder of any sort.

Rothstein wasn't the last mob figure to meet his fate at the Park Central. On Friday morning, October 25, 1957, gangster and hit man Albert "The Lord High Executioner" Anastasia was murdered by two gunmen as he sat lathered up for a shave at the hotel's first-floor barbershop. No one was ever charged for the crime, though Joey "Crazy Joe" Gallo was widely suspected of involvement. Anastasia was sufficiently evil so that the Diocese of Brooklyn denied him a Catholic burial. Gallo, himself, was famously bumped off at Little Italy's Umberto's Clam House (129 Mulberry Street) in April 1972. The barber chair in which Anastasia sat now resides at Las Vegas's "National Museum of Organized Crime and Law Enforcement" (aka, "The Mob Museum").

The Park Central Hotel in November 1928; "A" shows the location of Room 349.; "B" indicates where the murder weapon was found. (AUTHOR'S COLLECTION)

In December 1957, police detained former Rothstein narcotics procurer George Uffner and gambling kingpin Frank Erickson (another Rothstein protégé) for questioning in regard to Albert Anastasia's murder. Uffner denied knowing anything—even knowing Erickson!

From 1950 through 1953, while serving as the U.S. representative to the United Nations Commission on Human Rights, Eleanor Roosevelt maintained a suite here. She was not rubbed out.

The huge Park Central remains in business today.

120.

HOTEL GRENOBLE 886-890 Seventh Avenue at West 56th Street (Northwest Corner across from Carnegie Hall) Elizabeth F. Love, a thirty-one-year-old unmarried attending nurse at Polyclinic Hospital (*see* **POLYCLINIC HOSPITAL 335-361 West 50th Street**), lived here. Her December 17, 1928, New York Surrogates Court testimony helped capsize Maurice Cantor's claim that the alleged deathbed Rothstein will that Cantor had presented was indeed of the delirious dying man's volition:

> COUNSEL (DANIEL MADIGAN): And did you hear Mr. Cantor say, "Arnold, I have your will"?
>
> LOVE: Yes.
>
> COUNSEL: And did he have any other conversation with the patient of that kind, other than saying, "I have your will"?
>
> LOVE: Yes.
>
> COUNSEL: What was the other conversation?
>
> LOVE: "I am a little late in getting here, but I put in the things you told me to this morning."
>
> COUNSEL: What else?
>
> LOVE: He said, "Arnold, you know this is your will."
>
> COUNSEL: After that mark was made, as you stated, by Mr. Cantor holding Mr. Rothstein's hand, what else was done there at the time?
>
> [Objection raised by Mr. Isidor Gainsburg, Esq., attorney for contestants to the will. Discussion off the record. Mr. Madigan resumes]:
>
> COUNSEL: What do you mean by "wiggled his hand"?
>
> LOVE: Shook it like this and made the mark.
>
> COUNSEL: Is that the mark he made?
>
> LOVE: Yes, he made this wiggly mark here.
>
> COUNSEL: What did Arnold Rothstein do?
>
> LOVE: He didn't do anything.
>
> COUNSEL: Did Mr. Cantor say anything to you at the time?
>
> LOVE: Well, he told us not to tell what went on in the sickroom.

By April 1930, Love had relocated to 888 Seventh Avenue.

Elizabeth Love, by the way, wasn't the only nurse present (and disgusted) when Maurice Cantor had Arnold Rothstein "sign" his revised will. The other was Miss Margaret Goerdel. Goerdel and Love both witnessed the Cantor/Rothstein document, as Love recounted, and "I told [Cantor] the patient was very weak and that if I had to sign the paper, I would sign it in order to get him out of the room."

Opened in 1874, when the neighborhood remained at the upper fringes of Manhattan development, the seven-story Hotel Grenoble had once been the favorite of such dignitaries as Rudyard Kipling and the future Edward VII.

The establishment, nonetheless, seemed to specialize in suicides. In March 1925, thirty-eight-year-old Miss Margaret Pauline Lucas, a former *Ziegfeld Follies* girl, presently "a free lance advertising and feature writer," leapt to her death from atop the Grenoble's rooftop parapets.

In November 1919, William Livingston Flanagan, a nephew of former congressman DeWitt Clinton Flanagan, developer of the Cape Cod Canal, fired a bullet into his chest at his Grenoble room and died shortly thereafter at Bellevue Hospital.

In March 1912, washed-up actor Max Freeman, "the godfather of comic opera," taking no chances, took poison before hanging himself outside his window.

In declining fortunes for several years, the Grenoble finally committed suicide itself, closing its doors and windows in July 1931.

121. ARNSTEIN ELECTRIC SIGN BUSINESS 19 West 57th Street (Between Fifth and Sixth Avenues)

Nicky Arnstein's electric sign business, founded in partnership with Chicago jailbird Timothy D. "Big Tim" Murphy. A Rothstein-owned property.

As author Donald Henderson Clarke explained in *In the Reign of Rothstein*:

> Nicky and his co-defendants landed in Leavenworth, May 16, 1924 [following his second trial for bond theft]. Nicky emerged December 21, 1925, with seventy-two days off for good behavior.
>
> Fannie Brice was a constant visitor when he was a prisoner, and she thought the fact that he shoveled coal and worked as an electrician did him good. She remarked that he would be around the house in the future.
>
> After he had been free a few months Nicky blossomed out with an electric sign, which he himself had invented. He opened offices at 19 West Fifty-seventh Street, New York and acted as his own sales manager in a country-wide selling plan. The device was supposed to be for advertising purposes, and to be ideal because it was cheap to operate, requiring no motor.
>
> When this business died, Nicky's friends said that $75,000 passed away with it.

Longchamps Ad, 1927 (AUTHOR'S COLLECTION)

122. LONGCHAMPS RESTAURANT

19-21 West 57th Street (Between Fifth and Sixth Avenues) The address also hosted an outpost of the Longchamps restaurant chain, owned by Arnold's brother-in-law Henry Lustig. Originally, Rothstein had helped bankroll the operation, becoming Lustig's partner, but upon discovering Lustig cheating him through fraudulent billings, he ceased his involvement. "Buy me out," he threatened Lustig, "or I'll close up the place."

Lustig, also noted for his thoroughbred racing stable, lost control of Longchamps after his 1946 conviction on twenty-three counts of income tax and excise profits tax evasion. The chain—after numerous other changes in ownership—declared bankruptcy in June 1975.

123. JAY THORPE INC. 24 West 57th Street (Between Fifth and Sixth Avenues) A high-end women's fashion store founded here by Charles Oppenheimer in 1920 and heavily patronized by Carolyn Rothstein. In 1926, the store doubled in size, thanks to acquiring the building to its rear, which fronted on 56th Street.

On May 31, 1933, Jay Thorpe, Inc. sued Carolyn (now Mrs. Carolyn Rothstein Behar) for unpaid bills amounting to $1,299.35, with her City Court trial being held in October 1936. Justice Louis L. Kahn ruled in her favor and granted her $81.80 in court costs. Her defense had been that she never paid her own bills; they were husband's responsibilities and thus the liability of his estate.

Whatever the case, Carolyn had spent like a drunken sailor at Jay Thorpe. On March 14, 1927, alone she spent in the amount of $1,083.

1 Print Dress	$110.00
1 Dress	$85.00
1 Dress	$225.00
1 Green Dress	$350.00
1 Blue Dress	$165.00
Alterations	$3.00
1 Sport Dress	$145.00
	$1,083.00

Jay Thorpe, Inc. closed in May 1962.

124. ROTHSTEIN HEADQUARTERS 45–47 West 57th Street (Between Fifth and Sixth Avenues)

Rothstein (Redstone Building Co.) -owned. Offices for various Rothstein-controlled real estate and insurance companies: Rothstein, Simon Company, Inc.; the Hooper Realty Corporation; the Rothmere Mortgage Corporation, Inc.; the Juniper Holding Company, Inc.; the Lark Holding Company, Inc.; the Cedar Point Realty Corporation; the Rothstein Brokerage Corporation; the Redstone Building Company; and the Rugro Holding Corporation.

Commencing in September 1927, Rothstein attorney Maurice Cantor also maintained offices there—two floors above Rothstein's. Assessed at $665,000 for 1929. Rothstein offered space in the building to the Arbitration Society of America as a "Tribunal of Justice" in May 1922.

Here, Rothstein briefly employed down-on-his-luck songwriter and producer Con Conrad who convinced Arnold (a fan of Black entertainers) to bankroll the all-Black musical *Keep Shufflin'* (*see* **DALY'S THEATRE 22 West 63rd Street**).

In 1927, rumors floated of a kidnapping attempt at this site. The *New York Times* accordingly reported:

SILENT ON "KIDNAPPING."

ARNOLD ROTHSTEIN REPORTED

ATTACKED HERE BY CHICAGO GANGSTERS.

Arnold Rothstein of 45 West Fifty-seventh Street refused to discuss yesterday a published report that gangsters from Chicago attempted to kidnap him recently.

The report was that four men tried to force Rothstein into a taxicab as he was leaving his office. Rothstein broke away and ran back into the building. It was said that since the kidnapping attempt Rothstein had surrounded himself with guards. However, he left his offices yesterday unguarded.

No report had been received of the attempts to kidnap Rothstein at their Police Headquarters or at the West Forty-seventh Street Police Station.

In October 1928 a second kidnapping attempt transpired here. This time kidnappers mistakenly grabbed haberdasher Charles Winston, a fellow with the poor fortune to closely resemble A. R. Having soon discovered their error, Winston's kidnappers unceremoniously dumped him (shaken but mercifully alive) in Central Park.

Author Donald Henderson Clarke described Rothstein's work habits thusly:

When Rothstein arrived at his offices, which in later years were at 45 West Fifty-seventh Street, his first glance was at a sheet of paper on which had been written mysterious symbols. That paper revealed whether or not Rothstein's gambling and other regular enterprises had prospered the night before or not. If the news was good, Rothstein was most cheerful; if the news was depressing, he was extremely snappish with his employes, and put more than usual emphasis into the "God help you, if you don'ts" which he whipped into the telephone transmitter to delinquent promisers to pay.

Before him as he sat was a form on which were entered the details of business he wished to attend to that day. A receiver was clamped over one ear, leaving the other free to hear the words of the office workers. Rothstein didn't pay them too much, and he was a most exacting employer.

It was not unusual for him to apologize to some one for having sent a dunning letter, and to say that he would see that no more such letters were sent. Then he would turn to his secretary and say: "Keep on sending letters like that until they pay up."

125. DAVID'S FUR COUTURE 50 West 57th Street (Between Fifth and Sixth Avenues)

It's Sunday morning, January 21, 1951, and just across 57th Street from Arnold Rothstein's old headquarters, a brick flies through the side display window of David's Fur Couture. Two men hurriedly exit a bright red 1951 sedan and grab a $3,000 ranch mink coat from beyond the storefront's shattered glass. And then everything goes wrong: because two police detectives have (by coincidence) been standing nearby and have seen this sedan—this *bright red* sedan—circle the block several times beforehand, arousing their suspicions.

But even if they hadn't, the sight and sound of a brick smashing through a plate glass window surely would have. They open fire and shoot one of the men in his left thigh.

That man is none other than Jimmy Meehan. (*See* **CONGRESS APARTMENTS 161 West 54th Street.**)

Meehan's accomplice, fifty-seven-year-old Frank Chiaramonte (fourteen prior arrests, five convictions), speeds away. But Chiaramonte has a problem he may not be aware of. In Meehan's pocket is a slip of paper with Chiaramonte's name and address on it.

Chiaramonte, however, has given the situation *some* thought—not *enough* thought, but *some* thought. His plan: to ditch his bullet-riddled car and to brazenly report it stolen to the police.

The police—already on the lookout for Chiaramonte—promptly arrest him.

I shouldn't have to tell you this by now—but the moral is simply this: crime does not pay.

126. DOT KING APARTMENT 144 West 57th Street (Between Sixth and Seventh Avenues)

In her apartment in a three-story building owned by Rothstein, speakeasy hostess Dot "The Broadway Butterfly" King was found murdered on Thursday, March 15, 1923. Thirty-thousand dollars in jewelry was missing, including a $15,000 ruby necklace. Police questioned her Philadelphia socialite sugar daddy J. Kearsley Mitchell and her brutal live-in lover, a former

(above left) *Dot King* (above right) *Hilda Ferguson* (AUTHOR'S COLLECTION)

stockbroker named Alberto Santos Guimares, who alibied that he was with another girlfriend, the blonde socialite Mrs. Aurelia Fisher Dreyfus.

In October 1924, Dreyfus fell from a balcony at Washington, D.C.'s Potomac Yacht Club. On her deathbed, she confessed that she had perjured herself in providing Guimares's alibi. Remarkably, Guimares was still not charged with King's death.

Questioned, however, in connection with the murder was Harry Sitamore. (*See* **LORBER'S RESTAURANT 1420 Broadway.**)

Details of the case suspiciously foreshadow the plot of 1948's landmark film noir motion picture *The Naked City* (produced, by the way, by Mark Hellinger: *see* **MARK HELLINGER THEATRE 237 West 51st Street**).

Dot King's onetime roommate was fellow showgirl Hilda Ferguson, once voted to possess the most beautiful legs in America. Ferguson had arrived in New York in 1919 as a seventeen-year-old beauty, eventually running her very own speakeasy, Club Hilda, and boasting a number of well-heeled suitors including Atlantic City political and rackets boss Enoch "Nucky" Johnson (he of *Boardwalk Empire* fame). According to the *Daily Mirror*'s Jack Lait, Johnson featured Hilda "in an elaborate show in Atlantic City's Silver Slipper, a night club he bought for the sole purpose of providing a stage for his current reigning favorite.

"He gave her a $12,000 mink coat and a Rolls-Royce. They lived in half the second floor of the Ritz-Carlton. . . .

"When she went to Europe to duck a judgment she resented, for $270 for ten pairs of specially built shoes, she traveled incognito, with her Rolls-Royce, two maids and 27 trunks." She died in October 1933, at age twenty-nine, just as Prohibition was ending.

Hilda was present when her boyfriend, the former Rothstein body-guard Tough Willie McCabe, was knifed at the 61 East 52nd Street's Sixty-One Club in August 1931. Neither he nor Hilda had a word to say to police.

The building itself was built in 1920. It remains standing.

127. SITE OF FLOATING CRAP GAME 301 West 57th Street (Corner of Eighth Avenue, Fourth Floor

Apartment) On the night of January 19, 1919, Rothstein was among nearly two dozen gamblers at a floating crap game at this address. Abe Attell held the dice. Suddenly, there came a sharp rapping at the door and a demand to open up. It was a raid. But Arnold did not know that. Moreover, he reached a far different conclusion: it was a robbery, and with good reason for such an assumption. He had only recently been robbed of $11,000 at an earlier floating crap game.

Rothstein possessed amazingly sharp reflexes. He instantly fired three shots through the door, grazing detectives John McLaughlin, John J. Walsh, and Dick Oliver. With that, he then somehow vanished.

Police found him on a second-floor fire escape. But suddenly their case against him started falling apart. The wounded police could not testify who had fired the shots in question. They couldn't see through doors, after all. Every gambler on the other side of the door had his $1,000 bail provided from the huge bankroll A. R. carried with him. They remained steadfastly silent. By July 25, all charges had been dismissed against Arnold.

"I don't think," contended Carolyn Rothstein, "there is a better instance than this to offer as evidence of the very genuine influence which my husband exerted at the height of his career. He worshipped money and power, and he certainly had both for a short time.

"Practically every one knew that Arnold had fired the bullets in this case. In fact, the newspapers, on the first day, stated that he did. But the identity of the shooter never was mentioned definitely after that."

"It was rumored," wrote Herbert Bayard Swope biographer E. J. Kahn, "that [Rothstein] had paid thirty-two thousand dollars to have the case dropped. And Mayor [Red Mike] Hylan, who had no love for Swope, suggested to his Police Commissioner that he look into another, ancillary rumor—that Swope had been the payoff man.

NYPD Inspector Dominick Henry (AUTHOR'S COLLECTION)

Swope was subsequently absolved by a grand jury when he was able to point out that he had been abroad throughout the period under scrutiny."

A more probable rumor held that Rothstein had doled out $20,000 to his attorney, former magistrate Emil E. Fuchs (owner of the Boston Braves), to be distributed to Assistant District Attorney James E. Smith and the magistrate in the case, Francis X. McQuade (also treasurer of John McGraw's New York Giants).

But wait.

Rothstein was free, but the authorities now went after the raid's leader, Inspector Dominick Henry, eventually convicting him of perjury. His conviction was eventually overturned in 1921, but Henry's enemies prevented him from receiving his back pay until 1924.

128. BARBIZON-PLAZA HOTEL 101 West 58th Street (At the Corner of Sixth Avenue) Rothstein associate Lucky Luciano lived here following its May 1930 opening. Sold at

bankruptcy auction in 1933. Converted to the Trump Parc condominiums in 1988.

129. LILLIAN LORRAINE RESIDENCE 114 West 58th Street (Between Sixth and Seventh Avenues)

Miss Lorraine lived here in 1920, carousing to such an extent that it triggered neighbors' complaints. "Off Stage Gayety Laid to Actress," headlined the *New York Herald*. Found guilty of maintaining a "public nuisance," she paid a $200 fine and moved to 100-106 West 70th Street's Walton Hotel.

130. DR. PHILIP M. GRAUSMAN'S HOME AND OFFICE 130 West 58th Street (Between Sixth and Seventh Avenues)

The offices of Arnold and Carolyn's personal physician. The North Carolina–born Grausman enjoyed many show business clients

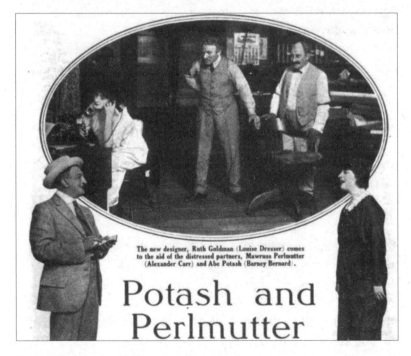

The new designer, Ruth Goldman (Louise Dresser) comes
to the aid of the distressed partners, Mawruss Perlmutter
(Alexander Carr) and Abe Potash (Barney Bernard).

Potash and Perlmutter

including Lillian Lorraine, George M. Cohan, producer Sam Harris, vaudevillian Lew Fields, the Metropolitan Opera's Rosa Ponselle, Jean Acker (the first Mrs. Rudolph Valentino), and Hammerstein Victoria manager William Hammerstein.

Grausman died of a heart attack at this office in November 1934 while treating a patient. He had made national news back in 1904, when, while operating on six-year-old Van Norden Fount, he discovered the boy's heart on the wrong side of his body. One would have thought a stethoscope might have revealed that.

Dr. Philip M. Grausman
(AUTHOR'S COLLECTION)

In 1914, Grausman sued producer Al Woods for 10 percent of the profits of the hit Broadway ethnic comedy *Potash and Perlmutter*—which Woods had promised Grausman in exchange for three years of medical care for him and his wife, actress Louise Beaton. When the play became massively profitable, Woods reneged. Arch Selwyn (*see* **SELWYN THEATER 229 West 42nd Street**) testified in Grausman's behalf.

At Polyclinic Hospital (where he once served as Assistant Professor of Surgery) in 1928, Grausman (who had known Rothstein since approximately 1913) had cautioned Carolyn to return home and rest, as there was nothing that could be done.

131. CLUB DURANT 232 West 58th Street (Between Seventh and Eighth Avenues) Opened by Jimmy Durante in 1924, featuring his madcap musical act "Clayton, Jackson, and Durante."

Patrons included Damon Runyon, Walter Winchell, Jack Dempsey, Billy Rose, actors John Barrymore, Richard Barthelmess, and Alfred Lunt, Broadway's W. C. Fields, Will Rogers, and Alfred Lunt and Lynn Fontanne, Babe Ruth, John Hay "Jock" Whitney, General Motors' Alfred P. Sloan—and George McManus.

One evening, well in his cups, the 6'2", 230-pound McManus got into a fight with a former jockey named "Tiny Cal." When "Tiny Cal" ducked, McManus's fist hit a wall, only further enraging the big Irishman who then vowed to shoot his little adversary. Only Durante's musical partner and business manager Lou Clayton (née Louis Finkelstein) slipping McManus a mickey saved Tiny Cal's life. Clayton was pretty good at slipping mickeys—he carried a supply in his purple tuxedo for whenever a hoodlum patron refused to hand over his firearm to the hatcheck girl for storage.

"The customers," wrote Durante biographer Jhan Robbins, "seemed willing to pay the prices Clayton set: twenty-five dollars for a bottle of champagne, five dollars for a highball, a dollar fifty for a glass of beer. Chicken Soup a la Creole was ten dollars—the cost to prepare was thirty cents; Supreme Fried Smelts Versailles, fifteen dollars—the cost including tartar sauce was thirty cents. Lynnhaven oysters—wholesale cost eight cents apiece—a plate of six brought five dollars."

Though a skilled dancer himself, Durante also hired George Raft—reputedly the best of all Charleston dancers (and the pal of mobster Owney "The Killer" Madden)—to entertain patrons. Raft's biographer, Stone Wallace, has written:

> Perhaps part of the reason for Club Durant's success was its fronting for one of New York's largest floating crap games. These crap games were held in a small garage beneath the club that could only be accessed by a connecting staircase through a back room. It was here that George [Raft] got to know many of the top names of the New York underworld most notably . . . Arnold Rothstein, a minor-league mobster [sic!] whose reputation exceeded his talents, Waxey Gordon, and a ruthless bootlegger named Larry Fay. It was always presumed that "A. R." (Rothstein) bankrolled Durante's Club.

132. THE *NEW YORK JOURNAL* 2 Columbus Circle (Between West 58th and West 59th Streets and

Between Broadway and Eighth Avenue) Two of Arnold's pals from Rector's toiled here for William Randolph Hearst as nationally known cartoonists—"Hype" Igoe and "Tad" Dorgan, both being not only known for their art but for being recognized experts on boxing. Dorgan's reputation now rests, however, on his phrase-making, being widely credited with crafting such phrases as "dumbbell," "drugstore cowboy," "the cat's pajamas," "dumb dora," "bunk," "for crying out loud," and "Yes, we have no bananas."

This area served as the heart of Hearst's New York holdings. Besides the *Journal* at 2 Columbus Circle, his Ziegfeld Cosmopolitan Theatre lay at 309–313 West 58th Street and the International Magazine Building resided at 951–969 Eighth Avenue (the west side of the Avenue; between West 56th and West 57th Streets). The latter building still serves as headquarters of the Hearst organization.

The *Journal*'s site later became (at various times) home to the Museum of Arts and Design, Huntington Hartford's much-derided Gallery of Modern Art, the New York Cultural Center, and the New York Convention and Visitors Bureau.

133. MAJESTIC THEATRE 5 Columbus Circle (Between West 58th and West 59th Streets) The

two-act operetta *The Duke of Duluth* opened here with Carolyn Green in the chorus on September 11, 1905, before later moving to Haverly's Fourteenth Street Theatre (107 West 14th Street), the American Music Hall (262 West 42nd Street), and the West End Theatre. This was Carolyn's first known stage appearance.

Theatre Magazine noted: "Very different is the 'Duke of Duluth,' book by George H. Broadhurst, music by Max S. Witte, now occupying the boards at the Majestic. The music is more than reminiscent, but the lyrics are bright and the book entertaining. There is more than the usual supply of good topical songs and each member of the company, from the star, Nat M. Wills, down, contributes to keep the audience in good humor. The piece is at least worth while. If we must have nonsense on the stage let it be of good quality. Dull musical comedy is an abomination."

Wills (aka "The Happy Tramp") would not continue to enjoy such good humor. In financial difficulties, compounded by alimony obligations to his third wife, Wills died of carbon monoxide poisoning in his Woodcliff, New Jersey, garage in December 1917. He left an estate of $23.00.

The Majestic had opened in 1903 and underwent a dizzying series of renamings including "Minsky's Park Music Hall." In the 1920s it was operated by William Randolph Hearst as the Ziegfeld Cosmopolitan Theatre, and in December 1925–January 1926 (following runs in Buffalo; Baltimore; Elmira; Springfield, Massachusetts; and at Werba's Brooklyn Theatre), it hosted the short-lived *Oh! Oh! Nurse* starring the late Bill Fallon's girlfriend Gertrude Vanderbilt (as "Lily White") in her final Broadway stage roll.

"Gertrude Vanderbilt," noted the *Times*, "with her boyish bob, assuredly made things hum in both senses of the word with 'I'm a Butter and Egg Baby.'" She had, in 1921, previously headlined David Belasco's 717-performance hit *The Gold Diggers*. "Dig sisters, while the digging is good" was among her most notable lines in that production. It is said that the great Belasco also asked Fallon to go on the stage.

NAT M. WILLS
In "The Duke of Duluth" at the Majestic

(AUTHOR'S COLLECTION)

Vanderbilt, however, was no mere gold digger when it came to her ardor for the married Fallon, proving unusually loyal. (*See* **BILLY LAHIFF'S TAVERN 156-58 West 48th Street** *and* **GERTRUDE VANDERBILT HOME 304 West 84th Street.**)

"Gertrude Vanderbilt," wrote Fallon's biographer Gene Fowler, "stuck by Fallon in a manner new and strange to Broadway, advancing money and otherwise shielding him. She knew well enough that he was irresponsible, fickle, and morally unreliable, but she loved him. Her every action in regard to this man was a refutation of the left-handed insinuations that she was 'on the make.' She had talent, beauty and wealthy admirers. The latter never got as far as mid-field with her."

Vanderbilt did, however, apply to be the administrator of what was left of his estate, finally losing her bid to Fallon's widow, Agnes Rafter Fallon, in April 1929.

Shortly after *Oh! Oh! Nurse* closed, Ziegfeld shifted his operations to West 54th Street, and the venue was leased to rival showman Earl Carroll. It was demolished in 1954.

134. CHILDS RESTAURANT 300-304 West 59th Street (Southwest Corner off Columbus Circle) When

Jack's restaurant would close at 1:00 a.m., Rothstein often repaired to this location of the famous restaurant chain. Later, he switched to Reuben's—and, after that, of course, to Lindy's.

In 1933, Sardi's famed hatcheck girl Renée Carroll gingerly described the clientele at Childs' various branches as follows:

> The Childs hostelries of the town are really the places to watch the various strata at work or play. Uptown around 116th Street the college boys throw butter squares to see if they'll stick on the ceiling. A little lower down on Broadway, the girls who have a beat between 59th and 72nd drop in for a snack. At the 59th Street Childs at any time after midnight you can see the bejeweled and be-ermined citizenry disporting itself in spite of Reuben's and Sardi's. The Childs under the Paramount used to be the hangout for the theatrical fraternity and the more squeamish of the uncertain sex. The latter had headquarters for a time in the Fifth Avenue Childs, near 48th Street, until police began warning them.

135. F. SCOTT FITZGERALD APARTMENT 38 West 59th Street (Between Fifth and Sixth Avenues)

Recent newlyweds Scott and Zelda Fitzgerald lived in a brownstone here commencing in October 1920 following residencies at the Biltmore and the Commodore Hotels.

Fitzgerald's 1925 novel, *The Great Gatsby*, famously featured a nefarious character, "Meyer Wolfsheim," based very loosely upon Arnold Rothstein.

Fitzgerald's "Wolfsheim" remains more than a bit of a relic of 1920s anti-Semitism, sporting cuff links fashioned from the "finest specimens of human molars" and spewing ghetto mispronunciations like "Oggsford University" and "business gonnection."

Fitzgerald described Wolfsheim and his role in the Series fix thusly:

"A small, flat-nosed Jew [with a] large head and . . . two fine growths of hair which luxuriated in either nostril."

"Who is he, anyhow, an actor?" asks the novel's narrator, Nick Caraway, regarding Wolfsheim.

F. Scott Fitzgerald (AUTHOR'S COLLECTION)

"No." answered Jay Gatsby.

"A dentist?"

"Meyer Wolfsheim? No, he's a gambler. He's the man who fixed the World's Series back in 1919."

"Fixed the World's Series?" asked the incredulous Caraway.

"The idea staggered me," pondered Caraway. "I remembered, of course, that the World's Series had been fixed in 1919, but if I had thought of it at all I would have thought of it as a thing that merely happened, the end of some inevitable chain. It never occurred to me that one man could start to play with the faith of fifty million people—with the single-mindedness of a burglar blowing a safe."

"How did he happen to do that?" Caraway finally asked Gatsby.

"He just saw the opportunity."

"Why isn't he in jail?"

"They can't get him, old sport. He's a smart man."

GANGSTERLAND NORTH
The Upper West Side

But wait! There's more . . .

Much more.

Due north of the Great White Way lies the Upper West Side, an area yielding another bountiful harvest of gangster-related locations. One might associate the Jazz Age Upper West Side with such literary and musical luminaries as George Gershwin (316 West 103rd Street), Dorothy Parker (252 West 76th Street), Alexander Woollcott (Hotel des Artistes, 1 West 67th Street), Edna Ferber (also the Hotel des Artiste plus 50 Central Park West, and 115 Central Park West), George S. Kaufman (14 West 94th Street), Oscar Levant (126 West 84th Street), Heywood Broun (333 West 85th Street), Franklin P. Adams (603 West 111th Street and 612 West 112th Street), and Paul Whiteman (539 Riverside Drive), but it contained more than its share of less artistic—and far less savory—characters.

Here are some of the many Upper West Side locations associated with Rothstein and company:

136. CIRCLE THEATRE 1825 Broadway (At West 60th Street) Facing the electric chair for Beansie Rosenthal's murder, Lt. Charles Becker recounted the tale of meeting

here with "Big Tim" Sullivan and receiving the green light (indeed, the order) to silence the talkative gambler.

"What about this Rosenthal affair?" Becker supposedly asked Sullivan. "There's nothing of it," Sullivan responded. "It must not be allowed to go any further. Rosenthal has gone so far now, he can't be stopped. He must be got away."

Built in 1901 for vaudeville, the Circle continually changed formats throughout its lifetime—to orchestra hall, legitimate theater, back to vaudeville, to burlesque, back to legitimate theater, vaudeville, and burlesque, and then finally to film in the late 1910s. During a 1935 labor dispute, a bomb wrecked the place.

Converted to the Columbus Circle Roller Rink in 1939. Demolished in 1954 to make way for the Coliseum Convention Center. Now the site of the Time Warner Center.

McManus Under Arrest (AUTHOR'S COLLECTION)

137. GEORGE MCMANUS HOME 51 Riverside Drive (Between West 77th and West 78th Streets)

McManus lived here at seven-room Apt. 10E at the time of Rothstein's shooting. On the evening of Rothstein's murder, police visited—but failed to search its contents—one of many lapses of judgment and procedure that marked their investigation. (See **Appendix A** for more details.) Police Commissioner Grover Whalen later noted that "a search warrant was [finally] obtained for George McManus's apartment and an entry gained on November 16th, 1928, at which time it was found that all of the photographs of George McManus had been removed from their frames. Although the apartment house at

51 Riverside Drive had been covered by detectives from November 6th, 1928, no attempt was made to seal the apartment occupied by George McManus, which was located on the tenth floor, so as to prevent the entrance of any persons to the apartment for the purpose of removing any evidence that might be found there."

Eventually, however, not only mere evidence vanished. During McManus's November–December 1929 trial for Rothstein's murder, he traveled to Yankee Stadium for Thanksgiving Day's NYU–Carnegie Tech football game. While he cheered (and probably gambled), robbers broke into his apartment, filching $20,000 worth of jewels and clothing. McManus called the cops.

138. GEORGE F. CONSIDINE HOME 10 West 61st Street (Between Central Park West and Columbus Avenue) With his brother William H. Considine, George F. Considine had owned the Metropole Hotel and, with yet another brother, John, had once served as manager to prizefighters "Gentleman Jim" Corbett and "Kid" McCoy. Previously, William, George, and John R. Considine had owned an earlier version of the Metropole on the south side of West 42nd Street between Broadway and Seventh Avenue. John R. Considine, the most famous of the three Considines, died in 1909.

In 1906, George F. Considine, then thirty-three, married the twenty-five-year-old actress Aimee Angeles, "[w]hom many Broadway theatergoers call one of the cleverest women on the stage." "Big Tim" Sullivan served as best man. Alderman "Little Tim" Sullivan performed the ceremony. Mrs. Frank Ferrell (wife of one the city's most prominent gamblers) was matron of honor.

In October 1912, just months after July 1912's Rosenthal murder, George Considine declared bankruptcy, alleging $258,698 in debts against only $5,442 in assets. He had, in fact, been in financial difficulties even prior to Rosenthal's slaying. Nonetheless, like Arnold Rothstein (and financier August Belmont II), he also held an interest in Maryland's Havre de Grace racetrack. Considine died at home here in August 1916.

A fourth Considine brother, James, was a convicted bank robber, pardoned by Theodore Roosevelt in July 1904.

139.

DALY'S THEATRE 22 West 63rd Street (just off Central Park West) Originally built in 1914 by the "People's Pulpit" and the "International Bible Student's Association" as a venue to exhibit biblical films and lectures, the 1,025-seat Daly's was the site of Rothstein's last Broadway venture, *Keep Shufflin'*, a 1928 all-Black musical featuring Fats Waller. Rothstein had been enticed into investing in the show by its author, director, and producer, Con Conrad ("Barney Google," "Margie," and "Ma! He's Makin' Eyes at Me"), a onetime Rothstein employee.

Keep Shufflin' turned out to be Conrad's last gasp as a Broadway producer. Moving to Hollywood, he commenced a career in films, culminating in a 1934 Oscar for Best Original Song, "The Continental," in the Fred Astaire–Ginger Rogers musical *The Gay Divorcee*—the first Oscar in that category.

Keep Shufflin' was not Broadway's first all-Black musical. That honor went to 1921's *Shuffle Along*, also produced at Daly's 63rd Street and featuring an all-star cast of Paul Robeson, Josephine Baker, Florence Mills, and Fredi Washington.

Nonetheless, *Keep Shufflin'*'s modest success (it ran for 104 performances) was hardly guaranteed. June 1925's production of *Lucky Sambo* (despite a glowing review from the *Times*) folded after just seven performances. William Grant Still's *Africana* played here to middling success (seventy-two performances) in 1927.

It was also here at Daly's in 1927 that police arrested thirty-three-year-old (she said she was twenty-six) Mae West on obscenity charges for her performance in the play *Sex*. The play's production company was ironically dubbed the "Morals Producing Company."

Daly's closed in 1941 and was demolished in 1957.

140. LILLIAN LORRAINE RESIDENCE 17 West 64th Street (Between Central Park West and Broadway)

When Lillian Lorraine moved back to New York City from visits to the West Coast and Atlantic City in late January 1941, she took a $15-per-week furnished apartment at this address. On February 18, 1941, however, after her davenport caught fire, she was forced into Bellevue's Psychiatric Ward under the name "Mary Ann Brennan"—her mother's maiden name. Following treatment for alcoholism, the now white-haired Lorraine was released—but not before press reports revealed her plight and how far a once-great star had fallen.

141. MONTICELLO HOTEL 35–37 West 64th Street (Between Central Park West and Broadway)

Legs Diamond's onetime headquarters. In 1930, at his suite here (Room 829), he survived a rub-out attempt despite having five bullets pumped into his pajama-clad body. The event, however, was hardly surprising because a lot of people wanted to kill him and he already had a habit of surviving such attempts, earning him the nickname "the clay pigeon of the underworld."

Diamond's mistress, Kiki Roberts, occupied the suite next door. His loyal wife, Alice Kenny Schiffer Diamond, heard the news (of the shooting, not the mistress) at the Diamonds' upstate Acra, New York home—an abode where (much to her husband's chagrin) she had installed an imitation electric chair. After having rushed back to Manhattan, Mrs. Diamond informed police: "I didn't do it."

Legs finally met his match as he slept in a seedy Albany apartment on December 18, 1931, following his acquittal on kidnapping charges in a Troy, New York, court, as unknown assailants shot him three times in the back of the head. The building (67 Dove Street) was later owned by Pulitzer Prize winner (and Albany native) William Kennedy, author of the 1975 novel *Legs*. A plaque, by the way, marks Kennedy's 640 North Pearl Street Albany home. No plaque adorns 67 Dove Street, which Kennedy offered for sale in March 2023 for $499,000. He had purchased the three-story property in partnership with Hollywood producer Gene Kirkwood in 1984 for a mere $80,000.

142. EUGENE REIMAN RESIDENCE 124 West 64th Street (Between Amsterdam Avenue and West End Avenue)

At 7:00 p.m. on the night of his shooting, Rothstein dispatched his forty-year-old Swiss-born chauffeur, Eugene Reiman, to retrieve some extra cash, either from the Fairmount Hotel or from his West 57th Street business office. By the time Reiman returned to Lindy's, he was informed that his boss had been "slugged" (whatever that meant) and taken to Polyclinic Hospital (*see* POLYCLINIC HOSPITAL 335-361 West 50th Street).

In 1914, Reiman gave this as his address in placing the following ad offering his services:

CHAUFFEUR, machinist, German; sober, reliable man; speaks English, German, Russian. and French; 10 years' experience with cars; go anywhere. Eugene Reiman, 124 West 64th.

(AUTHOR'S COLLECTION)

143. MICHAEL R. MARKS HOME 161 West 64th Street (Near Broadway)

In July 1928, "commission broker" (i.e., stockbroker) Michael R. Marks lent Rothstein $30,000. As collateral, Rothstein provided jewelry of an undisclosed value plus three thousand shares in the Automotive Standard Corporation. Rothstein later traded three $10,000 debenture notes of the Paramount Hotel Corporation to regain his Automotive Standard Corporation stock. Subsequently, Marks returned the Paramount notes to Rothstein leaving Marks with only the jewelry as collateral.

144. ISADORE RAPOPORT RESIDENCE 65 Central Park West (Between West 66th and West 67th Streets)

Isadore Rapoport, an all-around crook with a habit of getting caught, lived in this twelve-story, Emory Roth–designed apartment in the

1940s. His connections to Rothstein were at least two. In 1922, Saratoga County district attorney Charles B. Andrus raided premises operated by Rapoport, seizing a sizable quantity of liquor. Bill Fallon defended Rapoport, arguing that Andrus lacked a search warrant. The court upheld the seizure anyway—in the intriguingly named decision *People v. 738 Cases of Intoxicating Liquor.*

Fast-forward to 1946, when Jimmy Meehan (by now an ex-convict) found himself implicated in the embezzlement of $734,000 from Brooklyn's Mergenthaler Linotype Company—as (believe it or not) an innocent dupe of the actual culprits. It turned out that Rapoport was the brains of the operation—but not brainy enough to escape a two-and-a-half- to five-year sentence. Hearing his sentence, he suffered a heart attack.

In between those events, Rapoport operated an illegal brewery in Harrison, New Jersey, sold whiskey fraudulently labeled as to its age, and, while president of the "Ultima Optical Instrument Corporation," provided false information regarding a former employee to that employee's draft board. A 1935 press report noted that he "has been arrested and discharged in New York City for grand larceny five times."

145. BENNY KAUFF'S AUTOMOBILE ACCESSORIES BUSINESS 135 Columbus Avenue (Presently Across Lincoln Square from the Julliard School) Site of New York Giants outfielder Benny Kauff's automobile business. On February 19, 1920, Kauff was charged with selling an automobile stolen in front of 788 West End Avenue on Monday evening, December 8, 1919. As police arrested Kauff, they also arrested two of his former salesmen for a separate car theft, this one committed outside a restaurant at West 66th Street and Columbus Avenue very near to Kauff's auto business. Kauff won a quick acquittal on May 13, 1921, but was, nevertheless, permanently banned from organized baseball by Commissioner Kenesaw Mountain Landis. (*See* **HOTEL ASTOR 1511-1515 Broadway.**)

For decades, by the way, it was assumed that Benny Kauff was Jewish. Recent scholarship has, however, disproved this. He was German. So, who knew?

146.
FRANK E. CAMPBELL'S FUNERAL HOME (aka "THE FUNERAL CHURCH") 1970 Broadway (At West 66th Street) Site of Rudolph Valentino's frenzied 1926 funeral services, as well as those for Enrico Caruso, Roscoe "Fatty" Arbuckle, Frank Barrett Carman, and Texas Guinan. Texas had left instructions for an open casket, "so the suckers can get a good look at me without a cover charge." Well over ten thousand mourners filed past her casket. Seventy-five thousand had viewed Valentino.

Relocated to East 81st Street and Madison Avenue in 1938.

147.
HOTEL DES ARTISTES 1 West 67th Street Home to not only the Algonquin Circle's Alexander Woollcott and Edna Ferber but also to the studios of Alfred Cheney Johnston, official photographer to the *Ziegfeld Follies* and also portraitist of numerous other stars of the era. His subjects included Ziegfeld himself, Fanny Brice, Marion Davies, Billie Burke, John Barrymore, Ruby Keeler, Helen Morgan, Ann Pennington, and Ruby Keeler. A number of his Ziegfeld Girl portraits were decidedly undraped—most likely snapped either for Ziegfeld himself or for the girls in question's invariably wealthy male admirers.

Built in 1917, the eighteen-story Hotel des Artistes also proved a home to such notables as Rudolph Valentino; Noel Coward; illustrators James Montgomery Flagg, Howard Chandler Christy, and Norman Rockwell; dancer Isadora Duncan; actresses Alla Nazimova and Zasu Pitts; actor Joel Grey and Gary Oldman; author Fannie Hurst (who died here in 1968); director Mike Nichols; and Mayor John V. Lindsay.

148.
JIMMY MEEHAN'S HOME 128 West 67th Street (At Broadway) Meehan's home address when he was arrested in December 1937 for assaulting and robbing *Ziegfeld Follies* showgirl Diana Lanzetta, the thirty-ish widowed sister-in-law of former U.S. congressman James A. Lanzetta (Lanzetta had defeated Fiorello La Guardia to win his seat) and the future president of the National Women's Democratic Club, at her ninth-floor Ansonia Hotel apartment,

of cash and jewels. Meehan and an accomplice had tied the "blonde and hazel-eyed" Lanzetta to her bed with a bathrobe cord before ransacking the place. Meehan received a ten-to-twenty-year sentence but would be free a lot sooner than that.

149. **COLONIAL BANK Corner of West 68th Street** Here, in September 1928, Nate Raymond obtained a $6,000 loan based on two stolen stock certificates, triggering his January 1932 incarceration in Sing Sing.

150. **WILLIAM RANDOLPH HEARST RESIDENCE 91 Central Park West (Between West 69th and West 70th Streets)** Built in 1926, this sixteen-story neo-Renaissance apartment house contained Hearst's 3,000-square-foot penthouse (plus a 1,700-square-foot wraparound terrace) overlooking Central Park. Splendid as this residence was, it was by no means the largest Hearst abode in the city—that honor going to his older digs at The Clarendon at 37 Riverside Drive. (*See* **THE CLARENDON 137 Riverside Drive.**)

In late 2019, its then owner, T-Mobile CEO John Legere, disposed of Hearst's former digs here to his same-floor neighbor Giorgio Armani for a bargain $17.5 million. Legere's original asking price: $22 million.

151. **IRVING BERLIN RESIDENCE 30 West 70th Street (Between Central Park West and Columbus Avenue)** Songwriter Irving Berlin lived here with both his Swedish-born secretary and housekeeper (a married couple) according to the 1920 census. Arnold borrowed $20,000 from him in 1922—never repaying any of it.

152. **ROTHSTEIN HOME 120 West 70th Street (Between Columbus Avenue and Broadway)** Rothstein's home circa 1918–19; this may very well be the same residence referred to by author and screenwriter Edward Dean Sullivan when he wrote in 1930: "In [1910] or in 1911, Rothstein took a private house in the West Seventies, a most pretentious establishment containing—in perfect taste—treasures of art in painting, weaving and sculpture."

Of Rothstein at this time, Sullivan also observed: "He cultivated a wide circle of 'friends' who in no known instances ever got to know him intimately. He amused them, interested them, dined them, but withal and in every possible circumstance gave the impression that he was giving a performance, rather than mingling sociably. He had an abrupt way of indicating to guests that they were about to go; even as he had an abrupt way of terminating conversations with individuals the moment a sufficient pause made departure possible."

Also George Bauchle's home in November 1921. His third wife, Myrtle Goodrich Sloane Bauchle, resided there in January, when suing him in New York State Supreme Court for $4,996 regarding her jewelry that he had pawned and she had redeemed.

A year later, Bauchle vanished, having squandered his inherited fortune and owing $50,000 to various "hotels, restaurants, shops, and other creditors." Nat Evans speculated he might be in China. Arnold Rothstein theorized to Mrs. Bauchle that if her husband were still in the country, he would be contacting him in regard to moneys Bauchle claimed Rothstein owned him.

153. JOSEPH B. ELWELL HOME 244 West 70th Street (Between Broadway and West End Avenue) Scene

of the playboy bridge expert Joe Elwell's still-unsolved June 1920 murder, its great mystery being that while Elwell's body was found within his locked (from the inside) parlor, no murder weapon could be found within it. He was, by the way, a friend (or more properly an acquaintance) of Arnold Rothstein.

It was Elwell's demise that inspired novelist S. S. Van Dine to create the popular Philo Vance detective series. (*See* **DR. CHARLES NORRIS HOME 344 West 77th Street.**)

Demolished.

154. LILLIAN LORRAINE RESIDENCE 120 West 71st Street (Between Broadway and Columbus

Avenue) Lillian Lorraine's home on May 26, 1922, when it was raided by five private detectives hired by Mrs. Gladys Wagner in search of her wandering husband, Charles C. Wagner, half-owner of West 51st Street's Club Maurice. (*See* **THE CLUB MAURICE 209 West 51st Street.**) They found Wagner and Lillian—quite scantily clad. Miss Lorraine, at first fearing they were federal Prohibition agents, was heard to exclaim, "Charlie, save the hootch! Don't let them take my hootch!" Mrs. Wagner, of course, wasn't looking for booze. She was looking for alimony—$150 per week plus $5,000 annually. Nice work if you can get it in 1922.

155. HOTEL ALMANAC 160 West 71st Street (Between Broadway and Columbus Avenue) Here, on

February 8, 1924, Harry "The Hawk" Behan (aka "Harry Lasser") robbed, "slugged," and "nearly garroted" Mrs. Edna Leader Johnson, wife of noted composer Howard E. Johnson. Appropriately, Mr. Johnson had not only composed "I Scream, You Scream, We All Scream for Ice Cream" but also "There's a Broken Heart for Every Light on Broadway." His numerous other hits included: "Ireland Must Be Heaven for My Mother Came from There" and "When the Moon Comes Over the Mountains."

Behan's haul in robbing Mrs. Johnson: three diamond rings valued at $9,000.

Not long previously in Washington, Behan and master jewel thief Harry Sitamore had teamed up to relieve a congressman's wife of her cache of jewels.

"Sitamore," noted the *New York Times*, "positively identified by Mrs. Johnson as one of the two men in the apartment just before she was slugged and lost consciousness, admitted that he had attended the 'party.' He said that he had known the Behans and had accepted their invitation, but that he had left before the robbery was staged."

It's believed that Sitamore (identified to Edna Johnson as "Harry Victor") supplied police with tips regarding the Dot King and Louise

Lawson murders. In any case, while Behan received twenty years, Sitamore waltzed off, scot-free.

As usual, suspicious events surrounded the administration of justice in 1920's Manhattan. In March 1926, the *Kingston Daily Freeman* reported:

> Mrs. Howard Johnson . . . has been missing since early in February, when she left her apartment in the McAlpin [Hotel, Broadway and West 34th Street] to testify at the trial of Harry Sitamore, it was revealed by District Attorney [Joab] Banton of New York.

Nothing to see here, folks, move on . . .

Built in 1923, the nineteen-story Almanac later served as a home to Babe Ruth and in 1929 became the nation's first hotel to employ female bellhops. Now a nineteen-story apartment house known as the "South Pierre" owned by the Roman Catholic Church of the Blessed Sacrament (152 West 71st Street).

156. MAJESTIC APARTMENTS 115 Central Park West (Between West 71st and West 72nd Streets)

Rothstein protégé Frank Costello lived here in nine-room, two-bedroom,

Frank Costello Testifying Before Congress in 1951 (COURTESY OF THE LIBRARY OF CONGRESS)

two-bathroom apartment 18F. On Rothstein's death, an IOU from Costello in the amount of $40,000 was found in Arnold's papers.

In the Majestic lobby in May 1957, Costello narrowly escaped assassination by Vincent "The Chin" Gigante, a member of the rival Genovese family. Costello survived but decided retirement from the rackets might finally be in order.

Gossip columnist Walter Winchell also lived here. The Majestic stood on the site of another hotel that once accommodated both composer Gustav Mahler and novelist Edna Ferber.

The Deceptively Peaceful-Looking Foyer of the Majestic Hotel (COURTESY OF COLUMBIA UNIVERSITY LIBRARIES)

157. FAIRFIELD HOTEL 20-28 West 72nd Street (Between Central Park West and Columbus Avenue)

Owned by Rothstein and assessed at $1,470,000 for 1929; residence of Ciro "The Artichoke King" Terranova; residence of Inez Norton; home of Samuel Brown, Rothstein's business partner; Irish-born chambermaid Bridget Farry once worked there—as she did at the Park Central on the evening of Rothstein's murder. As one reporter noted: "She had been injured while in his employment and he had paid her personally and made a very good impression on her by his consideration."

The hotel opened in 1925-26 following the demolition of five existing row houses. Early tenants included the infamous "Peaches" and "Daddy" Browning. Edward W. Browning, a successful fifty-one-year-old real estate developer, had married the fifteen-year-old Frances Belle "Peaches" Heenan in June 1926. "He showered me with flowers," she later recalled, "deluged me with candy and gifts, my boy friends were forgotten, I had glances for none save Mr. Browning, my silver-haired knight, his gentle caresses, his quiet dignity, his savoir faire."

The Former Hotel Fairfield in the 1940s (Second Building from the Left) (AUTHOR'S COLLECTION)

When Peaches sued for divorce a year later, the tabloids had a field day, and following his bride's lurid testimony (a non-lurid detail: Mr. Browning kept a live goose on the premises) he became a national laughingstock.

A 1955 interview with Peaches included this tidbit:

Q - Were you in love with him?
A - Not at all.
Q - Why did you marry him?
A - I haven't the faintest idea. How can you account for the actions of a 15-year-old?

Rothstein acquired the fifteen-story Fairfield in 1927 and promptly sued the city to reverse its ban on guests/tenants cooking in the rooms, contending "that the tenement house law prohibiting cooking in serving pantries was ineffective because city officials have permitted it since 1901." Representing him was Maurice F. Cantor, a Fairfield resident until moving to either 225 West 106th Street or 225 West 108th Street (accounts vary), in September 1928.

Following Rothstein's death, authorities scoured the Fairfield for evidence of his activities. In December 1928, *the New York Evening Post* noted, "Another safe of Rothstein's has been discovered . . . in a storeroom on the roof of the Hotel Fairfield. . . . Representatives of the District Attorney and of the United States Attorney will be co-operating in going over these documents carefully." A few months later, the Fairfield's furniture (once valued at $100,000) was auctioned off for $40,000.

In January 1930, Inez Norton testified in New York State Supreme Court that she and Rothstein had planned to live in an apartment on the Fairfield's sixteenth floor.

Renamed the Hotel Franconia in 1929.

158. REUBEN'S RESTAURANT Broadway and West 73rd Street From 1916 through 1918, this was the site of Arnold Reuben's "Reuben's Restaurant" and a Rothstein haunt.

Rothstein once phoned Reuben's, impersonating Lillian Lorraine, and ordered three hundred sandwiches and a barrel of herrings to be dispatched to West 49th Street. The excited Reuben rustled everything up, personally delivering it to the address Rothstein had provided him with—the horse's entrance to Madison Square Garden.

Eventually, Reuben requested that Rothstein no longer darken his doors, and A. R. relocated to Lindy's.

Reuben also relocated several times. While operating at 2270 Broadway (between West 81st and West 82nd Streets) on September 6, 1922, police raided his restaurant on alcohol charges. Defending him in West Side Court was none other than Bill Fallon.

159. THE ANSONIA HOTEL 2109 Broadway (At West 73rd Street) The newly married Mr. & Mrs. Arnold

Rothstein resided here briefly following their marriage during the 1909 racing season at Saratoga Springs. Carolyn Rothstein recalled it as "a large single room . . . with a sort of partition which separated the bed from what might be called the dressing section, but it was, in no sense of the word, a suite." Although they soon secured lodgings above Arnold's 108 West 46th Street gambling house, they (for some reason—probably not a good or legal one) retained this room until 1913.

The Ansonia was a luxury hotel, built by the scandal-plagued copper fortune heir (and eugenicist) William Earl Dodge Stokes, featuring shared servants and kitchen facilities but more spectacularly a lobby fountain graced with live seals and a rooftop farm featuring chickens, pigs, ducks, and geese. In 1907, on orders from city officials, said pigs, ducks, and geese were packed off to the Central Park Zoo, but the chickens survived to take up residence in Stokes's own "French flat" apartment.

Scandal seemed baked into the address.

On October 1, 1906, the recently retired "king of the policy dealers," Al Adams, beset by $2 million in financial losses and increasingly in ill health, committed suicide in his fifteenth-floor apartment.

In May 1916, forty-eight-year-old Highland Park, Illinois, business-man Edward R. West, the millionaire vice president of C. D. Gregg Tea and Coffee Co., found himself arrested at the Ansonia by three "warrant"-wielding "detectives" charging him with violation of the federal Mann Act, i.e., transporting twenty-seven-year-old brunette beauty Buda Godman across state lines for immoral purposes. In fact, they weren't detectives at all but rather part of a "badger game," designed to blackmail West out of $15,000. The scheme failed when the widowed West finally decided to "accept personal humiliation" and contacted the police.

"It was," noted the *Chicago Tribune*, "at [Buda's] tearful entreaties [West] had paid the swindlers $15,000 to shield her, as he supposed, from disgrace. Since then he had met her frequently. Despite her treachery which had betrayed him into the hands of thieves she had been able to hold his regard. The stage evidently lost a star when Miss Godman turned to blackmail."

Two of her accomplices went to jail. Godman herself jumped bail, and authorities dropped charges against her in 1921.

"She was never brought back to Chicago for prosecution," noted Jack Lait and Lee Mortimer. "She remained in the East and was often seen with Rothstein, Owney Madden, New York's boss killer-bootlegger, and Bill Fallon."

Godman's Ansonia Hotel sting was hardly her first fling at the badger game. She had been active in the scam for years, often abetted by future Rothstein rumrunning ally Dapper Don Collins. (*See* **DAPPER DON COLLINS RESIDENCE 242 West 48th Street**; **CHARLES A. STONEHAM APARTMENT 110 West 55th Street**; *and* **BUDA GODMAN APARTMENT 161 West 54th Street**.)

Author Theodore Dreiser, singers Enrico Caruso and Lily Pons, composer Igor Stravinsky, conductor Arturo Toscanini, and empresarios Sol Hurok and Florenz Ziegfeld all lived here.

As did *Ziegfeld Follies* star Lillian Lorraine, dubbed "The Most Beautiful Girl in the World." Ziegfeld had installed Lorraine—his mistress—at an Ansonia tower suite, just two floors below where Ziegfeld and his current wife, actress Anna Held, resided. Lorraine had a connection to Arnold Rothstein as well, occasionally serving as a "steerer" of wealthy suckers to Rothstein's gambling house.

"She never wore any make-up," said Fanny Brice of Lorraine. "Everything about her was glowing and fresh, a sort of blooming newness like you see in a very young girl. Her hair rolled off her forehead in simple lines and swung into lovely folds. I have never seen a woman in the theatre with so little artificiality."

Which was her good side. Brice's biographer Herbert Goldman added this assessment of Lorraine: "She had made her stage debut at four and had lost her virginity at thirteen. Willful, childishly selfish and coquettish, Lillian also had a voracious sexual appetite that seldom focused on one man for long."

Jack Dempsey and Babe Ruth also lived at the Ansonia, but the hotel's most prominent—i.e., most infamous—sporting connection unfolded on September 21, 1919, when members of the American League champion Chicago White Sox met to conspire fixing that fall's

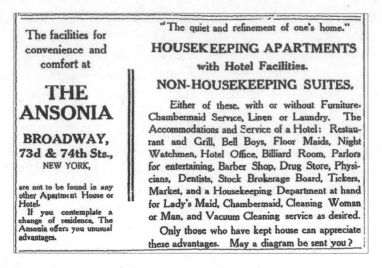

A 1922 Ad for the Ansonia (AUTHOR'S COLLECTION)

World Series. On that date shortstop Charles "Swede" Risberg, third baseman George "Buck" Weaver, outfielder Oscar "Happy" Felsch, infielder Fred McMullin, and pitchers Eddie Cicotte and Claude "Lefty" Williams assembled in first baseman Charles "Chick" Gandil's room to plot the fix.

Three days earlier, Gandil and Cicotte had approached former prize-fighter Billy Maharg and Maharg's friend the former major league pitcher "Sleepy Bill" Burns in the Ansonia's lobby, offering to throw the Series for $100,000.

Maharg later testified that he "heard Cicotte say that if the Sox won the pennant the world series could be thrown for $100,000. Gandil said the players would throw the games in any order desired.

"After Cicotte and Gandil left, Burns repeated the conversation to me, as I had heard all of it. He said Cicotte and Gandil had agreed to see that the Series was thrown for $100,000. He asked me if I could get some one to put up $100,000.

"When I got back to Philadelphia [Maharg's home] I went to see a man named Rossie."

Rossie and his associates, Maharg also later revealed, "told me it was too big a proposition for them to handle, and they recommended me to

Arnold Rothstein." Eventually, Rothstein did supply funding to Maharg and his partner-in-crime, former major league pitcher "Sleepy Bill" Burns.

The following also transpired at the Ansonia, with Attell and Des Moines gambler David Zelser (posing as former Rothstein bodyguard "Curley" Bennett) on one side and the hapless Burns and Maharg on the other (also present were New York Giants first baseman Hal Chase and pitcher Jean Dubuc).

In court in Chicago, Sleepy Bill Burns later testified:

Q - When was the conversation?
A - Two days before the series [opened on October 1, 1919].
Q - What did they [Attell and Zelser/Bennett] meet you for?
A - They came to arrange the fixing of the series.
Q - What did Attell say?
A - He asked me to go to Cincinnati to see the players. Bennett also wanted to see what kind of a deal he could make with them. I told him I would go and see.
Q - Did Bennett say anything about whom he represented?
A - Yes, he said he represented Rothstein and was handling the money for him. Bennett also wanted to go to Cincinnati to confer with the players.
Q - Was anything else said?
A - I asked Attell how it was that he had been able to get Rothstein in when I had failed?
Q - What did he say?
A - He said he had once saved Rothstein's life and that the gambler was under obligations to him.
Q - At that time you were at the hotel was any mention made of money?
A - Yes, $100,000.
Q - In what way?
A - Bennett said Rothstein had agreed to go through with everything.
Q - Just what was said in reference to the $100,000?
A - They were to pay that to the players for the series.
Q - What was said?

A - Bennett said he would handle the money and that Attell would arrange for the betting.

It was also at the Ansonia where, as Lefty Williams later averred in a sworn statement, Chick Gandil first approached him regarding the fix:

> This situation was first brought up to me in New York. Mr. Gandil called me to one side, out in front of the Hotel Ansonia, and asked me if anybody had approached me about the world series, and I said: "Just what do you mean?" He says: "That the series be fixed; if they were fixed what would you do about it? Would you take an active part, or what?" I says, "I am in no position to say right now." I says, "I will give you my answer later, after thinking it over."

The Ansonia's Rothstein/criminal persona continued on September 23, 1937, when, as a press report narrated, Jimmy Meehan and his accomplice, Solomon Engel, robbed Mrs. Joseph C. Lanzetta, a sister-in-law of former congressman James Lanzetta and "obtained $2,500 in jewelry and $12 in money in her suite in the Hotel Ansonia, . . . after forcing their way

(AUTHOR'S COLLECTION)

into the suite and beating and kicking Mrs. Lanzetta, a former actress, as they bound and gagged her.

"She identified Meehan from his Rogues' Gallery picture and his arrest followed. He had been convicted in Mineola, L. I., in 1932; and served a six-month term in the county jail for 'doping' a horse in a race at Belmont Park. There is a warrant pending against him in New Rochelle in connection with a burglary."

But, in an all too familiar story, the Ansonia eventually slowly skidded into shabbiness and then notoriety—first hosting the homosexual bathhouse the Continental Baths (the very young Bette Midler was a star there) and then the infamous 1970s swingers venue Plato's Retreat.

(AUTHOR'S COLLECTION)

Following a dizzying series of tenant lawsuits and rent strikes, the Ansonia was finally converted to condominiums in 1990.

160. HOTEL PRISAMENT 2120-2122 Broadway (At West 74th Street) Opened in 1922 by the Prisament brothers, with former treasury secretary William Gibbs McAdoo as a featured speaker.

Inez Norton (originally Inez Smythe and then Mrs. Claude W. Norton) was by 1928 really "Mrs. Miles Reiser," and Mr. Miles E. Reiser had to be gotten rid of if any Rothstein-Norton romance were to fully blossom.

By now, you're probably thinking that Reiser (a salesman for his father, the wealthy cabinetry manufacturer Ely J. Reiser, and a part owner of the Prisament) was one step away from being bumped off.

"Bumping off" had its charms, but divorce was a less messy option.

It was not, however, without its complications. First and foremost being the fact that one—and *only* one—ground for divorce existed in New York: adultery.

Hotel Prisament (COLUMBIA UNIVERSITY LIBRARY)

Thus, adultery needed to be forcefully demonstrated, and thus it was at the Prisament on the evening of April 8–9, 1928, that Inez's two agents "surprised" Mr. Reiser in the indiscreet company of who the *New York Sun* tastefully noted as "a woman, not his wife, who had retired for the night." Arnold Rothstein's attorney Maurice Cantor represented Norton in the divorce proceedings that followed. The wheels of justice often ground slowly in New York, but Inez received her decree barely three months later, on July 16, 1928.

Another personage connected with the Prisament was Sidney Stajer, described by the *Brooklyn Times-Union* in November 1928 as "a boyhood pal of Rothstein—a protégé educated at Columbia University by the gambler. . . .

"On July 17 1928], Staijer [sic] was arrested with four other men at the Hotel Prisament . . . on [a] narcotics charge. It was reported that Rothstein, breaking an iron clad rule never to appear in court personally, appeared at the bar and gave $10,000 bond for his boyhood friend, and, some say, business manager extraordinaire for the gambler's undercover operations.

"Staijer [sic], at the time, gave the name of Samuel Stein, which police report, is his real name."

Damon Runyon described Stajer as "a rotund young man who was one of Rothstein's closest friends." At George McManus's trial, Runyon observed Stajer thusly: "Sidney Stajer scowled at [the press photographers] fiercely, but Sidney really means no harm by his scowls. Sidney is not a hard man and ordinarily would smile very pleasantly for the photographers, but it makes him cross to get up before noon."

161. EDNA WHEATON APARTMENT 39 West 76th Street (Between Central Park West and Columbus Avenue) Here, at 4:00 a.m. on the morning of November 27, 1921, George D. Uffner, a twenty-eight-year-old salesman for the "Universal Film Manufacturing Co." (Universal Studios), planned to spend what little remained of the night with his lover, the *Ziegfeld Follies* showgirl and budding motion picture actress Edna Wheaton.

Wherein lay a problem, for Miss Wheaton had not only a lover but also a recent husband, Mr. Irving H. Stark (they had wed only that June), who harbored, shall we say, suspicions. A newspaper account revealed what followed:

> Accompanied by four men friends and a policeman, [Stark] waited for his wife to come home. He hired a taxicab and waited in the closed car outside the apartment house.
>
> About 4 a. m. Miss Wheaton arrived home with another man. After waiting a time Stark started for his wife's apartment, accompanied by the policeman and four witnesses. They pounded on the door and Miss Wheaton asked: "Who is there?" The policeman called: "I've got a message for you." Miss Wheaton asked the policeman to wait a moment.
>
> After she steadfastly refused to open the door, it took the four men and the officer a few minutes to kick the door in. Stark discovered his wife with another man, whom he names as M. [sic] Uffner, connected with a moving picture firm.

Edna was soon in the news once more on December 28, 1921, seeing her apartment robbed of $1,500 in jewels by "telephone burglars." As the *New York Evening World* explained:

"Telephone burglars" enter an apartment after assuring themselves by repeated calls over the wire that no one is at home. Miss Wheaton had several calls that evening just before she left at 6:30 o'clock. When she came home again at 1 o'clock she found that the front door had been forced and her property taken. The thieves had spent time enough in the apartment to make tea, coffee and cocoa, and had played several records on the phonograph.

But back now to Mr. Irving Stark. Divorce was certainly in the offing for him and Edna, and you might surmise that wedding bells remained in the offing for Edna and George Uffner. They weren't. They never did tie the knot. Instead, in October 1924, Edna wed her dance act partner, Bert Gordon (née Barney Gordetsky), later famed for his "The Mad Russian" character on Eddie Cantor's popular radio show. "I love George [Uffner]," she nonetheless told the press, "very dearly. I have loved him a long time—even before I was married."

George Uffner forged a far more sinister path.

As the '20s progressed, Rothstein saw two of his prime sources of income—the Wall Street "bucket shops" and gambling—under increasing attack. He also grew wary of the liquor trade's inherent risks—hijackings, murder, and police raids. But he saw new opportunities, wonderful opportunities, in narcotics and set out to build (and control) the international drug trade.

As Rothstein biographer Leo Katcher revealed:

Until 1925 Rothstein limited his drug purchases to European sources. Late that year he turned to Asiatic sources and sent Sid Stajer, a narcotics addict himself, to Asia. Stajer visited China, Formosa and Hong Kong. He was able to make "buys" in all three places.

The next year Rothstein sent George Uffner to Asia. Uffner was to continue to act as a buyer long after Rothstein was killed. He would work for [Lepke] Buchalter, for Luciano and for others who needed supplies. He would become a favorite of such as Frank Costello and Frank Erickson.

Crime writer Christian Cipollini has further explained that:

Uffner's role was primarily in the establishment and maintenance of opium trade routes that began in China, carved through various points in Europe, and ended in New York City. . . .

Uffner and Sidney Stajer were the dynamic duo of dope, working as a pair since at least 1923, when they boarded ships to Europe for month-long stays. The roundup of countries on their itinerary included England, France, Germany, Italy and Switzerland, then to Shanghai and Formosa. . . .

Rothstein's "dope men" visited contacts throughout Western Europe who either provided shipping of pure opium tar, or had access to laboratories to process the opium into morphine and heroin. Uffner, Stajer and [Jacob "Yasha"] Katzenberg, when venturing into China, also met with the opium magnates to discuss price, quality and quantities. . . . Usually, the quantities were quite large, often shipped in steamer trunks or similar containers; the dope men went "big" because Rothstein wanted total market share.

Rothstein's involvement became immense. He increasingly associated with those in the trade. Following his death, when United States Attorney Charles H. Tuttle poured through his Rothmere Mortgage Corp. records, the information therein enabled him to seize $2 million in pure opium, cocaine, morphine, and heroin in early December 1928. Said information also resulted in a March 1929 $1 million seizure. (*See* **PARK CRESCENT HOTEL 351-357 West 87th Street**.)

162. RIVERSIDE MEMORIAL CHAPEL 180 West 76th Street (At Amsterdam Avenue) Site of Rothstein's

1928 funeral. His coffin was of bronze trimmed in mahogany. Charles Rosenthal served as undertaker.

Also, the site of Charles Entratta's July 1931 service, Sidney Stajer's in December 1940, Benny Leonard's in April 1947, Bald Jack Rose's that same October, *Zit's Weekly* publisher Carl F. Zittel, and—for that matter—that of Minnie Marx, mother of all three, four, five, or six (depending on how you count them) Marx Brothers in September 1929.

163. ARNSTEIN-BRICE RESIDENCE 306 West 76th Street (Between Riverside Drive and West Side Avenue)

Nicky Arnstein and Fanny Brice resided here from 1920 through 1927. Purchased from Gilbert Colgate of the Colgate Soap family. A five-story, twenty-room townhouse. The Arnsteins lived on the lower three floors and rented the rest of the building to theatrical friends; A. R. forced Brice to buy furniture for it from him at exorbitant prices.

"Fanny's immediate plans for the townhouse," wrote her biographer Herbert Goldstein, "were settled, not by her, but by Arnold Rothstein [who] insisted Fanny buy her furnishings from him. He himself, what's more, would make all the selections.

"Rothstein was most insistent.

"Within a day, the furnishings arrived, together with a bill for fifty thousand dollars. Fanny called in an appraiser, who told her the stuff was worth from ten to thirteen thousand dollars.

"Fanny paid Rothstein the fifty thousand dollars and said nothing. But she knew the difference between the payment and value of the furnishings was simply Rothstein's interest on Nick's $100,000 bail money."

Nicky Arnstein and Fanny Brice (COURTESY OF THE LIBRARY OF CONGRESS)

164. "THE MONASTERY" (Apartment House) 22 West 77th Street (Between Central Park West and Columbus Avenue)

In February 1924, a twenty-five-year-old Texas-born gold digger, Louise Lawson, was murdered here—suffocated in her fifth-floor, two-bedroom apartment.

"That morning," the *New York Daily News* would later write, "at about 8 a.m., two 'roughly-dressed' men had called on Lawson . . . to deliver some bootleg hooch, the building's elevator operator told cops. A sleepy Lawson, still groggy from whatever shenanigans she had partaken in the night before, let them up to her fifth-floor apartment, he said.

"It was a fatal mistake. The men were vicious robbers who tied Lawson up while they ransacked her home. She died horribly and needlessly, suffocated from the towel taped tightly to her face as the fiends made off with jewelry worth upwards of $15,000 . . . and furs."

Her finances were decidedly mysterious. Investigators could only discern a grand total of $245 of income during her stay in New York: $75 a week for three weeks as a *Ziegfeld Follies* girl and $20 for two days as a $10-per-day extra on D. W. Griffith's melodramatic film *Way Down East*.

Her outgoing exceeded that exponentially—even by 1920s' standards. A newspaper account noted in the days following her death:

> The administrator of her estate discovered that her monthly budget for the maintenance of the apartment was as follows:

Rent	$175
Maid	$85
Liquor	$150
Delicatessen	$75
Laundry and Cleaning	$100
Total	$585

In addition, there were her music lessons, her taxi bills and incidentals which brought her expenses up to approximately $650 a month, as against over $2,000 a month that she deposited in the bank.

When she died, there was a balance of only a few dollars in her favor! Where did the money come from, and how did she spend more than $100,000 which her bank book showed she had deposited during her two years in New York?

Among Miss Lawson's well-heeled admirers was the married multimillionaire Gerhard M. Dahl (aka "Jerry Doll"), chairman of the board of the BMT (Brooklyn–Manhattan Transit Corp.). "I told [police]," Dahl wrote years later, "that I knew Miss Lawson well, not in a way even remotely connected with romance but as a talented young musician half my age."

Sure.

A. R. had insured the diamond and platinum jewelry stolen during Miss Lawson's murder for $15,000. The policy lapsed just before her death.

Held in connection with her death was jewel thief Harry Sitamore. (*See* **LORBER'S RESTAURANT 1420 Broadway.**)

In August 1925, New York City mayor "Red Mike" Hylan (vociferously opposed to raising subway—i.e., BMT—fares) linked the names of Dahl and Rothstein as supporters of his Tammany-backed primary challenger, State Senator James J. Walker.

165. THE BLOSSOM HEATH INN Basement of the Park Plaza Hotel 50 West 77th Street (Between Central Park West and Columbus Avenue) Owned by Hump McManus's brother Frank, an official of the Children's Court. Frank McManus lived in Room 252 at the Park Central Hotel. From Frank's Blossom Heath Inn, Frank and Hump actually broadcast a radio program featuring their singing voices. Frank was a tenor. An Irish tenor, come to think of it.

On May 21, 1931, Brooklyn mobster and bootlegger Vannie Higgins, a Legs Diamond ally, was stabbed here "twice in the left side of the chest and once in the right side." One wound penetrated his lung.

For some reason, Higgins gave out the story that he had been stabbed in Flushing, Queens. Observers found the story absurd since he was then dropped off in a Packard sedan at Polyclinic Hospital (site of Rothstein's death—*see* **POLYCLINIC HOSPITAL 335-361 West 50th Street**) by

Andrew Marotta, manager of Union City, New Jersey's Abbey Inn.

"Higgins," noted one press report, "stuck to his story that the stabbing affray had been in Flushing. The doctors said they doubted this because he was bleeding profusely when he was brought to Polyclinic and would have bled to death had he come all the way from Queens."

But, according to the *New York Daily News*, what actually happened was this:

Vannie Higgins and Frank McManus (AUTHOR'S COLLECTION)

Half an hour after the Higgins party had been seated Vannie arose in anger—a brunette girl friend, since interviewed by detectives, was dancing a rhumba with brother Frank McManus. Vannie rose in a rage. He dashed to the middle of the floor. Then the fun began.

George and Frank McManus (AUTHOR'S COLLECTION)

The outcome! Vannie and his mob tossed into the wash-room. Higgins stabbed. A Blossom Heath waiter with slashed wrist. A McManus mobster with a broken nose. Then silence.

Or, rather, a trip to the Polyclinic—followed by silence—or rather lies.

"Who are you?" inquired Detective Bert Maskell, at Polyclinic Hospital.

"You know who I am," Higgins stonewalled.

"Who are you?"

"I'm Vannie Higgins—right name Charles."

"What happened to you?"

"I was in a cab in the Bronx and we drove to Flushing."

"Do you know you're going to die?"

"What of it?" Vannie retorted.

But Higgins didn't die—at least not for a while.

Coincidentally, just shortly before all this transpired, another Brooklyn mobster, twenty-six-year-old John Kempt, was shot in the right arm by one of four unidentified men in "Sloppy Joe's Cabaret" (133 West 51st Street).

———————————

As with so much of the city, by the 1970s, the twelve-story Park Plaza Hotel had trundled seriously downhill, degenerating into a particularly squalid single-room-occupancy facility.

In October 1974, twenty-six-year-old ex-convict Calvin Jackson was indicted for the murder of eight female Park Plaza residents in their respective rooms from April 1973 through September 1974. He was also indicted for a ninth slaying, committed two doors down in the victim's luxury apartment.

"Subsequently," as the *New York Times* noted in February 1975, "the police of the 20th Precinct reported that during a nine-month period the hotel had been the scene of two murders, nine robberies, one rape, 18 burglaries, three assaults and one case of sodomy."

Distraught neighbors complained that the hotel was "a home for prostitutes, transvestites, narcotics addicts and alcoholics" and that their activities "threaten to destroy the community."

That same February of 1975, New York State Attorney General Louis
J. Lefkowitz damned the place as a "chamber of horrors" and moved to
dissolve its operating corporation.

The site is now the much more respectable "Parc 77 Apartments."

166. HOTEL BELLECLAIRE 250 West 77th Street (Between Broadway and West End Avenue) Here

on Thursday, August 12, 1926, in Room 815, a woman described as his former admirer, threw acid (perhaps Lysol) in Bill Fallon's face and right eye.
"That afternoon," reported the *New York Daily News*, "shortly after 3:30
the lawyer was entertaining some friends at the hotel. He had been living
there since Monday. In the room when the woman entered were Fallon,
Miss May Kenny, an attractive former actress, a man named [Joseph]
Baker ["well known on Broadway"] and another girl. The intruder, clutch-
ing a dog whip in her hand, sprang forward and began striking the girl
who was with Baker about the face and body. Fallon jumped up and as
he sought to grapple with the woman, she emptied a bottle of acid in his
face. The lawyer instinctively turned his head and the fluid struck the side
of his face, part of it reaching his eye."

Despite first refusing treatment at Port Chester's United Hospital,
Fallon escaped not only blindness but also any scarring whatsoever.

A very simple thing sometimes makes a reputation for a man or an institution.

When The Hotel Belleclaire advertised Apple
Pie two years ago, people immediately began to
talk about the hotel and patronize it. This simple dish appealed to them.

Other advertisements followed in which the
hotel talked about ham and eggs, griddle cakes
and country sausage, picked-up Cod Fish, in
cream and baked potatoes, salt mackerel for Sunday morning breakfast, rice pudding, etc.—all
simple dishes that everybody likes.

The Belleclaire now enjoys a reputation all
over the world as being a fine home hotel in
which home cooking of simple dishes is a feature,
and people come to the hotel to get "good grub."

ROBERT D. BLACKMAN, *Proprietor.*

A Hotel Belleclaire Ad from 1918 (AUTHOR'S COLLECTION)

Reporters contacted Fallon's girlfriend Gertrude Vanderbilt regarding the incident, and she denied having seen her paramour for weeks, exploding, "I don't ever want see him or any of that gang again. Of course, I don't know anything about it. I wasn't at the Hotel Belleclaire and I'll make it hot for any one who says I had anything to do with it. No, I don't know where Fallon is now, and I don't care."

Despite such words, reporters did spy a framed portrait of "The Great Mouthpiece" atop the piano at her West 50th Street apartment.

Built in 1903. Ten stories, 197 rooms. Designed by architect Emery Roth.

167. WILLIAM FALLON HOME 304 West 77th Street (Between West End Avenue and Riverside Drive)

While still riding high, Bill Fallon purchased this white stone mansion for $40,000 for his wife, Agnes Rafter Fallon, and their daughters, Ruth and Barbara. At roughly the same time, he purchased 304 West 84th Street for Gertrude Vanderbilt.

168. DR. CHARLES NORRIS HOME 344 West 77th Street (Between West End Avenue and Riverside Drive)

Dr. Norris died here of a heart attack (following "acute dysentery") on September 11, 1935. As Chief Medical Examiner of the City of New York from January 1918 until his own passing, he issued the autopsy report not only on Rothstein but also on numerous other celebrated slayings or suicides, such as that of showgirl Dot King, whom Norris determined had been set upon by a person of extreme strength who had applied a "hammerlock hold" on her while chloroforming her. (*See* **DOT KING APARTMENT 144 West 57th Street.**)

Other high-profile cases (both still unsolved) involved the June 1920 murder of "bridge expert, sportsman, society gambler and amorist" Joseph B. Elwell and the June 1931 slaying of twenty-five-year-old socialite and model Starr Faithfull. Both, at first, might have been judged suicides but, in the case of Elwell, Norris proved that Elwell could not have held the .45 caliber death pistol far enough away to have pulled the trigger himself.

In the drowning death of Faithfull (an underaged sexual victim of former Boston mayor Andrew J. Peters), Norris found that while the technical cause of death was, indeed, drowning in the Long Island surf, her [bruised] body contained nine grains of luminol . . . indicating she reached the water in an unconscious condition."

The Faithfull case eventually reached the screen as 1960's Elizabeth Taylor–Eddie Fisher effort *BUtterfield 8*. Taylor hated the film but that did not prevent her turning down the Best Actress Oscar she won for her portrayal of the doomed "slut of all time Gloria Wandrous."

A Rendering of Dr. Charles Norris (Looking a Bit John Barrymore-Ish) at Work (AUTHOR'S COLLECTION)

In 1932, Norris (praised by the *Times* as "almost a legendary figure in the life of the metropolis") commented to an interviewer:

> I am not a detective! I am the chief medical examiner of New York. I am a man who finds out what made dead people die. I am an old fool who has spent 14 years poking around in cadavers. I am a physician, a bacteriologist, a toxicologist. But by the great jumping Jehosaphat, I am not a criminologist!
>
> People seem to think I go around like a combination Dr. Watson and Sherlock Holmes, solving mysteries. Do I care who murdered that floater they brought into the morgue today? I do not.
>
> All I care about is the fact that it was not a suicide, but a homicide; that death was caused by strangulation before the body was thrown in the river; and that the body was in the water five days. Now the mystery belongs to the police; my job is ended.

169. A. R. STERN HOSPITAL (aka Dr. A. R. Stern's Sanitarium) 365 West End Avenue (At West 77th Street) Lillian Lorraine spent weeks here in a full-body cast as she recuperated from her January 1921 fall. (*See* FIFTY-FIFTY CLUB 119-121 West 64th Street.) Stern's Sanitarium was a thirty-eight-bed full-service hospital treating everything from severe fractures to births to appendectomies and tonsillectomies—and was a particular favorite of theater folk.

Dr. Stern (home address: 440 West 87th Street) attended actor Barney Bernard when he died of pneumonia at his 215 West 90th Street home in March 1924. The forty-six-year-old Bernard had portrayed "Abe Potash" more than three thousand times in the *Potash and Perlmutter* series of plays originally bankrolled by Dr. Philip M. Grausman. (*See* DR. PHILIP M. GRAUSMAN'S HOME AND OFFICE 130 West 58th Street.)

Replaced by a fifteen-story apartment house in 1925.

170. ARTHUR DAVEY PAYROLL ROBBERY West 81st Street and Central Park West Here, on October 5, 1928, two armed men stopped the Premier Fireproofing company's Arthur W. Davey's chauffeur-driven car, stuck a gun in the sixty-year-old Davey's face, and relieved him of the $8,474 he had just secured at the nearby Colonial Bank branch on the ground floor of the Colonial Hotel, West 81st Street at Columbus Avenue. (*See next location* THE ALDEN 225 Central Park West.)

171. THE ALDEN 225 Central Park West (Between West 82nd and West 83rd Streets) Police raided a dice game at George D. Uffner's fifth-floor apartment here on November 17, 1928. While they were at it, they took Uffner into custody regarding the above-mentioned October 5, 1928, $8,474 Arthur Davey payroll robbery. Arrested with the thirty-three-year-old Uffner were former longtime Rothstein bodyguard Fats Walsh (also age thirty-three) and the thirty-one-year-old Rothstein-connected hoodlum Charles Lucania (aka

Lucky Luciano—and then residing at 266 East 10th Street). Their arrest on robbery charges, however, was a mere pretext. Police were far more interested in grilling the trio regarding Rothstein's murder. Investigators dropped the robbery charges on November 29.

The fifteen-story Alden opened as an apartment hotel in 1926. Converted into co-ops in 1984.

172. HERBERT BAYARD SWOPE HOME 130 Riverside Drive (At West 85th Street) Swope resided here in 1920 with his wife, Pearl Honeyman "Maggie" Powell Swope, a former legal secretary, and their two children, Jane and Herbert Jr. "I liked Herbert as a gambling fellow," recalled Maggie Swope. "I was always on his side and sort of rooting him on. It was exciting not to know whether we had ten cents or a million dollars." One form of gambling is, of course, the stock market. In October 1929, Swope enjoyed holdings of $14 million. After the October 1929 Crash, far less than $14 million. Bernard Baruch had warned him to get out. He didn't.

173. GERTRUDE VANDERBILT HOME 304 West 84th Street (Between West End Avenue and Riverside Drive) The brick five-story home of Gertrude Vanderbilt, purchased for $10,000 in cash plus a $5,000 mortgage at 6 percent interest. The property had been valued at $31,000 with a $16,000 mortgage.

Noted the *New York Daily News* in 1927:

During Fallon's trial in the summer of 1924 on a charge of jury bribery, in which he won an acquittal by a brilliant defense in his own behalf, the actress was not only his most intimate friend but almost his only friend.

She sold her five-story house in West 84th St., and it was understood that the money she realized from the sale went to Fallon's defense. She stuck to him when his practice dwindled to less than a livelihood and it is believed that her money, in loans, made it possible for him to keep up appearances. For all his fame as a criminal lawyer, Bill Fallon died broke and was never able to pay back any part of Gertrude Vanderbilt's loans.

174. THE CLARENDON 137 Riverside Drive (Between West 85th and West 86th Streets) Commencing

in 1905, William Randolph Hearst, the publisher of three New York dailies—The *Evening Journal,* the *New York American,* and, starting in 1924, the tabloid *Daily Mirror*—dwelt in this twelve-story apartment house, occupying thirty rooms on the top three floors.

"It was here," noted Hearst biographer David Nasaw, "that he held his business meetings, entertained friends, family, and publishing colleagues, and exhibited his favorite artworks. Hearst had originally leased the top three floors of the building and the roof garden, but as his family and art collection expanded, so did his need for additional space. In 1913, he asked his landlord for permission to lease the eighth and ninth floors and make extensive renovations throughout, including raising the ceiling on the top floors to accommodate a new oversized tapestry he had brought back from Europe. When the landlord refused Hearst permission to make these changes, he bought the building from him. The price was reportedly close to $1 million."

From the 1920s onward, however, Hearst spent most of his time in California with his mistress, the actress Marion Davies (née Marion Douras), leaving his wife, Millicent Veronica Willson Hearst (yet another of the seemingly unending stream of ex-showgirls we meet on this tour), to rattle around these digs on her own.

For all his faults, however, Mr. Hearst proved to be a fairly consistent (as these things go) opponent of Tammany Hall and, by extension, of Arnold Rothstein and company.

It was his *New York American*'s investigation into Bill Fallon's suspicious legal (or, rather, extra-legal) maneuvers during 1922's Fuller & McGee Wall Street fraud cases that triggered Fallon's 1924 indictment for jury tampering. The case against Fallon was strong. Fallon's counterattack was stronger still, shredding the reputation of opposition witnesses and most spectacularly—and bizarrely—placing Hearst himself on trial, alleging that the entire prosecution had been triggered on orders from Hearst ("Fallon must be destroyed!") because Fallon had proof (birth certificates) of a set of twins fathered by Hearst and mothered not by Mrs. Hearst but by Miss Davies (whose father, by the way, was a Brooklyn magistrate, Bernard J. Douras). Fallon's tale was pure hogwash from start to finish. There were no birth certificates. There were no twins. But Fallon's strategy worked. He stayed out of the slammer—and Hearst's affair (because it had reached court records) now embarrassingly reached the public eye.

No good deed, in fact, does pass unpunished.

With his financial empire tottering and with neither he nor Millicent spending much time there, Hearst sold the building in the mid-1930s.

(above left) *Mr. and Mrs. William Randolph Hearst in 1923* (above right) *Marion Davies* (COURTESY OF THE LIBRARY OF CONGRESS)

175. BELNORD HOTEL 209 West 87th Street (Between Broadway and Amsterdam Avenue) In 1929,

Broadway columnist Mark Hellinger recounted (in great detail) a strange tale. Rothstein, it seems, was getting a shave in the Belnord barbershop. It was a slow, rainy day, and for some reason, the barber, Sam Lester, providing Arnold's shave, proposed establishing a "suicide club," at a dollar a head with the proceeds going to the last survivor. A dozen persons joined, but Rothstein demurred. Lester persisted, and Rothstein (invariably unable

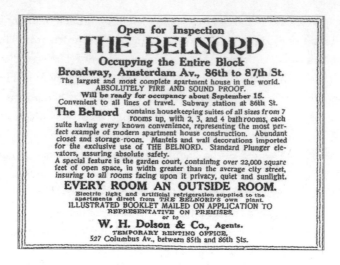

A 1922 Ad for the Belnord (AUTHOR'S COLLECTION)

to resist a bet) finally became unlucky number thirteen. By the time of
Rothstein's death, eight members had already perished—six (five barbers
and a manicurist) were outright suicides, plus two would-be bank robbers:
one shot during the robbery; the second executed for murdering a teller.

Concluded Hellinger:

It is Mr. Lester's argument that all of them have died by their own
hand. Even the bank robbers and Arnold Rothstein.

"You see," he argues. "The two chauffeurs who tried to hold
up that bank walked into death deliberately. They knew the odds
were very much against them. The one that killed the cashier knew
he was going to his death if they were caught. Those two fellows
were absolute suicides."

We looked at Lester.

"But how," we asked him, "do you figure Rothstein a suicide?"

"Very easily," he responded. "When Arnold Rothstein lost the
money in that huge poker game, he was asked to pay. He evidently
refused.

"Again, he was asked to pay. Again, he refused. He was finally
threatened with death unless he paid.

"He laughed at them. And with that laugh he committed suicide."

Opened in 1922. A branch of the Gertner's Restaurant opened there in 1924. (*See* **HOTEL ALBANY 1446-1450 Broadway.**) In 2021, the Belnord temporarily hosted a men's homeless shelter.

176. PARK CRESCENT HOTEL 351-357 West 87th Street (aka 150-153 Riverside Drive) Inez Norton resided here following Rothstein's murder.

On March 5, 1929, police, acting on information seized from Rothstein's Rothmere Mortgage Corp., raided the room here of Bonny Grant, seizing $1 million in cocaine and opium.

Also arrested: Irving "Little Itch" Halpers, Bennie "The Sweeper" Walker, and Harry Stern, formerly a body for both Kid Dropper and Little Augie Orgen. As both Dropper and Orgen were both eventually rubbed out, it may be assumed Stern was no more successful at body-guarding than at drug-dealing.

Fifteen stories. Built in 1926–27. Now The Riverside, a rehabilitation center.

177. HOTEL OXFORD 205 West 88th Street (Between Amsterdam Avenue and Broadway) Bill Fallon died of alcoholism and heart disease here at his wife's apartment on the late morning of April 29, 1927. He was just forty-one.

"Bill Fallon is dead," eulogized columnist Mark Hellinger. "And in those four words rests the greatest sob story Broadway ever knew. He played Broadway until Broadway finally got him. When he tried to pull out, it was too late. It always is. And so, Fallon, who was still a young man, is dead. Perhaps, after all, he was satisfied to go. For his early days had been filled with love and happiness and fame. And when the future holds hope for none of these, it is time to go."

178.

WAXEY GORDON'S RESIDENCE 590 West End Avenue (Between West 88th and West 89th Streets) Location of the ten-room apartment of Arnold's bootlegging associate Waxey Gordon (Irving Wexler). Wrote authors Craig Thompson and Allen Raymond in *Gang Rule in New York*: "His West End Avenue home consisted of ten rooms and four baths, and he paid $6,000 a year rent for it. He paid an interior decorator $2,200 to construct a combination bookcase and bar in his library, and the bookcase was stocked with sets of the classics in magnificent bindings." He later lived on Central Park West.

Waxey Gordon (on the left) in a May 1933 NYPD lineup, following his capture in upstate Sullivan County on tax charges. His sidekicks: his bodyguards the Austrian-born Hymie Pincus (alias Harry Klein) and Albert Arndt. (COURTESY OF THE LIBRARY OF CONGRESS)

179. SPENCER TRACY RESIDENCE 153 West 96th Street (Between Columbus and Amsterdam

Avenues) Tracy, who portrayed Rothstein in 1934's *Now I'll Tell* (*see* **THE ROXY THEATRE 153 West 50th Street**), occupied a $2.00-per-week "two steep, shaky flights up" room here as a poverty-stricken young actor in the early 1920s. His roommate was the equally impoverished fellow future star Pat O'Brien. "Twelve-by-twelve, with two iron bedsteads taking up nearly as the space," it was "about the size of a jail cell and furnished like one, with a shared toilet and a shared bath that cost extra."

The duo had relocated from an equally miserable room on West 56th Street.

180. HOLY NAME OF JESUS CHURCH 307 West 96th Street (At Amsterdam Avenue) Here on April 20,

1955, was Lillian Lorraine's funeral Mass. Only her common-law husband, John W. O'Brien; her accountant; and two friends attended, and she was at first buried in a pine box in a pauper's grave at Queens' Calvary Cemetery. Also buried at Calvary is Ciro "The Artichoke King" Terranova.

Just a month later, Lorraine's remains were transferred to a marked gravesite at a friend's plot in St. Raymond's Cemetery, the Bronx.

Built in 1900. Now merged with the Parish of St. Gregory the Great, 138 West 90th Street.

181. LILLIAN LORRAINE RESIDENCE 255 West 97th Street (At Broadway) Lillian Lorraine's home at the

time of her death from "natural causes" at 10:00 a.m., April 17, 1955. Just sixty-three, she had been in ill health since shattering her spine in January 1921. (*See* **FIFTY-FIFTY CLUB 119-121 West 64th Street**.)

In 1945, *New York Daily News* reporter Ruth Turner had tracked down the now-obscure Lorraine and interviewed her, and she confessed (if that is the word):

"What do you think happened, Miss Lorraine?" asked Turner. "Ziegfeld said you were the greatest beauty he ever had in the *Follies*. What went wrong?"

"He was *right*," Lorraine shot back. "And he was crazy about me. He had me in a tower suite at the Hotel Ansonia and he and his wife lived in the tower suite above. And I cheated on him, like he cheated on [his wife] Billie Burke. I had a whirl! I blew a lot of everybody's money, I got loaded, I was on the stuff, I got the syphilis, I tore around, stopped at nothing, if I wanted to do it I did it and didn't give a damn. I got knocked up, I had abortions, I broke up homes, I gave fellers the clap. So that's what happened."

"Well, Miss Lorraine," her interlocutor responded, perhaps, a bit shocked, "if you had it to do over would you do anything different?"

"Yes," came her response. "I never shoulda cut my hair."

"The filth and gutter talk most probably continued," noted Lorraine's biographer Nils Hanson. "No good purpose can be served in continuing to further relate this drunken diatribe from an embittered and hapless shadow of a woman who had once been the adored and undisputed toast of Broadway. Lillian had committed the unpardonable cardinal sin by disgracing not only herself and the *Ziegfeld Follies* name but, most importantly, maligning the character of the most important figure in Broadway musical history—the man who had in every sense of the word been her creator. Her name, her photographs and innumerable other memorabilia were subsequently all removed from the Ziegfeld Club [an alumni association of *Follies* showgirls] archives. Now, the question I had raised early on—why no one in the Ziegfeld Club would return my calls or discuss her association with the Ziegfeld—was finally answered. Lillian Lorraine had quite simply been excommunicated by her own peers. The Ziegfeld Diva successfully brought down the curtain on any good memories associated with a lustrous, albeit tumultuous career."

The Ziegfeld Club, by the way, served not only social and historic purposes, but also a charitable one, looking out for old comrades in need. At one point, Gertrude Vanderbilt served as president. Its actual headquarters were maintained on the fifth floor of the Central Presbyterian Church at Park Avenue and East 64th Street.

182. HYMAN BILLER HOME 315 West 99th Street (Between West End Avenue and Riverside

Drive) Biller was indicted alongside his boss "Hump" McManus for Rothstein's murder. He provided this address when he checked into Havana's Plaza Hotel, when he was on the lam for that crime. Biller never went to trial, and after McManus's acquittal, the charges were dropped.

(AUTHOR'S COLLECTION)

183. CHURCH OF THE ASCENSION 221 West 104th Street (Between Broadway and Amsterdam

Avenue) Site of Bill Fallon's May 1927 Solemn High funeral Mass. Eight priests assisted. Arnold Rothstein, Abe Attell, Nicky Arnstein and Fanny Brice, Gene McGee (Fallon's former law partner), John J. McGraw, and Charles A. Stoneham were among the seven hundred mourners. So was the deceased's nephew—also named William J. Fallon and looking a bit scruffy. He had an excuse, though, being just sprung on $1,000 bail on bootlegging charges. Thirty-five cars accompanied the body to Cavalry Cemetery. John McGraw paid for Fallon's mahogany casket. Conspicuous by her absence was Gertrude Vanderbilt.

184. **W. J. DARGEON FUNERAL PARLOR West 107th Street (At Amsterdam Avenue)** Site of Bill Fallon's wake, May 1927. "A rosary [was] twined about his fingers," noted the *New York Daily News*. "At each end of the casket [was] a single lighted candle flickering in a silver holder."

In 1912, Dargeon's advertised itself in the *New York Herald*:

W. J. DARGEON, INC.
Any First-Class Funeral With Grave, $115
Hearse, three coaches to any cemetery or depot within ten miles services and attendance, including deed of grave for the interment of three adults, complete.
NEVER ONE DISSATISFIED PATRON.

185. **CARRIE ARNSTEIN HOME 200 West 109th Street (Between Amsterdam Avenue and Broadway)** Nicky Arnstein's estranged first wife, Carrie Greenthal Arnstein, resided here with her daughter in October 1917 when she sued Nicky for divorce. "I am now informed," she charged, "the defendant [Nicky] was receiving visits from Fannie Brice while . . . in jail, and whom he represented as his lawful wife. . . . [He] rides around in an automobile and meets said Fannie Brice nightly after her performance at one of the New York theatres."

186. **MONONGAHELA DEMOCRATIC CLUB 292 Manhattan Avenue (Between West 112th and West 113th Streets)** The 11th Assembly District's Tammany clubhouse—led by George McManus's powerful protector, James J.

"Jimmy" Hines. Hines also served as Dutch Schultz's ally in safeguarding the city's burgeoning numbers racket, for which Hines snagged an estimated $200,000 in payoffs. In 1939, District Attorney Tom Dewey convicted Hines of complicity in the numbers racket, and he received a four-to-eight-year sentence.

Among the Monongahela Club's less nefarious activities was Hines's Central Park "June Walk," described by the *New York Times* as follows:

> Thousands of residents of the old Eleventh Assembly District recall Hines' June Walk, which he staged in Central Park annually for twenty-six years before he went to jail. As many as twenty-five thousand women and children listened to half a dozen brass bands, put on paper hats and gorged themselves on ice cream, hot dogs and pop furnished by Hines, who used to take part in the fun wearing the gay green bucket hat of the stage Irishman.

The four-story building housing the club was built in 1900. Now apartments.

187. SUBWAY SAM ROSOFF HOME 179 West 113th (Between Seventh Avenue [Adam Clayton Powell Blvd.] and St. Nicholas Avenue) According to 1920's census, the home of contractor "Subway Sam" Rosoff, a rough-hewn, largely illiterate Russian immigrant who eventually ascended from the rags of the East 42nd Street's Newsboys' Home to the multimillionaire who constructed a full quarter of New York's subway lines and as a habitué of Rothstein's elegant Saratoga Springs casino, The Brook. One night, there, in August 1920, the colorful Rosoff's luck was running $400,000 to the good. Prudence might have suggested that Rothstein shutter The Brook for the night, but Arnold merely phoned his friend Charles A. Stoneham to borrow $300,000 in cash Stoneham had stashed in his nearby Saratoga safe. By evening's end, however, Sam's luck had U-turned. By the time, Rosoff finally departed The Brook, he was $100,000 in the red.

"He was a long shot player," noted the *New York Times*'s Red Smith, "who, it was said, would bet on the bull at a bull fight. . . . A more lovable character would be hard to imagine."

Lovable or not, in February 1937, Rosoff found himself a suspect in the fatal shooting of Norman Redwood, business manager of the Compressed Air, Tunnel, and Subway Workers Local 102—aka, the "sandhogs" union. "I will kill you stone dead," Rosoff had supposedly threatened the future late Mr. Redwood. "I have two guns, if I don't use them, I will get the men who will use them."

Rosoff denied all, and nothing came of the matter.

188. MAURICE CANTOR HOME 312 Manhattan Avenue (Between West 113th and West 114th Streets)

Cantor's address when he won election to the New York State Assembly in 1926. After losing his Assembly seat in 1930, he moved to Long Beach, Long Island.

(above left) *The "Hon." Maurice F. Cantor* (above right) *Dr. Nathaniel F. Cantor* (AUTHOR'S COLLECTION)

It is possible that he lived here earlier than that, however, including when his younger brother Nathaniel attended Columbia University graduate school, and just as possible that Nathaniel lived with him at that time. In December 1925, following studies under Franz Boas and John Dewey, Nathaniel received his doctorate in anthropology—and then quickly moved on to a professorship in sociology and anthropology at the University of Buffalo. He was just twenty-six.

What is more remarkable, however, is this: despite (or, perhaps, because of) being the kid brother of one of the underworld's most disreputable mouthpieces, Nathaniel soon established himself as one of the nation's foremost criminologists—even publishing such well-regarded treatises as *Crime, Criminals and Criminal Justice* and having himself voluntarily incarcerated in a Prussian jail to study foreign prison conditions.

It all sounds like a movie Warner Brothers should have made starring Edward G. Robinson as Maurice and Paul Muni as Nathaniel!

189. BALD JACK ROSE HIDEOUT THE RIVIERA APARTMENT HOUSE West 157th Street and Riverside Drive OK, this one is a bit north of the Upper West Side, but it's too grand a story not to share.

Here at the apartment of his friend Harry Pollok, Bald Jack Rose hid out following the Rosenthal murder, leading to this development:

MRS. HARRY POLLOK SUES
WOMAN JACK ROSE MET WAS
NOT SHE.

Mrs. Mary Emily Pollok, who was married to Harry Pollok, the promoter of sporting events, in Buffalo in 1909 and lived with him only a short time has filed for divorce.

The case arises out of the testimony of Jack Rose, who says he was in Pollak's apartments in the Rivers, 157th Street and Riverside Drive, after the killing of Herman Rosenthal.

Rose mentioned the name of "Mrs. Pollok," but it wasn't the real Mrs. Pollok, and when she learned of the testimony she instructed her attorneys to bring suit.

Rose, by the way, had a wife of his own, who he had pimped out as a prostitute.

Bald Jack Rose (AUTHOR'S COLLECTION)

APPENDIX A:
THE WHALEN REPORT

There are definitely a helluva lot of murders recounted in these bullet-riddled pages and a wealth of *theoretically* unsolved slayings. But the Big Enchilada (or, perhaps, in this case, rather the "Big Blintz") of said murder mysteries is, of course, that involving Arnold Rothstein's demise. The authorities did their darndest to keep it unsolved, but an awful lot of tantalizing clues seeped into the NYPD's official (but never before published) report on the subject. And so, for all you armchair detectives out there, here goes. Enjoy.

Police Department

CITY OF NEW YORK

In the matter of the charges preferred against various members of the Police Department, in connection with the shooting

— of —

ARNOLD ROTHSTEIN

OPINION BY
HONORABLE GROVER A. WHALEN
POLICE COMMISSIONER

IN THE MATTER OF CHARGES PREFERRED AGAINST VARIOUS MEMBERS OF THE POLICE DEPARTMENT, IN CONNECTION WITH THE SHOOTING OF ARNOLD ROTHSTEIN

Arnold Rothstein, a notorious gambler, was shot on the night of November 4th, 1928 and died on the morning of November 6th from his gunshot wounds.

Following Rothstein's death, an investigation was conducted relative to the action taken by the police authorities regarding this crime. As a result, charges were preferred against various members of the Police Department involving violations of the rules and regulations of the department and neglect of duty.

In order that the public might know of the action which had been taken by the members of the Police Department with respect to the shooting of Rothstein, public hearings were conducted and every phase of police activity in any way connected with the solution of this crime was thoroughly investigated. A number of witnesses were interrogated upon these hearings, including former members of the Police Department and representatives of the District Attorney's Office.

In disposing of the charges preferred against the members of the department, I have reviewed the reports made by the officers connected with the case, as well as all the testimony and evidence adduced at the trial and have made my findings with respect to these charges based upon the evidence presented.

The first information received by the police authorities regarding the shooting of Rothstein was by Patrolman William S. Davis, who was performing patrol duty in the vicinity of the Park Central Hotel located at 56th Street and 7th Avenue. He arrived there about 10:40 P. M. and was the first member of the Police Department to reach the scene of the shooting. A watchman at the hotel informed him that a man had been

"Shot in the hotel" and upon receiving this information, Patrolman Davis proceeded immediately to the employees' entrance of the hotel on 56th Street where he saw Arnold Rothstein holding his side.

Although the police officer questioned Rothstein as to the identity of the person who had shot him, Rothstein refused to give him any information nor would he state where he had been shot. This silence was continued by Rothstein up to the time of his death and at no time would he divulge any information to the police authorities to assist them in apprehending the person responsible for the crime. This refusal, on the part of Rothstein to furnish the police authorities with any information regarding the circumstances under which he had been shot, made it necessary for the police to act independently in its investigation of the crime, handicapped by the stubbornness on the part of the wounded man to lend any assistance.

The first action taken by Patrolman Davis was to telephone to Police Headquarters that a shooting had taken place at the Park Central Hotel and requesting that an ambulance be sent. This message was telephoned at 10:45 P. M. on November 4th, 1928, and was supplemented by a telephone message sent by Patrolman Davis to the old 9th Precinct Station House located in West 47th Street in which precinct the Park Central Hotel is located.

Lieutenant John Collins, who was assigned to signal monitor duty at the station house received this message at about the same time that he was informed by the Telegraph Bureau at Police Headquarters by Patrolman Reilly, since retired from the department, that an ambulance was on the way to the Park Central Hotel. The records of the old 9th Precinct Station House show that this message was received at 10:49 P. M. on November 4th, 1928.

At the time that Patrolman Davis arrived at the hotel, he found Thomas Calhoun, a watchman, and Lawrence Fallon one of the hotel detectives, in the employees' entrance with Rothstein, both of whom informed Detective Patrick Flood, who subsequently arrived at the hotel, that they had seen Rothstein coming from "a stairway leading from an upper floor."

While Patrolman Davis was waiting for the arrival of the ambulance, Patrolman Robert J. Rush also performing patrol duty in the vicinity came in with Alfred Bender a taxicab driver, who had found a revolver on the east side of 7th Avenue, between 55th and 56th Streets, between the northbound car tracks, while he was operating his taxicab on 7th Avenue. The taxi driver accosted Patrolman Rush and turned over the revolver to him, stating the circumstances under which he had found it. At the time the revolver was found, it had one discharged shell and five empty chambers. At about the same time, Patrolman Rush was called into the hotel by one of the employees thereof and went with the taxi driver to the employees' entrance where they met Patrolman Davis.

Shortly thereafter, Detective Flood who was assigned to the 9th Squad Detectives, arrived accompanied by Detective Green (who has since died) and Patrolman Rush turned over to Detective Flood the revolver which had been given to him by the taxi driver, stating the circumstances under which it had been found.

Within a few moments, Dr. Malcolm J. McGovern who was assigned to ambulance service at the City Hospital, arrived at the Park Central Hotel. The testimony of Dr. McGovern was to the effect that he had received the ambulance call at 10:50 P. M., on November 4th, 1928, and arrived at the hotel within approximately five or six minutes thereafter.

Although Detective Flood in his reports submitted to his superiors stated that he was first informed of the shooting at 11:15 P. M., this statement is erroneous for it was undisputed that Detectives Flood and Green were at the hotel prior to the arrival of the ambulance.

An examination of Rothstein by Dr. McGovern, disclosed that Rothstein had been shot in the right lower abdomen, but was not bleeding externally. After making a superficial dressing of the wound, Rothstein was taken in the ambulance to the Polyclinic Hospital at the request of Dr. Hoffman, the house physician of the hotel, Rothstein having refused to go the City Hospital.

After the taxi driver had pointed out the spot where the revolver had been found, a further investigation made the same night, resulted in the finding of five unexploded shells which fitted the revolver.

The investigation relative to the commission of the crime was undertaken by Detective Flood. He was assigned to night duty in the 9th Squad Detectives, and it therefore, was his case.

The preliminary investigation made by Detective Flood produced no results. The elevator boys and employees of the hotel were interrogated but none would state that Rothstein had been seen in the hotel. Detective Flood then proceeded to the Polyclinic Hospital hoping that Rothstein might tell him of the facts surrounding the shooting, but was unsuccessful as Rothstein refused to give him any information.

Thereupon Flood returned to the 9th Squad Detective office where he received a call from Detective Joseph A. Daly, who was attached to the Headquarters staff of Inspector John D. Coughlin, who was then the Commanding Officer of the Detective Division, both of whom have since retired from the Police Department.

As a result of information received by Detective Daly, he went to Lindy's Restaurant located at 50th Street and Broadway, accompanied by Detective Flood. There they interviewed Abe Scher the cashier at Lindy's and were informed that he had received a message asking that Rothstein come to Room 349 of the Park Central Hotel. This was the first information that had been obtained about Room 349, which was almost two hours after the shooting. Immediately upon receiving this information, Detectives Flood and Daly proceeded to the Park Central Hotel, where they met [Burdette N.] Divers the house detective, and obtained from him a key to Room 349.

Prior to going to Room 349, however, the detectives had learned that Frank McManus had occupied Room 252 in the hotel, and they entered this room with a pass key furnished by Divers the house detective. There, they found Mrs. Frank McManus in bed and interrogated her as to the address of George McManus. She did not give them his address, but did furnish them with his telephone number, Endicott 2649, which Daly subsequently ascertained was an unlisted private wire.

No effort, was made, however, to obtain the address at which this telephone number was listed until nine o'clock the following morning.

Detective Flood testified that Daly had told him that he would obtain this address through Inspector Coughlin, and apparently the other detectives assumed that this would be done, as none of them made any effort to secure the same.

In spite of the fact that there was a delay of almost ten hours in ascertaining the address of George McManus, Inspector Coughlin, Commanding Officer of the Detective Division, admitted in his testimony that he did not interrogate any of the detectives as to the reason for this delay nor did he prefer any charges against those responsible for this obvious neglect.

An examination of Room 349 disclosed an overcoat in the clothes closet with the name "George McManus" on the label and a key to Room 349 in the coat pocket of said coat. There was also found in the room several handkerchiefs with the initials "G. McM," and a shirt size 16.

It further appeared that a wire screen on one of the windows facing 7th Avenue had been forced down from the upper end, indicating that the pistol which had been found on the north-bound tracks on 7th Avenue by Bender, the taxi driver, had been thrown from that window.

Further investigation disclosed that Room 349 had been registered in the name of "George A. Richard, Newark, N. J." since November 2nd, 1928, and that a call had been made from Room 349 on the night of November 4th, 1928, to Circle 3842, which was Lindy's Restaurant.

The condition of Room 349 indicated that the persons occupying the room had been drinking, as four glasses and bottles of ginger ale and white rock and empty liquor bottles were found in the room. These were carefully preserved and turned over to Detective Ramirez assigned to the Homicide Squad, for the purpose of examining them, in order to obtain any fingerprints that might appear thereon. Although the fingerprints of every person employed in the hotel who might have entered that room, as well as the fingerprints of all members of the Police Department who might have had any contact with these glasses were taken, none compared with the fingerprint impression which was found on one of the glasses.

The only fingerprint which was not compared with the impression found upon the glass was that of Arnold Rothstein, which might have resulted in definitely establishing that he had been in Room 349. During his lifetime, the fingerprints of Rothstein were not obtained. After his death, it was the duty of the Homicide Squad, under the regulations of the department, to have obtained these fingerprints. This, however, was not done and the body of Rothstein was buried, without his fingerprints ever having been secured.

At that time, the Homicide Bureau was in charge of Inspector Arthur Carey, who has since retired from the department.

The information received as a result of the investigation indicated that George McManus had occupied Room 349 and from the descriptions furnished of "George A. Richards" by Bridget Farry the housemaid, Patrick Grace and Emanuel Cabonus, waiters who had brought meals to Room 349, it fitted that of George McManus.

While the investigation was being conducted in Room 349, the telephone rang and Divers, the house detective, was permitted to receive the message over the phone. He stated that someone was inquiring for "George," and was told by the detectives to have the persons telephoning come up to the room. Immediately thereafter, Tom and Frank McManus, brothers of George McManus, and Hyman Biller known as the "payoff man" for George McManus, entered Room 349.

Detectives Flood and Daly interrogated these visitors and asked them where their brother George could be located. At that time George McManus's coat which had been found in Room 349, was in full view and Detective Flood told them that their brother George would have to explain the presence of his overcoat in this room.

Although the investigation which had been conducted, indicated that the shooting of Rothstein had occurred in Room 349 and that George McManus was in some way connected with the shooting, no attempt was made to detain Tom and Frank McManus and Hyman Biller when they entered Room 349 but, on the contrary, they were permitted to leave upon their assurance to Detective Flood that they would bring their brother George to the 47th Street Station House for questioning.

Since that night Hyman Biller has not been apprehended. More than fifty detectives were subsequently assigned to the apprehension of Hyman Biller at an expense to the Police Department of approximately $9,000, and their investigations have taken them to all parts of the United States, to Mexico, to Havana and other parts of the world. All this would have been avoided if Detective Flood had been awake to the situation which faced him in the early morning hours following the shooting of Rothstein.

Detective Flood had no right to rely upon the assurance given to him by Tom and Frank McManus that they would bring in their brother George. His friendship with the McManus family undoubtedly influenced him in the confidence which he placed in the pledge made to him by Tom and Frank McManus that they would locate their brother George.

Although Detective Flood knew that the call to Lindy's Restaurant had been made from Room 349, he permitted the house detective to answer the telephone call that came into that room while they were there, which would have obliterated any possible fingerprints that might have been left upon the telephone by the person making the call.

When the detectives left Room 349 everything was removed from the room except the screen, which was taken by Detective Green the following day. No member of the Police Department investigation was left in charge of the room, although the investigation indicated that that was the place where the crime had been committed. The explanation of Detective Flood is that he arranged with the manager of the hotel that no one would be permitted to enter the room and that the names of any persons calling that room would be furnished to Detective Flood. That, however, does not excuse the failure of Detective Flood to have placed a member of the department in charge of Room 349.

In spite of the fact that the investigation indicated that George McManus was in some way connected with the crime, his name was not placed upon the report submitted by Detective Flood under the list of "Description of Persons Wanted." Detective Flood testified that this was at the direction of Inspector Coughlin. Neither was there any general alarm sent out for George McManus, although such action was recommended by Detective Louis Ramirez who reported that

From our investigation we believe that George McManus was in the room where Rothstein was shot, and is either a party to the crime or a witness to its commission.

As a result of the shooting of Rothstein, George McManus was indicted and charged with murder and tried in the Court of General Sessions. Upon the trial, Detective Flood testified and was interrogated relative to the revolver which had been handed to him by the taxi driver. In his report submitted to his superior officers, Detective Flood stated that Bender had told him that when he found the revolver it was "still hot," but at the trial of George McManus in General Sessions, he testified that he made no observation of the temperature of the gun at the time it was handed to him.

Nowhere in the reports submitted by Detective Flood is there any mention made of the appearance of Tom and Frank McManus and Hyman Biller in Room 349 in the early hours of the morning of November 5th, 1928, although he claims that he gave this information to Inspector Coughlin. Neither is there anything in the report of Detective Flood to indicate that he had interrogated any persons occupying any rooms on the third floor, although he testified that he had given this information to his superior officers and also to Assistant District Attorney [P. Francis] Marro, who was investigating the case.

Upon the trial in General Sessions, Detective Flood testified that he went to all of the rooms on the third floor, although as a matter of fact, he did not enter all of the rooms, particularly Room 320 which was occupied by a Mrs. Putnam who was one of the witnesses produced by the prosecution in the trial of George McManus.

Although the address of George McManus was not ascertained until about 9:00 o'clock on the morning of November 5th, 1928, and an unsuccessful effort was made to enter the same, no application for a search warrant was made until November 16th, 1928. This delay of almost eleven days was another blunder on the part of those directing the activities of the detectives in the solution of this crime. That responsibility rested upon Inspector Coughlin, the Commanding Officer of the Detective Division, and the only explanation made by him upon the trial for this delay was that, "We probably overlooked it."

Detective Flood testified that he had been given no instructions to apply for any search warrant until he made the application to Chief Magistrate [William] McAdoo, a day or two before it was granted. Even at that time the seriousness of the delay was apparent to Chief Magistrate McAdoo who, in commenting upon the delay said, "I am afraid the apartment has been searched and cleaned out."

This criticism becomes particularly apparent when it is realized that the investigation made at 51 Riverside Drive disclosed that the superintendent had seen George McManus and his chauffeur "Willie" [Essenheim] about midnight of November 4th, 1928, and that McManus had sent his chauffeur up to the apartment to bring down to him his heavy overcoat. This was the last seen of McManus until he was taken into custody on November 27th, 1928.

Detective Sergeant Cordes was assigned to the case at 8:50 A. M. on November 5th, 1928, by Inspector Coughlin, and he was instructed to meet Detective Daly. He went with him to the Park Central Hotel where various persons were interviewed.

Nate Raymond, one of those interviewed, was taken to Police Headquarters where he was questioned by Assistant District Attorney Marro, and gave the information regarding a poker game that had taken place at the home of James Meehan in September 1928. At this game it was claimed that George McManus and Rothstein had participated together with other known gamblers, and that Rothstein had lost a large sum of money and had given his I. O. U. for $219,000 in payment of some of his losses.

As a result of this information, Detective Cordes and Daly and Mr. Marro, went to Madison Square Garden that evening looking for the McManus Brothers and those who had participated in the game at Meehan's. The search for McManus was continued at 51 Riverside Drive without avail. In fact, the residences of all the members of the McManus family were covered by detectives and every effort made to apprehend George McManus, but without success.

On the following morning, Detective Cordes was instructed by Inspector Coughlin to report to Mr. Banton, District Attorney of New York County. Mr. Banton testified that he had requested Detective Cordes' assignment to his office to work on the Rothstein case, because Cordes knew George McManus, Hyman Biller and William Essenheim (McManus's chauffeur) by sight, and would recognize them if he saw any of them. Cordes devoted his time in an effort to locate George McManus, Hyman Biller and others who were wanted for questioning by the District Attorney's office regarding the Rothstein case.

In the meantime, a search warrant was obtained for George McManus's apartment and an entry gained on November 16th, 1928, at which time it was found that all of the photographs of George McManus had been removed from their frames. Although the apartment house at 51 Riverside Drive had been covered by detectives from November 6th, 1928, no attempt was made to seal the apartment occupied by George McManus. which was located on the tenth floor, so as to prevent the entrance of any persons to the apartment for the purpose of removing any evidence that might be found there.

Realizing the importance of obtaining a photograph of George McManus, a number of detectives visited photograph galleries and other places where pictures of outings might be examined, for the purpose of finding one which included the picture of George McManus. Finally, such a picture was obtained and a photograph of McManus made therefrom which was so blurred, that even Cordes who knew McManus, admitted that it would be difficult to identify him from that photo.

It was not until November 27th, 1928, that George McManus was taken into custody by Detective Cordes, who testified that on the previous evening he had received an anonymous telephone communication asking that he be at 242nd Street and Broadway in The Bronx on the following morning. Although no information was given to him as to what the matter had reference to, he appeared at the place mentioned on the morning of November 27th, 1928, and there saw George McManus in a barber shop in company with Mr. [James D. C.] Murray, his lawyer. It was then that Mr. Murray told Cordes that he had phoned him the previous night, having made arrangements with Mr. Banton to have George McManus brought to the office of the District Attorney for questioning.

Detective Cordes, instead of bringing McManus to the old 26th Precinct Station House (which embraces the location at 242nd Street and Broadway) for record and booking as required by the regulations of the Police Department, took him to the office of the District Attorney. Cordes' explanation for this procedure is that he was acting under prior instructions received from his superiors.

Inspector Coughlin testified that he told Cordes to report to Mr. Banton and "to go down to his office and work on the Rothstein case" and that he instructed Cordes to work under the direction of Mr. Banton.

Mr. Banton testified that he did not tell Cordes where he was to bring McManus, if he was apprehended. It was also assumed by Assistant District Attorney Marro who testified at the hearing, that Cordes would first take McManus to the station house and that Mr. Marro would be sent for, in order to question him.

Detective Cordes claimed that after taking George McManus into custody at 242nd Street and Broadway, he telephoned to Inspector Coughlin for instructions. Although Detective Cordes contended that he had asked Inspector Coughlin for instructions on the morning of November 27th, 1928, and received instructions from his commanding officer, he admitted that he thereafter telephoned to the District Attorney's office for instructions which he explains by the statement, that he did it "to assure myself that I would not do anything that would conflict with his judgment."

In any event, there were no specific instructions given to Detective Cordes that precluded or prevented him from taking McManus to the 26th Precinct Station House, in accordance with the rules and regulations of the Police Department. Even this was admitted by Inspector Coughlin who testified that he did not understand that the instructions meant that the rule regarding the taking of prisoners to the station house for booking and record was abrogated or that any instructions received from the District Attorney's office prevented the rule being followed and then bringing the prisoner to the District Attorney's office for questioning.

After George McManus was brought to the District Attorney's office accompanied by his lawyer, he refused to reply to any questions put to him by Mr. Banton. It was then that Mr. Banton directed Cordes to place McManus under arrest and he was brought before Judge Mancuso in the Court of General Sessions on the charge of murder and held without bail. At that time, fingerprints of George McManus were obtained, although these had already been obtained from the War Department prior to his apprehension.

A photograph of McManus, however, was not secured by reason of the fact that his lawyer objected to such procedure. It was not until December 29th, 1928 that George McManus was brought to Police Headquarters for the purpose of having him photographed which was accomplished through the assistance of Richard Patterson, Commissioner of Correction.

During the time that Detective Cordes was assigned to the District Attorneys's office, no reports were made by him to his commanding officer in the Police Department. This was the result of a custom that had grown up in the department, that men assigned to the District Attorney's office would report direct to him and not to their commanding officer in the Police Department.

That such a custom prevailed is unfortunate, but that it did exist was testified to by Inspector Coughlin who stated that he did not know what the men assigned to the District Attorney's office were doing, that "Those men were sent down there and whose work I knew nothing about, they were reporting direct to him (District Attorney) which has always been the case when men are assigned to the District Attorney's office to work on any particular case. They report to the District Attorney and the commanding officer never knew what they were doing or what the work consisted of."

Inspector Coughlin also admitted that he did not know if any of the superior officers in charge of the detective district were present on the night of the shooting of Rothstein, nor did he interrogate them as to their activities on the case on the night of November 4th, 1928. He also admitted that he did not know what direction was given on that night by any officers of the detective division.

Although Inspector Coughlin denied any knowledge of the shooting of Rothstein until the morning of November 5th, 1928, the records of the Telegraph Bureau show that his office was notified at 11:22 o'clock on the night of November 4th, 1928, and that Lieutenant Quinn of his office did notify Inspector Coughlin. If Inspector Coughlin had not been notified as he testified, it was his duty to have preferred charges against those who were charged with the responsibility for such failure. This was never done.

As a matter of fact, however, there was no Superior officer present at the scene of the shooting or during the early hours of the investigation which took place. The work was undertaken by the detectives working on the case.

Acting Lieutenant Samuel Dribben, who was temporarily in charge of the 3rd Detective District from 6:00 P. M. to midnight on November 4, 1928, testified that he received no notification of the shooting of Rothstein during his tour of duty, and did not know about the case until the following morning. Captain Henry Duane, who was in charge of the 3rd Detective District, testified in that he was not present during the early hours of November 5th, 1928, not having been notified during the night of the commission of the crime.

The records of the Telegraph Bureau did not show that any notification was given to the 3rd Detective District prior to midnight, nor to Captain Henry Duane during that night.

Under the regulations of the Police Department then in force, it was the duty of the Telegraph Bureau to notify the detective district office of the commission of this crime during the day time, and to communicate with the commanding officer's residence during the night time. The records of the Telegraph Bureau show that it failed to function properly on the night in question, and that no notification was given to the 3rd Detective District Office or to Captain Duane at his home.

It was most unfortunate that there was no superior officer directing the activities of the members of the detective division immediately following the shooting of Arnold Rothstein. There was an evident lack of coordination and supervision on the part of the commanding officer of the detective division, that had its effect throughout the entire case.

While the investigation was under way, Captain Duane who was in charge of the 3rd Detective District, left on his vacation. While it is true that his application was made on November 3rd, 1928, prior to the shooting and approved on November 5th, 1928, he should have felt a moral responsibility to have voluntarily canceled his vacation and to have remained at his post so that he might supervise and direct the work under his command. Particularly is this so, in view of his failure to have been present on the night of November 4th, 1928, to direct the activities of his subordinates.

While Captain Duane was on his vacation, the 3rd Detective Division was in charge of Captain John Lagarenne, and the evidence indicates that he was reporting to the commanding officer of the detective division, as to the efforts of those working out of his district on the Rothstein case.

Charges were also preferred against several members of the uniformed force. While these charges were not the result of wil[l]ful misconduct nor of action prompted by ulterior purposes, they did involve technical violations of the regulations of the department. Although technical violations, proper discipline requires that they be taken cognizance of by the Police Commissioner.

Lieutenant John Collins was assigned to the telephone signal monitor at the 47th Street station house on November 4th, 1928, and it was his duty to enter in the telephone record book all messages received from patrolmen assigned to duty in that precinct. There was no entry of the telephone message of Patrolman Davis at 10:50 P.M. on November 4th, 1928.

Failure to record this message was merely an oversight, because the same message was entered by Lieutenant Collins which he received from the Telegraph Bureau about the sending for the ambulance.

Lieutenant Edward J. Moran was assigned to desk duty at the station house and was charged with the responsibility for the entry of all messages received by Lieutenant Collins over the telephone signal monitor. Failure, therefore, of Lieutenant Collins to make the aforesaid entry becomes the responsibility of Lieutenant Moran, who was the desk officer.

Lieutenant Francis A. Stainkamp was assigned as desk officer at the station house from midnight November 4th, 1928 to 8 o'clock of the following morning. Under the regulations, it was the duty of Lieutenant Stainkamp to examine the memorandum books of Patrolmen Davis and Rush, who returned to the station house at the expiration of their tours of duty.

Patrolman William S. Davis and Robert J. Rush were required, under the regulations, to have presented their memorandum books to Lieutenant Stainkamp for the purpose of having him initial the entries made regarding the shooting of Arnold Rothstein.

The neglect of the patrolmen to present their books to the desk officer, and the latter's failure to have examined their books were due to an oversight and were not prompted by any ulterior purpose, for the information regarding the shooting of Rothstein was contained upon the forms which were required to be filled out and forwarded to Police Headquarters.

Accordingly, I have disposed of the Charges and Specifications as follows:

PATROLMAN PATRICK FLOOD

1. **GUILTY.** Flood should have detained Tom and Frank McManus and Hyman Biller when they entered Room No. 349, instead of permitting them to leave under the pretense of bringing George McManus to the Station house for questioning.
2. **GUILTY.** Flood was careless and negligent in his examination of the rooms located on the third floor of the Park Central Hotel, particularly in view of the fact that the investigation indicated that Rothstein had been shot while in Room No. 349.
3. **GUILTY.** Under the regulations of the department, it was the duty of Flood to incorporate in the reports submitted by him, all important information which he obtained as a result of his investigation.

   While the information not included in the reports is alleged to have been furnished orally to the Commanding Officer of the Detective Division, that did not justify a disregard of the regulations.
4. **NOT GUILTY.** Prior to Rothstein's death, his fingerprints could not be obtained by reason of his physical condition, as a result of the shooting. After Rothstein's death, it was the duty of the Homicide Bureau to have secured his fingerprints.
5. **GUILTY.** Flood exercised poor judgment as a detective of long years of experience in the manner in which he investigated the crime immediately following the shooting.

Detective Flood has been a First Grade Detective for a great many years. These charges have resulted in his demotion and his transfer to patrol duty. I have also taken into consideration, his record in the department. I find him **GUILTY** as aforesaid and it is ordered that he be **FINED THIRTY DAYS PAY.**

DETECTIVE SERGEANT
JOHN H. CORDES

1. **GUILTY.** Cordes could have brought McManus to the station house for search and record as required by the regulations of the Police Department, before bringing him to the District Attorney's office for questioning. While there was an obvious conflict as to the instructions given to Cordes, there was nothing in those instructions, that would have prevented him from complying with the regulations of the department.

2. **NOT GUILTY.** As a result of the charge made against McManus by the District Attorney and his arraignment in the Court of General Sessions where he was held without bail, Cordes was precluded from bringing McManus to Police Headquarters for finger printing and photographing.

3. **NOT GUILTY.** It was the established custom in the Police Department that men who were assigned to the District Attorney's office were to report direct to the District Attorney and were not required to make any report to the Commanding Officer of the Detective Division. This custom relieved Cordes from filing any reports until directed by his Commanding Officer to do so.

4. **NOT GUILTY.** There was no evidence to sustain the charge against Cordes that he failed to report all information obtained by him from his investigation of the Rothstein case. He was almost in daily contact with the District Attorney to whom he reported all information which he had obtained.

5. **NOT GUILTY.** It was not the duty of Cordes to obtain the finger prints of Rothstein during his life time. After the death of Rothstein, it was the duty of the Homicide Bureau to obtain these fingerprints.

6. **NOT GUILTY.** There was no evidence indicating Cordes failed to take all necessary police action which was required of him in the investigation of the Rothstein case. Nor was he guilty of any conduct which prevented or impeded the arrest and apprehension of George McManus, or in his prosecution for the shooting of Rothstein.

Cordes has an exemplary record in the Police Department having received the Medal of Honor on two (2) occasions, this being the highest award for bravery conferred by the Police Department. I am of the opinion that his failure to comply with the regulations was due to a misunderstanding of the instructions given by his superior officers and the District Attorney's office. In view of that fact, I believe that a **REPRIMAND** would suffice and it is so ordered.

LIEUTENANT JOHN COLLINS

1. **GUILTY.** This was a technical violation, as a message of similar import, which was received by the Telegraph Bureau was entered in the Telephone Record of the Precinct.

It is therefore ordered that said Lieutenant John Collins be REPRIMANDED.

LIEUTENANT EDWARD J. MORAN

1. **GUILTY.** This charge is based upon a technical violation. Under the regulations of the department, as Desk Officer, he was charged with the responsibility for the proper recording of all entries received by the officer assigned to Signal Monitor duty.
2. **NOT GUILTY.** There having been no change of posts, the regulations did not require that any entry be made of the sending of the patrolman to the Park Central Hotel.

It is therefore ordered, that said Lieutenant Moran be REPRIMANDED.

LIEUTENANT
FRANCIS A. STAINKAMP

1. **GUILTY.** Lieutenant Stainkamp should have examined the entry made in the memorandum book of Patrolman Davis. His failure to do so was not influenced by any improper motive, as the records which were sent to Police Headquarters contained the information which appeared in the memorandum book of Patrolman Davis. **GUILTY.** The same applies to the entry made in the memorandum book of Patrolman Rush.

It is therefore ordered that said Lt. Stainkamp be REPRIMANDED.

PATROLMAN WILLIAM S. DAVIS

1. **GUILTY.** Davis should have submitted his memorandum book to the Desk officer for inspection when he completed his tour of duty. His failure to do so was not prompted by any ulterior purpose but the result of an over-sight, the same information having been recorded on the forms which were sent to Police Headquarters.

It is therefore ordered that said Ptl. Davis be REPRIMANDED.

PATROLMAN ROBERT J. RUSH

1. **GUILTY.** Rush should have submitted his memorandum book to the Desk Officer for inspection when he completed his tour of duty. His failure to do so was not prompted by any ulterior purpose but the result of an over-sight, the same information having been recorded on the forms which were sent to Police Headquarters.

It is therefore ordered that said Ptl. Rush be REPRIMANDED.

ACTG. LIEUTENANT
SAMUEL DRIBBEN

1. **NOT GUILTY.** It was the duty of the Telegraph Bureau to notify the Acting Commanding Officer of the Detective District of this shooting. The official records of the Telegraph Bureau do not show that any notice was given to Lt. Dribben, who was then Acting Commanding Officer of the Third Detective District.

2. **NOT GUILTY.** There was no evidence to prove that Lt. Dribben had any knowledge of the shooting of Rothstein until the following morning.

It is therefore ordered, that the Charges and Specifications filed against Lt. Samuel Dribben be DISMISSED.

CAPTAIN HENRY DUANE

1. **NOT GUILTY.** It was the duty of the Telegraph Bureau to have notified Captain Duane, Commanding Officer of the Third Detective District, at his home after midnight of this shooting. The official records of the Telegraph Bureau do not show that any notice was given Capt. Duane at his home during the night of the shooting.

2. **NOT GUILTY.** There was no evidence to prove that Capt. Duane had any knowledge of the shooting of Rothstein until the following morning.

3. **NOT GUILTY.** Prior to leaving on his vacation, Capt. Duane properly directed the men who were working out of his district on the Rothstein case.

4. **GUILTY.** Although Capt. Duane made his application for his vacation prior to the shooting of Rothstein and the same was approved by his Commanding Officer, Capt. Duane should have felt a moral responsibility to have cancelled his vacation and to have remained at his post, in order to assume proper

supervision over the investigation of the shooting of Rothstein which occurred within the Third Detective District and over which Capt. Duane was in command.

In view of the record of Captain Duane in the department, I believe that a REPRIMAND would suffice and it is so ordered.

CAPTAIN JOHN LAGARENNE

1. **NOT GUILTY.** Capt. Lagarenne reported to the Commanding Officer of the Detective Division, with respect to the efforts of the men working out of his district on the Rothstein case.
2. **NOT GUILTY.** Capt. Lagarenne directed the activities of the detectives working from his district in the investigation of the Rothstein case.

It is therefore ordered that the Charges and Specifications filed against Capt. Lagarenne be DISMISSED.

CONCLUSION

The shooting of Arnold Rothstein has occupied the columns of the newspapers throughout the country for over a year. Many strange, fantastic tales have been woven around his shooting. The impression has been sought to he created that some person in high authority was responsible for the failure of the Police Department to apprehend and convict the perpetrators of that crime.

At the outset, I should like to make this observation. The trial of the several police officers who were charged with neglect of duty in connection with the investigation of the Rothstein case, was not for the purpose of determining who killed Arnold Rothstein but, rather from the viewpoint of the Police Commissioner, to fix the responsibility for any failure on the part of the police in connection with the case and to apply such corrective measures as would prevent a recurrence of such failure.

The greatest obstacle experienced by the Police Department in the Rothstein case was the refusal on the part of Arnold Rothstein to furnish the police authorities with any information as to the person who had shot him.

Although conscious for several days prior to his death, Rothstein stubbornly refused to aid the authorities by divulging the names of his assailants and, with lips sealed, went to his grave. Obviously if helpful clues are missing, or if victims or their associates obstruct or do not cooperate with the police, then culprits may not be apprehended, or their arrest and conviction may be delayed.

With the difficulties presented at the trial of George McManus in the Court of General Sessions on the charge of homicide, the public is well familiar. Witnesses, who had been produced by the prosecuting attorney based upon the testimony given by them before the grand jury failed to testify at the trial in accordance with the testimony previously given by them. The weakness of the law in failing to provide punishment for recalcitrant witnesses of this character, has provoked considerable comment in the daily newspapers, resulting in the recommendation to the State Legislature for an amendment to the Penal Law of our State, so as to provide punishment for "false swearing." That problem is the responsibility of the State Legislature and not that of the Police Department of the City of New York.

The widest latitude was permitted in the trial of the charges preferred against members of the Police Department arising out of the investigation of the Rothstein case. The hearings before the Police Commissioner which embraced an investigation into every phase of activity on the part of the members of the Police Department in the solution of this crime, consumed over a month's time. Every effort was made to bring to light any failure or neglect on the part of any member of the Police Department, regardless of the person who was responsible for such error, in order that the public might be informed of all the developments in the case.

First and foremost, among the developments in the investigation conducted by the Police Commissioner, was the fact that there was no mysterious powerful figure in the background, who in any way counseled or interfered with the police investigation of the Rothstein case or its ultimate solution. There is, however, abundant evidence of the fact that the persons directly responsible for the official conduct of the detectives assigned to the case were grossly neglectful of their duty and that the responsibility for any failure in the police work on the case must be charged to them.

The evidence presented at the trial indicated a breakdown in the efficient operation of the detective bureau, due to the lack of intelligent and capable direction on the part of the commanding officer of the detective division at the time that the Rothstein shooting occurred. All through the trial, the evidence indicated a lack of supervision by commanding officer of the detective division or any coordination of the work of the detectives engaged in the investigation.

As a matter of fact, the commanding officer of the detective division frankly admitted, upon the hearings, that although he was the responsible head in charge of the investigation, he did not keep himself informed of the reports made by the detectives working on the case, known as supplementary reports "D. D. 5." The commanding officer of the detective division also admitted that he did not know the nature and character of the work that was being performed by the detectives assigned to the district attorney's office. That such a condition existed is most reprehensible. Although it was contended that it was the practice of detectives assigned to the district attorney's office to report direct to the district attorney, that offers no excuse for such a condition to have been permitted to exist. As the commanding officer of the detective division. it was his duty and responsibility to know of the work that was being done by every member of the Police Department assigned to the Rothstein case. That, perhaps, was more responsible for the lack of coordination of the various units of the Police Department working on the case, than anything else.

The absence of any superior officer at the scene of the crime on the night of November 4th, 1928 is most significant. The official records of the telegraph bureau of the Police Department show that the main desk of the detective division was notified of this shooting at 11:22 P.M. on November 4th, 1928. The records of the detective division show that Inspector Coughlin was notified, and it is difficult to understand his statement, that he had no knowledge of the shooting of Arnold Rothstein until his arrival at Headquarters the following morning. Particularly does this seem incredible, in view of the fact that Detective Joseph A. Daly who was working on the personal staff of the commanding officer of the detective division, was present at the scene of the crime shortly after the shooting, and participated in the preliminary investigation.

Moreover, the evidence revealed that it was Detective Joseph A. Daly who stated to the other detectives present at the scene of the shooting, that he would undertake to secure the address at which the private unlisted telephone number was located, which was the residence of George McManus. That information was not ascertained until the following morning and then there was a delay of almost eleven days before a search warrant was obtained from the Chief City Magistrate for the purpose of entering the home of George McManus.

The failure to require the commanding officer of the 3rd Detective Division in which this crime was committed to refrain from taking his vacation, although previously approved, so that the ranking detective officer in that district could be assigned to the investigation, is another evidence of the indifference on the part of the commanding officer of the detective division with respect to the Rothstein case.

This attitude of carelessness, of lack of direction and supervision, of lack of coordination of the various forces of the Police Department working on the case, found its repercussion throughout the entire work of those engaged in the solution of this crime. Undoubtedly, the fact that Arnold Rothstein was a despised common gambler, and that George McManus to whom the evidence pointed as the person responsible for the shooting of Rothstein, was regarded in a better light, as a common gambler, resulted in no extraordinary effort being put forth in this case.

This is confirmed by the testimony of Detective Flood, that the name of George McManus was not placed upon the report submitted by him under the list of "description of persons wanted" at the direction of Inspector Coughlin, in spite of the fact that the investigation indicated that George McManus was in some way connected with the crime. Neither was there any general alarm sent out for George McManus, although such action was recommended by Detective Louis Ramirez, who reported that

> From our investigation we believe that George McManus was in the room where Rothstein was shot, and is either a party to the crime or a witness to its commission.

The whole spirit of the investigation which took place after Rothstein's death, reflected the attitude of total indifference on the part of the commanding officer of the detective division to the ordinary routine which should have followed in a case of this kind.

Inspector John D. Coughlin was the Commanding Officer of the Detective Division at the time of the shooting of Arnold Rothstein. As such, the failure of the department to function properly is his responsibility. Since the commission of this crime, however, Inspector Coughlin has been **retired** from the Police Department.

What direction was given by the commanding officer of the detective division to the homicide bureau did not appear at the trial. But the evidence presented indicated that the activity of the homicide bureau was practically nil. Prior to Rothstein's death, fingerprints had been found on one of the glasses in Room 349 and, although fingerprints of every member of the Police Department that might have had any contact with this glass, as well as the fingerprints of every person who might have been in Room 349 was obtained, none compared with the fingerprints found upon the glass. The only person's fingerprints that were not compared with those found upon the glass were those of Arnold Rothstein. It was the duty of the homicide bureau to have secured the fingerprints of Arnold Rothstein prior to the removal of his body from the morgue. If that had been done, it would have settled the question as to whether Arnold Rothstein was or was not in Room 349. This fact, the police were unable to establish even at the trial of George McManus.

Inspector Arthur Carey was the Commanding Officer of the Homicide Bureau at the time of the Rothstein shooting, and the failure, on the part of his bureau to have secured these fingerprints, was his responsibility. He, too, has since been **retired** from the Police Department.

Detective Joseph A. Daly who was working on the personal staff of Inspector Coughlin and who was looked upon as the representative of Inspector Coughlin, was one of the first detectives present at the scene of the shooting. He was present while the investigation was being conducted in Room 349 by Detective Flood, and his activity also indicated a lack of intelligent police work. Detective Daly has since been **retired** from the Police Department.

Detective **John Green** who was the partner of Detective Flood, assigned to night duty in the 47th Street station house, has **died**.

Patrolman Joseph Reilly of the Telegraph Bureau, whose records show that he failed to notify the 3rd Detective District office or the commanding officer of the 3rd Detective District on the night of the shooting, has since been **retired** from the Police Department.

Detective Patrick Flood has been tried and found guilty of carelessness and laxity in the manner in which he investigated the crime after he appeared on the scene. He has already been demoted and has been found guilty and **fined 30 days' pay**.

Detective Sergeant John H. Cordes has been tried and found guilty of failure to bring George McManus to the station house after his apprehension, in compliance with the rules and regulations of the Police Department and has been **reprimanded**.

Captain Henry Duane, Commanding Officer of the 3rd Detective District in which territory, the shooting of Arnold Rothstein occurred, has been tried and found guilty of failing to remain on duty while the investigation of the Rothstein case was being undertaken, even though his application had already been approved for a vacation. He has been **reprimanded**.

Lieutenants John Collins, Edward J. Moran and Francis Stainkamp, who were assigned to the 47th Street station house on the night of November 4th, 1928, have been tried and found guilty of failing to comply with the regulations of the Police Department, regarding the proper entries which should have been made in the records of that precinct with respect to the shooting of Arnold Rothstein. They have been found guilty and have been **reprimanded**.

Patrolman William J. Davis and Robert J. Rush have been tried for failure to comply with the regulations of the Police Department, in regard to exhibiting their memorandum books to the desk officer on duty at the 47th Street Precinct station house at the expiration of their tour, of duty. They have been found guilty and have been **reprimanded**.

The experience which has been gained as a result of the investigation in the Rothstein case, has not been without its beneficial advantages to the Police Department. The rules and regulations, particularly those affecting the detective division, have been revised. The lack of supervision and coordination which were manifest in the department at the time of the Rothstein case, have been eliminated. Today, there could be no similar situation as was present in the Rothstein case, for there would be a superior officer upon the scene as soon as the Police Department was informed of the commission of any crime. The present commanding officer of the Detective Division, is in constant touch with his office in order that he may be kept informed of the commission of any serious or unusual crime. That same spirit of devotion to duty finds its reflection on the part of the commanding officers in charge of the subordinate units of the Police Department.

The detective division, as well as the entire Police Department, has benefited by the errors which were brought to light in the Rothstein investigation. The new procedure prevailing in the department as the result of the revised rules and regulations which were issued, has resulted in an intelligent management of the detective division and a closer coordination between the uniformed force and the members of the detective division. Whatever weaknesses were presented in the hearings of the members of the Police Department above referred to, have been corrected.

The Police Commissioner wishes to express his appreciation to Counsel on both sides of this case for their impartial, painstaking and judicial presentation of the evidence.

Nelson Ruttenberg, Fourth Deputy Police Commissioner, who acted in the capacity of Prosecuting Officer for the Police Department, exhibited unusual intelligence and fine legal knowledge during the entire conduct of the case. James I. Cuff, attorney for the defendant police officers, brought to this task his rare ability as a lawyer as well as an unusual understanding of the Police Department routine.

For the information of the Public, this review of the Rothstein case and opinion shall be printed as a record of the Police Department.

Dated, New York, March 24, 1930.

GROVER A. WHALEN,
Police Commissioner.

APPENDIX B:
A GANGSTERLAND
CHRONOLOGY

You can't tell the players without a scorecard—and you can't recall what transpired in each at bat or inning—or to who or by whom—without putting that scorecard on your lap, retrieving your trusty no. 2 pencil, and keeping score. And, so (in a manner of speaking), we've worn our pencils to their nubs, keeping a play-by-play score by compiling this chronology of Arnold Rothstein and his chums and their chums. We view their origins, their crimes, their milestones, and eventually their fate.

It turns out that if you don't get rubbed out, you can live a good long time beyond the roar of the Roaring Twenties.

Maybe, somebody should have told Arnold that.

1899
- Rothstein leaves home; takes job as traveling hat and cap salesman.

1901
- The Considine Brothers assume operation of 42nd Street's Metropole Hotel. (March 7)

1903
- Jules "Big Julius" Formel's 226 West 16th Street apartment robbed. (February 4)
- Jules Formel-Philip Black gun battle at Broadway and West 28th Street. (February 12)

1904

- Rothstein makes first trip to Saratoga Springs aboard the Cavanagh Special; strands Abe Attell.

1908

- Rothstein meets showgirl Carolyn Green at the Hotel Cadillac. (September)

1909

- Rothstein marries Carolyn Green at Saratoga Springs; pawns her jewelry. (August 12)
- Rothstein borrows $2,000 from his father-in-law to open his West 46th Street gambling house.
- Rothstein wins $4,000 against Jack Conaway at John McGraw's pool hall on Herald Square. (November 18)

1910

- Charles G. Gates loses $40,000 in one night at Rothstein's. (November)
- Rothstein buys out his West 46th Street gambling house partner, Tammany ward leader Willie Shea.
- Rothstein's upper teeth are replaced by false teeth—"a marvel of workmanship . . . said to have cost $3,000."

1911

- Herman Rosenthal opens a gambling house at 104 West 45th Street. (November)

1912

- Gambler Herman Rosenthal meets with Manhattan district attorney Charles Whitman. (July 15)
- Murder of Herman Rosenthal at West 43rd Street's Metropole Hotel. (July 16)
- NYPD Lt. Charles Becker indicted for ordering Herman Rosenthal's murder. (July 29)
- Charles Becker found guilty of ordering Rosenthal's murder. (October 24)
- Becker condemned to death. (October 30)
- Tammany leader Charles Francis Murphy increases Rothstein's influence in politics.

1913

- American Tobacco Co. president Percival S. Hill loses $250,000 at Rothstein's gambling house.
- Rothstein's bankroll reaches $300,000; closes gambling house on West 46th Street.
- Rothstein opens gambling house at Hewlitt, Long Island.
- Rothstein begins relationship with showgirl Bobbie Winthrop.
- Charles A. Stoneham forms Charles A. Stoneham & Co. at 41 Broadway.
- George Graham Rice publishes *My Adventures with Your Money*.
- Anna Held divorces Florenz Ziegfeld as a result of his affair with Lillian Lorraine. (January 9)
- George Young Bauchle attends Woodrow Wilson's first inauguration. The *Chicago Tribune* describes him as "a Manhattan plutocrat . . . arrayed like the lilies of the field." (March 4)
- Lillian Lorraine and Frederick M. Gresheimer remarry at Hoboken. (April 25)
- Outside Louis Martin's Restaurant, Frederick Gresheimer attacks Florenz Ziegfeld. (June 28)
- Death of "Big Tim" Sullivan. (August 31)

1914

- Rothstein begins laying off bets for fellow bookmakers.
- Rothstein moves into real estate and insurance.
- Charles Becker's conviction overturned. (February 24)
- Florenz Ziegfeld marries actress Billie Burke. (April 11)
- "Dago Frank" Cirofici, Whitey Lewis (Jacob Seidenshner), Lefty Louie (Louis Rosenberg), and Harry "Gyp the Blood" Horowitz executed for the murder of Herman Rosenthal. (April 13)
- Becker again found guilty of ordering Rosenthal's murder. (May 22)
- Rothstein suffers heavy losses on the 1914 World Series. (October)

1915

- As president of the "Humanology Film Producing Company, Bald Jack Rose releases the five-reel autobiographical film *Are They Born or Are They Made?*
- Harry Sitamore arrested in Newark for grand larceny—not convicted. (April 6)
- New York State Court of Appeals affirms Becker guilty verdict. (June 18)

- Becker delivers a ten-thousand-word statement on the Rosenthal murder, drags the late "Big Tim" Sullivan into the case. (July 21)
- Becker executed at Sing Sing for ordering Rosenthal's murder. (July 30)
- Fred Gresheimer arrested at Jack's for fraud. (September 4)
- Fred Gresheimer convicted in San Francisco of fraud. (December 7)
- Charles A. Stoneham invests in Havana's Oriental racetrack.

1916
- Fred Gresheimer sentenced to eighteen months at San Quentin. (January 10)
- Morris Reisler convicted of burglary in the third degree for robbing a Bronx haberdasher. (February 28)
- Edward R. West and Buda Godman register at the Ansonia Hotel. (May 9)

1917
- Rothstein begins bankrolling Saratoga Springs gambling house owner Harry Tobin.
- A $10,000 mortgage is granted to the "Carolyn Holding Co." for a property on Broadway in Hewlett (Long Island). Presumably, this is Rothstein's gambling house. (March 13)
- Rothstein is robbed at a Hotel St. Francis crap game. (May 16)
- Arch Selwyn opens the Selwyn Theater at 229 West 42nd Street; bankrolled by A. R. (October 2)
- Rothstein wins $300,000 on Hourless at Laurel. (October 18)

1918
- Fanny Brice and Nicky Arnstein wed.
- Charles A. Stoneham and Buda Godman take up residence at his 110 West 55th Street apartment.

1919
- Rothstein opens The Brook gambling house in Saratoga Springs.
- Rothstein robbed of $11,000 in floating crap game. (January)
- Rothstein serves as middleman for Charles A. Stoneham's purchase of New York Giants. (January 19)
- Rothstein is charged with assault after police raid crap game at 301 West 57th St. (January 19)
- Rothstein bankrolls first edition of *George White's Scandals*. (June 2)
- Charges dropped against Rothstein in the 301 West 57th Street police shooting matter. (June 5)

- Rothstein allegedly speaks to fellow New York City gambler Jules Formel and then to District Attorney Charles B. Andrus to keep his Saratoga Springs gambling resort, The Brook, open. (August 7)
- Frederick Gresheimer arrested on narcotics charges. (August 12)
- Rothstein fixes 1919 World Series between Chicago White Sox and Cincinnati Reds.
- Rothstein intervenes in garment industry labor disputes; places Little Augie Orgen in charge.

1920

- Benny Kauff charged with selling an automobile stolen in front of 788 West End Avenue. (December 8, 1919)
- Rothstein henchman Nicky Arnstein (husband of Fanny Brice) in hiding for Wall Street Liberty Bond thefts. (February–May)
- Nicky Arnstein surrenders to police after riding down Fifth Avenue in the annual police parade. (May 15)
- Rothstein furnishes bail for Nicky Arnstein; Monk Eastman steals Fanny Brice's car, returns it on mention of Rothstein's name. (May 16)
- Frederick Gresheimer committed to the Riverdale Sanitarium. (May 18)
- Gresheimer escapes. (May)
- Edna Wheaton arrives in New York from her home in Ithaca.
- Fred Gresheimer captured at Broadway and West 76th Street. (June 15)
- Joseph F. Crater joins the staff of State Supreme Court justice Robert F. Wagner. (June)
- "Subway Sam" Rosoff loses $100,000 in one night at The Brook.
- Rothstein bankrolls Waxey Gordon's rumrunning operation.
- Rothstein begins work with Meyer Lansky and Lucky Luciano.
- Rothstein wins between $850,000 and $900,000 on Sailing B at Saratoga. (August 27)
- Grand jury convenes in Chicago to investigate baseball gambling. (September 7)
- Billy Maharg implicates Attell and Rothstein regarding the 1919 World Series fix in a *Philadelphia North American* article. (September 27)
- A Chicago grand jury indicts eight Black Sox players. (September 28)
- Rothstein announces retirement from gambling. (October 1)
- Rothstein testifies before Chicago grand jury investigating World Series fix. (October 26)
- George D. Uffner is reported working for the "Universal Film Manufacturing Co." (Universal Studios) (October)

- Mistrial for Jules Formel on charges on running a gambling house at 201 South Broadway, Saratoga Springs in the summer of 1919. (December 23)
- Monk Eastman, formerly a Rothstein debt collector, is found shot to death outside the Blue Bird Café (62 East 14th Street). (December 26)

1921

- Second Jules Formel trial—and a second hung jury. (January 4–5)
- Buda Godman arrested in Chattanooga on counterfeiting charges. (February 2)
- Black Sox confessions and waivers missing. (February 14)
- American League President Byron "Ban" Johnson alleges Arnold Rothstein told him that Benny Kauff offered to help fix the 1919 World Series. (March 8)
- Ban Johnson charges that Rothstein stole confessions from the Chicago State's Attorney's office; Rothstein threatens to sue Johnson for $100,000. (March 14)
- Edna Wheaton wins the *Daily News* beauty contest and a film role. (March 19)
- In his third trial, Jules Formel is finally convicted and is sentenced to a minimum of one year in Clinton State Prison at Dannemora. Bill Fallon is no longer part of the defense. (March 25)
- Nat Evans (aka "Nate Evens"), Sidney Stajer, and two other men identified as Hyman Cohen and Elias Fink arrested in St. Louis in connection with the Series fix. Both Evans and Stajer claim they had lost large sums betting on the White Sox. (April 2)
- Dominick Henry's conviction on perjury charges is reversed. (April 8)
- Birth of a son, William, to Fanny Brice and Nicky Arnstein; he is named after Bill Fallon. (April 23)
- Benny Kauff acquitted of auto theft. (May 13)
- Black Sox trial commences in Chicago. (June 27)
- Federal authorities indict Edward M. Fuller and Frank McGee. (June)
- The prosecution in the Black Sox trial announces Sleepy Bill Burns has turned state's evidence. (July 1)
- Rothstein wins $850,000 on Sidereal at Aqueduct. (July 4)
- All defendants acquitted in the Black Sox scandal trial. (July 28)
- Baseball commissioner Kenesaw Mountain Landis reprimands Charles A. Stoneham for allowing Rothstein into his private Polo Grounds box. (July)

- Bill Fallon represents Isadore Rapoport who had a quantity of liquor seized by Saratoga County district attorney Charles B. Andrus. The court upholds the seizure (July)
- Baseball commissioner Kenesaw Mountain Landis bans all eight Black Sox players from Organized Baseball. (August 3)
- Rothstein wins $500,000 on Sporting Blood in Saratoga's Travers Stakes. (August 20)
- Insolvency of "Dandy Phil" Kastel's Dillon & Co. bucket shop (32 Broadway). (September 1)
- Maurice Cantor defends Joseph Curry of the September 28, 1921 murder of patrolman Joseph A. Reuschle. (September)
- Rothstein loses $270,000 on single race at Aqueduct. (Fall)
- George Uffner caught at Edna Wheaton's 39 West 76th Street apartment. (November 27)
- Uffner named in Edna Wheaton divorce suit. (December 3)
- Edna Wheaton's 39 West 76th Street apartment is robbed of $1,500 in jewels. (December 28)
- Rothstein enters Bahamian rumrunning scheme with Dapper Don Collins.
- Rothstein begins his association with Frank Costello.
- With attorney Gene McGee, Rothstein discovers the "padlock" loophole in New York's Mullen-Gage Law.
- Jimmy Meehan first arrested.
- Charles Stoneham shutters his firm Charles A. Stoneham & Co.

1922

- George Young Bauchle disappears.
- Rothstein sells The Brook to Nat Evans. (Alternate date: 1925)
- Collapse of the Rothstein/Charles Stoneham–connected E.D. Dier & Company bucket shop. (January)
- Rothstein helps promote Benny Leonard–Rocky Kansas lightweight fight at Madison Square Garden. (February 10)
- *Collier's Eye* reports Rothstein may take over operation of Madison Square Garden from Tex Rickard. (February 18)
- Rothstein pays income tax of $35.25 for 1921; declares gross income of $31,544.48, net of $7,257.29. (March 15)
- Texas Guinan visits the Hardings at the White House. (April 22)
- Fire erupts at Abe Attell's Ming Toy Bootery; Attell is questioned by police. (May 21)

- Five detectives raid Lillian Lorraine's West 71st Street apartment in search of Charles C. Wagner. (May 26)
- Vincent Terranova, brother of Ciro "The Artichoke King" Terranova, is found shot to death on East 116th Street. (May 22)
- Premiere at the New Victory Theater of Anne Nichols's *Abie's Irish Rose*, which Rothstein helped finance. (May 23)
- Fifty-Fifty Club (119–121 West 54th Street) raided and closed. (June 8)
- Collapse of the E. M. Fuller & Co. bucket shop. Investors lose $5 million. (June 26)
- Fearing kidnapping, Rothstein engages Eugene "Red" Moran, Thomas "Fats" Walsh, and Jack "Legs" Diamond as bodyguards.
- Rothstein fences $285,000 in jewels stolen by Moran from Mrs. Hugo A. C. Schoellkopf.
- Rothstein borrows $20,000 from Irving Berlin.
- Irving Bitz arrested on firearms charges.

1923

- In New York State Supreme Court, Myrtle Goodrich Sloane Bauchle sues her husband for $4,996 regarding her jewelry pawned by him and which she had redeemed. (January 8)
- Owney Madden released from Sing Sing. (February 1)
- Joyce Hawley "Champagne" incident at the Earl Carroll Theatre. (759 Seventh Avenue). (February 23)
- Showgirl Dot King found murdered in a Rothstein-owned apartment. (March 15)
- Morris Reisler, defended by George Z. Medalie, a onetime Rothstein attorney, convicted of the murder of his aunt Miss Bertha Katz. (March 19)
- William Randolph Hearst's *New York American* links Rothstein to bucket shop scandals.
- Rothstein closes Long Beach gambling house.
- *Collyer's Eye* insinuates Rothstein might be involved with the Cincinnati Reds in throwing games. (August 18)
- Bill Fallon and Gene McGee ousted from their law offices in the Knickerbocker Hotel for non-payment of their July rent. (August 29)
- Charles A. Stoneham indicted for perjury for denying his secret partnership in E. M. Fuller & Co. (August 31)
- Rothstein testifies before Referee in Bankruptcy re: E. M. Fuller & Co.; interrogated by the firm's clients' attorney William M. Chadbourne. (June 25 and October 8)

- Jack Dempsey–Luis Firpo heavyweight fight at the Polo Grounds; A. R. helps Lucky Luciano pick out a new wardrobe for the event. (September 14)
- Charles A. Stoneham indicted for mail fraud. (September)
- Boston attorney William J. Kelly sues Rothstein for $53,000 ($50,000 in fees; $3,000 in expenses) for defending him regarding charges of fixing the 1919 World Series. (October)
- Owney Madden charged with the theft of two hundred cases of whiskey from a New York warehouse. (December 3)
- Rothstein bankrolls swindler "Jake the Barber" Factor.

1924

- Charles A. Stoneham indicted. (January)
- Harry Sitamore involved in the robbery of Mrs. Edna Johnson at the Hotel Almanac. (February 8)
- Rothstein indicted for concealing E. M. Fuller assets (Fuller's Pierce-Arrow automobile). The case never goes to trial. (April)
- El Fey Club opens. (May 1)
- Nicky Arnstein, convicted of conspiracy, enters Leavenworth. (May 16)
- Bill Fallon, charged with bribing a juror, jumps bail. (June 2)
- Bill Fallon captured by police in a seedy uptown apartment. (June 14)
- Judge Charles C. Nott suspends sentencing for Fuller & McGee. (July)
- Frank Tinney assaults *Daily News* photographer Nicholas Peterson.
- George Ringler serves summons upon Frank Tinney.
- Fallon acquitted. (August 8)
- Billy Rose opens West 56th Street's Back Stage Club. (Fall)
- Fallon defends New York Giants coach Cozy Dolan. (October–November)
- Rothstein sends Sid Stajer to Asia for drug buys in China, Formosa, and Hong Kong.
- Edna Wheaton marries comedian Bert Gordon in New Orleans. (October 1)
- On Fifth Avenue, Legs Diamond is wounded by a shotgun blast; drives himself to a hospital. (October)
- George Uffner is convicted on a minor narcotics charge; receives a suspended sentence.

1925

- Edna Wheaton is back upstate, living with her parents and stepsister in Syracuse.

- Bill Fallon's law partner Eugene F. McGee is disbarred for failing to attend to a case for which he accepted a $210 fee. (February 6)
- Charles A. Stoneham acquitted of mail fraud. (February 26)
- Rothstein loses money on the Mickey "The Toy Bulldog" Walker–Harry Greb bout at the Polo Grounds. (July 2)
- Judge Aaron J. Levy signs order barring further raids on Teepee Democratic Club. (July 29)
- In Jamaica, Queens, Mayor John F. "Red Mike" Hylan accuses A. R. of being a "gambler," backing James J. Walker for mayor. (August 26)
- At Brooklyn's Prospect Hall, Gov. Alfred E. Smith derides Hylan's charges. (August 27)
- Tammany chief George Olvany denies "that my alleged poolroom king and big gambler adviser is Arnold Rothstein and that my B. M. T. [Brooklyn–Manhattan Transit Corporation] lawyer adviser is a man whom he calls Tom Chadbourne." (August 27)
- Rothstein wins $80,000 on the suspicious Mickey "The Toy Bulldog" Walker–Dave Shade fight at Yankee Stadium. (September).
- Harry Sitamore arrested in Kingston, New York, in connection with the Edna Johnson robbery. (November 7)
- Izzy Einstein and Moe Smith dismissed from the federal Prohibition Bureau. (November 18)
- Nicky Arnstein is released from Leavenworth. He had received seventy-two days off for good behavior. (December 22)
- Rothstein ranked as high agent in sales for the Norwalk Insurance Co.
- Rothstein bankrolls Jake Factor again.
- Jimmy Meehan arrested after a failed robbery attempt. His accomplice receives a prison sentence. Meehan goes free.

1926

- Rothstein, Inc. employee Irving Sobel arrested on charge of selling heroin.
- Irving Bitz arrested on narcotics charges.
- Rothstein mediates garment industry strike—allegedly influences police on behalf of the Communist-dominated faction.
- Rothstein sends George Uffner to Asia for further drug purchases— these will continue following Rothstein's death.
- Rothstein gives power of attorney to both L. P. Mattingly and Rolland Nutt to represent him against additional tax assessment lodged against him for the years 1919, 1920, and 1921. Mattingly was the son-in-law of

Col. Levi G. Nutt, chief of the Federal Narcotics Bureau. Rolland Nutt was Col. Nutt's son.

- Death of gambling house owner "Honest John" Kelly. (March 26)
- "Dandy Phil" Kastel convicted of mail fraud. (April 17)
- Rudolph Valentino appears at "Tommy Guinan's Playground" on West 52nd Street. (July 25)
- Murder in Brooklyn of Miss Bertha Katz, sister-in-law of "John the Barber" Reisler. (July 26)
- Convicted gambler Jules Formel charges A. R. had paid Saratoga County district attorney Charles B. Andrus $60,000 in "protection" money. (August 10)
- Acid attack on Bill Fallon at the Hotel Belleclaire. (August 12)
- A letter from Rothstein to Saratoga County district attorney Charles Andrus is made public in which Rothstein denies any wrongdoing. (September 9)
- Rothstein is at ringside at the controversial first Jack Dempsey–Gene Tunney fight in Philadelphia. He wins $500,000. (September 23)
- The Citizens Union (a good government group) deems Maurice Cantor "qualified and preferred . . . an intelligent and well-informed candidate who is entitled to preference" in the Eleventh Assembly District but holds back from granting an outright endorsement. (October)
- Rothstein sets aside a trust fund of $100,000 in securities for his girl-friend Bobbie Winthrop. (December)

1927

- Carolyn Rothstein informs Rothstein that she desires a divorce.
- Rothstein meets showgirl Inez Norton.
- Rothstein urges Little Augie Orgen to lay off strong-arm tactics in unions and to opt for infiltration of their management—Orgen refuses.
- Trial commences of three Rothstein drug smugglers—William Vachuda (a former policeman), Charles Webber, and John C. Webber. They are defended by Bill Fallon, Leonard Snitkin, and future U.S. Attorney George Z. Medalie. At stake was six hundred pounds of morphine, cocaine, and heroin with a street value of $4,000,000. (February 17)
- William Vachuda, Charles Webber, and John C. Webber found guilty—receive long sentences. (February 23)
- Carolyn Rothstein spends $1,083 at Jay Thorpe, Inc. (March 14)
- Bill Fallon appears in court for the last time, defending John J. McGraw in an action brought by the estate of the late E. R. Thomas. (April 25)

- Death of Bill Fallon at the Hotel Oxford, 205 West 88th Street. (April 29)
- Two federal indictments against Charles A. Stoneham dropped. (April)
- The American Federation of Labor (AFL) accuses Arnold Rothstein of "fixing the police in behalf of the Communists"; in recent furriers' strike. (June 11)
- Legs Diamond arrested on narcotics charges; rumors fly Rothstein had tipped off authorities on him. (July 9)
- Rothstein loses roughly $47,000 on the Jack Dempsey–Jack Sharkey heavyweight title fight at Yankee Stadium. (July 21)
- George Young Bauchle's daughter Jorice marries banker Clifford B. Schaffer at Christ Church, 111 East 87th Street. Bauchle is absent. (August 17)
- Gangster Joey Noe appointed a special Bronx deputy sheriff. (August 17)
- Legal separation granted to Carolyn Rothstein. (August 27)
- Fanny Brice divorces Nicky Arnstein. (September 27)
- Death of Bobbie Winthrop from "alcoholic polyneuritis" at the Hotel Langdon (southeast corner of Fifth Avenue and East 56th Street). (September 5)
- Legs Diamond is wounded, while fellow mobster "Little Augie" Orgen is shot to death at Delancey and Norfolk Streets. Louis Lepke and Gurrah Shapiro are suspected. (October 15)
- Rothstein is profiled in the *Brooklyn Daily Eagle* by reporter Zoe Beckley. "My code of life is absolutely simple," he claims. "Help a friend, be a friend, use your brains and fear nothing. Happiness? Hm! I haven't a material wish ungratified. That isn't happiness. What is? Being a good scout, keeping busy and helping people." (November 27)
- Helen Morgan opens in Flo Ziegfeld's *Show Boat* at West 54th Street's Ziegfeld Theatre. (December 27)
- Federal agents raid the Helen Morgan–fronted nightclub, the Chez Morgan. (December 30)
- Arnold Rothstein emerges in virtual control of U.S. drug trade.

1928

- Police raid the Paramount Building, seizing $20,000 in stolen furs; also arrest Legs Diamond on murder charges. (February 2)
- Legs Diamond released. (February 3)
- Rothstein bankrolls Con Conrad's all-Black Broadway review *Keep Shufflin'*. (Opens February 27)

- A federal judge orders Chez Morgan's furnishing restored to Helen Morgan. (February 28)
- Rothstein's Cedar Point Realty Co. sells Woodmere, Long Island's 260-acre Cedar Point Golf Club to a syndicate headed by Billy LaHiff. (Late February or early March)
- At Rothstein's behest, Maurice Cantor becomes the attorney for Inez Norton. (March 31)
- Rothstein loses $130,000 at Belmont Park. (May 31)
- Rothstein's "Rothmere Mortgage Corporation" "loans" $19,940 to City Magistrate Albert H. Vitale. (June 18)
- Helen Morgan again arrested. (June 29)
- Frankie Yale murdered in Brooklyn. (July 1)
- Albert Vitale repays the "Rothmere Mortgage Corporation" loan. (July 2)
- Rothstein loses $300,000 at a poker game at Jimmy Meehan's 161 West 54th Street apartment. (September 8–10)
- Rothstein applies for a $10,000 life insurance policy (policy #232126) from the Manhattan Life Insurance Company. (September 29)
- Gangster Joe Noe associate Tony Marlow gunned down outside the Hotel Harding (205 West 54th Street). (October 5)
- Bessie Poole dies of injuries most likely inflicted on her by Tommy Guinan. (October 8)
- Joey Noe shot by Louis Weinberg outside the Chateau Madrid (234 West 54th Street). Weinberg is killed in the exchange. (October 16)
- Maurice Cantor revises Rothstein's will. (October 22)
- Rothstein reviews his revised will at Maurice Cantor's office; does not sign it, however. (October 29)
- Rothstein shot in Room 349 of the Park Central Hotel, 200 West 56th Street. (November 4)
- Rothstein lingers at Polyclinic Hospital (335–361 West 50th Street); he signs a revised will prepared by Maurice F. Cantor. (November 5)
- Rothstein dies at 10:15 a.m. at Polyclinic Hospital. (November 5)
- Eddie Diamond is unharmed when his car is strafed by machine-gun fire in Denver. Police arrest Eugene Moran and Joseph Piteo (alias "James J. Nolan"), both former Rothstein bodyguards. Piteo will jump his $5,000 bail. Some say Rothstein ordered the hit. (November 6)
- Lucky Luciano, George Uffner, and "Fats" Walsh are charged with robbery by New York police. (November 17)

- Andrew J. Sheridan, Samuel Brown, and Abraham E. Rothstein are appointed temporary administrators of the Rothstein estate. (November 17)
- "Dandy Phil" Kastel convicted of grand larceny in connection with a Dillon & Co. transaction. (November 18)
- The Silver Slipper and the Club Frivolity are padlocked for one year by federal court order. (November 19)
- Death of Joey Noe at Bellevue Hospital. (November 21)
- George McManus surrenders to police. (November 27)
- Sidney Stajer and Jimmy Meehan testify before Rothstein murder grand jury. (November 28)
- In The Tombs, Park Central chambermaid Bridget Farry and two others identify gambler George McManus as the occupant of Room 349. (November 28)
- Robbery charges dismissed against Lucky Luciano, George Uffner, and "Fats" Walsh. (November 29)
- George McManus, Hyman "Gillie" Biller, "John Doe," and "Richard Roe" are indicted for A. R.'s murder. (December 4)
- Eight surviving members of the late Joey Noe's gang are arrested at a 542 Brook Avenue, Bronx speakeasy for the recent $104,500 robbery of the First National Bank of Yonkers. They include Joseph Piteo and Vincent "Mad Dog" Coll. (December 13)

1929

- Queens bootlegger Harry Vesey, another former Rothstein associate, is found shot to death on the Hoboken waterfront. Police suspect Legs Diamond. (January 10)
- Tommy Guinan found guilty of liquor violations at the Club Florence. (January 25)
- Tommy Guinan sentenced to four months in federal prison. His sentence will later be suspended. (February 5)
- Body of former Rothstein and Eugene Moran associate Frank "Blubber" Devlin found at a Somerville, New Jersey, farm. Devlin had accompanied Moran and Joseph Piteo to Denver in November 1928. (March 3)
- Bonny Grant arrested at the Park Crescent Hotel (351–357 West 87th Street at Riverside Drive); $1 million in cocaine and opium seized. (March 5)
- Former Rothstein bodyguard Thomas "Fats" Walsh shot to death at Miami's Biltmore Hotel. (March 6)
- George McManus freed on $50,000 bail. (March 27)

- Gertrude Vanderbilt loses suit to gain control of Bill Fallon's estate. She had claimed to have lent Fallon $25,000; also claimed that John J. McGraw owed the estate $15,000. (April 2)
- Park Central chambermaid Bridget Farry released on a $15,000 bond. (April 11)
- Rothstein's deathbed will is voided by Surrogate Court Judge John P. O'Brien; he instead probates Arnold's March 1, 1928, will. (April 15)
- Helen Morgan acquitted of June 1928 liquor charges. (April 18)
- In Atlantic City, the nation's crime lords meet to divide up the spoils. Among Rothstein's associates present are: Meyer Lansky, Dutch Schultz, Lucky Luciano, Owney Madden, Frank Costello, Larry Fay, and Frank Erickson. (May 13–15)
- Legs Diamond held for questioning re: Tony Marlow's 1928 murder. (May 20)
- In London, Carolyn Green Rothstein, forty-one, marries Robert Behar, twenty-eight; resides in London at 85 Portland Place for the next year and a half. (June 23)
- Frankie Marlow murdered outside a Flushing, Queens, Cemetery. (June 24)
- Legs Diamond and Charles Entratta involved in fatal gun battle at the Hotsy Totsy Club. (July 13)
- William Wolgast, formerly a Hotsy Totsy Club waiter, is found murdered at Bordentown, New Jersey. (July 19)
- Jack Rothstone and John J. Glynn appointed administrators of the Rothstein estate, superseding Andrew J. Sheridan, Samuel Brown, and Abraham Rothstein. (July 26)
- Body of former Rothstein bodyguard Eugene "Red" Moran found in a Newark dump. (August 10)
- Republican mayoral candidate Fiorello La Guardia rips the annual police department report issued by Commissioner Grover Whalen; charges "Rothstein was the financier of Tammany Hall itself." (August 26)
- La Guardia reveals A. R.'s 1928 loan to Judge Albert H. Vitale. (September)
- Vitale confirms the Rothstein loan; denies knowing Rothstein. (September 27)
- Helen Morgan's *Applause* premieres at Paramount's Criterion Theater (1514-16 Broadway at West 44th Street). (October 8)

- Judge Charles C. Nott refuses to try McManus before the upcoming mayoral election. (October 10)
- Lucky Luciano is abducted and beaten on Staten Island. (October 17)
- James J. Walker wins reelection; defeats Fiorello La Guardia 865,000 to 368,000; Thomas C. T. Crain elected district attorney. (November 5)
- George McManus's trial postponed because of illness of witness. (November 12)
- McManus trial begins. (November 18)
- George McManus's home is robbed while he attends the NYU–Carnegie Tech football game. (November 28)
- Judge Nott directs acquittal of George McManus. (December 5)
- Judge Albert H. Vitale robbed at a banquet for the Tepecano Democratic Club at the Bronx's Roman Gardens Restaurant (2407 Southern Boulevard at 187th Street). (December 7–8)
- In Surrogates Court, attorney Nathan Burkan applies for $75,000 in counsel fees for work on Rothstein's estate; temporary administrators Andrew J. Sheridan, Samuel Brown, and Abraham Rothstein had estimated the estate's assets at $2,512,993.07. (December 13)
- In Surrogates Court, Maurice Cantor applies for $115,000 in counsel fees for work on Rothstein's estate. (December 23)
- Police raid John Reisler's barbershop (now at 156 West 44th Street), discovering 162 bottles of liquor at its rear. (December 27)
- Buda Godman is reported as no longer living at Charles A. Stoneham's 110 West 55th Street apartment.

1930
- Eddie Diamond dies of tuberculosis at Saranac Lake, New York. (January 14)
- Judge Nott quashes charges against Hyman Biller. (January 16)
- In NYS Supreme Court, Inez Norton loses a bid to have a $20,000 Rothstein life insurance policy transferred to her. (January 24)
- Ciro Terranova arraigned before Magistrate Bernard J. Douras (Marion Davies's father) in connection with the Vitale Robbery at the Bronx's Roman Gardens Restaurant.
- Inez Norton returns from Florida, announces she will appear on Broadway in a play based on Rothstein. (February 1)
- Grand jury issues report on the NYC federal narcotics office. (February 19)
- Legs Diamond surrenders to police. (March 10)

- Magistrate Albert Vitale is removed from office over the Rothstein loan. (March 14)
- Governor Franklin D. Roosevelt pardons Morris Reisler. (March 20)
- Charges against Legs Diamond dismissed by Judge Max Levine. (March 21)
- Police Commissioner Grover Whalen issues an official report on police mishandling of the Rothstein murder probe. (March 24)
- Joseph F. Crater appointed to the New York State Supreme Court by Governor Franklin D. Roosevelt. (April 8)
- The late Fatty Walsh's brother James is shot in the spine while attempting to rob the South Bronx Homing Pigeon Club (at Chisholm and Freeman Streets). (April 20)
- Inez Norton opens in *Room 349* at the National Theater (now the Nederlander). (April 21)
- Sandy Ford, a long-shot four-year-old gelding owned by Willie Shea (Rothstein's old partner), wins Pimlico's $25,000 Dixie Handicap; Shea also collects $6,000 on bets. (April 28)
- *Room 349* closes after fifteen performances. (May)
- Willie Shea suffers "a broken wrist and some bad cuts" from an auto accident at West 72nd and Broadway on his way to Belmont Park, where his filly Novena, a 3-1 favorite, wins in her first outing for him. (June 2)
- William Powell's film *For the Defense* premieres at The Paramount Times Square (1501 Broadway at West 43rd Street). (July 18)
- Judge Crater attends *Artists and Models* at the Majestic Theatre in the company of Mrs. Constance Braemer "Connie" Marcus, a "model in a 5th Ave. gown shop." (July 24)
- Judge Crater vanishes. (August 6)
- Judge Samuel Seabury appointed to investigate Magistrates Courts; the move begins end of Walker administration. (August 25)
- Mrs. Stella Crater finally asks friends to locate her missing husband. (August 27)
- A grand jury commences an inquiry into the Judge Crater mystery. (September 15)
- Legs Diamond sails for Europe. (September)
- Death of John J. "John the Barber" Reisler at Lebanon Hospital, the Bronx. (September 15)
- Philadelphia authorities arrest Legs Diamond as a "suspicious character." (September 22)

- Legs Diamond is wounded but escapes death at the Hotel Monticello (35-37 West 64th Street). (October 22)
- Joseph Piteo, once suspected of trying to bump off Eddie Diamond, is shot dead during a botched jewel robbery in Philadelphia. He was thirty-two. (October 23)
- Amanda E. McManus, wife of George McManus, is killed in an auto accident; McManus suffers a heart attack as a result. (October 29)
- Magistrate Francis X. McQuade resigns under fire. (December 9)
- Stephen McManus retires from the police force at age forty-six. (December)

1931

- The bullet-riddled body of Antony Indelicato is found in a Paterson, New Jersey, field. (January 11)
- Samuel Levy, Jack Rothstein's future father-in-law, is named Manhattan Borough President by the Board of Alderman with the backing of Mayor James J. Walker and Tammany leader John F. Curry. (January 16)
- Dutch Schultz and his bodyguard Charles "Chink" Sherman are wounded at a brawl at West 54th Street's Club Abbey. (January 21)
- New York State Supreme Court justice Edward J. Gavegan rules against the claim of the Rothstein estate versus The Manhattan Life Insurance Company regarding its $10,000 life insurance policy issued on Rothstein, finding that the policy's initial $406.70 premium remained unpaid at Rothstein's death. (February 24)
- Legs Diamond is wounded at upstate Acra, New York. (April 27)
- Brooklyn mobster and bootlegger Vannie Higgins, a Legs Diamond ally, is stabbed at the Blossom Heath Inn owned by George McManus's brother Frank McManus. (May 21)
- Vincent "Mad Coll" Coll kidnaps Frenchy DeMange at West 48th Street's Argonaut Club. (June 15 or July 15)
- Patrolman Andrew J. McLaughlin surrenders to police to face perjury charges. (June 22)
- In Los Angeles, Inez Norton (aka "Inez Mitchell") is purported to have attempted suicide from poison. (August 19)
- Supposedly, the suicide victim in question was not Inez Norton but an "Inez Mitchell" who had borrowed Norton's automobile. (August 19)
- "Tough Willie" McCabe is knifed at the Sixty-One Club (61 East 52nd Street). He refuses to name his assailant. With McCabe was former *Ziegfeld Follies* showgirl Hilda Ferguson, a onetime roommate of Dot King. (August 26)

- Nate Raymond fixes a race at the Havre de Grace track. (October 3)
- Jimmy Meehan, charged with "sponging" racehorses at Belmont Park, is released on bail. (October 11)
- The Maryland Racing Commission rules Nate Raymond off all of the state's tracks. (November 18)
- Legs Diamond is shot to death (finally!) at 67 Dove Street, Albany, New York. (December 18)

1932

- Larry Fay shot to death outside his nightclub, the Casa Blanca (33 West 56th Street), by Edward Mahoney, a club doorman disgruntled by a recent pay decrease. (January 1)
- Nate Raymond surrenders to authorities in Florida regarding charges of stock fraud involving his September 1928 loan from New York's Colonial Bank. (January 8)
- Trial commences of Nate Raymond. (January 12)
- Nate Raymond found guilty of stock fraud. (January 14)
- Triangle Club (formerly the Club Abbey) raided. (January 14)
- Robbery of $305,000 in jewels from Harry C. Glemby (22 East 67th Street). (January 21)
- Nate Raymond sentenced to five years. (January 26)
- Nate Raymond freed on bail on order from Supreme Court Justice Aaron J. Levy.
- Rothstein murder grand jury dismissed. (February 2)
- Buda Godman arrested in a taxicab at Broadway and West 63rd Street for attempting to fence the stolen Glemby jewels. (April 13) Samuel "Sammy the Hook" Entratta (aka Sam Ippolito) commits suicide at Buda Godman's 161 West 54th Street apartment. (June 14)
- Vannie Higgins shot to death following his daughter's tap dance recital at Bay Ridge's Knights of Columbus Hall. (June 19)
- Salvatore Spitale and Tough Willie McCabe sought for questioning in the slaying of mobster Vannie Higgins. (June 20)
- Death of Florenz Ziegfeld in Hollywood. (July 22)
- Jimmy Walker resigns as mayor. (September 1)
- Suicide (gunshot to temple) of broker Edward M. Fuller. (October 8)
- Buda Godman pleads guilty to fencing the stolen Glemby jewels. (November 1)
- Decree of divorce granted in New York Supreme Court to Herbert Van Blarcom and Margot Colin. (November 9)

- Buda Godman is sentenced to four-to-eight years at Auburn prison. A probation report reveals Buda Godman to have been the mistress of Charles A. Stoneham. (November 10)
- Nate Raymond sentenced to five years.
- At Mineola, New York, Jimmy Meehan convicted of "sponging" a horse at Belmont Park; sentenced to six months in the Nassau County jail.

1933

- Harry Sitamore arrested in his Miami bungalow. (March)
- Jay Thorpe, Inc. sues Carolyn Rothstein Behar for unpaid bills in the amount of $1,299.35. (May 31)
- Harry Sitamore begins forty-year sentence. (April 1)
- Harry Sitamore escapes from Florida's Raiford State Prison. (June 2)
- Legs Diamond's widow, Alice Kenny Schiffer Diamond, is found shot to death at her 1641 Ocean Avenue, Brooklyn apartment. (June 30)
- Suicide of Henry Sherman, brother of "Chink" Sherman, at 1333 Bronx River Avenue, the Bronx. (October 12)
- Death of Hilda Ferguson from peritonitis at New York Hospital. (October 3)
- Trial commences of Waxey Gordon for income tax evasion; Thomas E. Dewey is the prosecutor. (November 20)
- Waxey Gordon convicted of income tax evasion. (November 29)
- Prohibition is repealed. (December 5).
- George Uffner convicted on check forging charges. Sent to Sing Sing.

1934

- Death of John J. McGraw in New Rochelle, New York. (February 25)
- George McManus arrested on gambling charges. (March)
- In Los Angeles, Inez Norton's fifteen-year-old son, Claude Norton Jr., is placed on probation for reckless driving. (April 10)
- Carolyn Green Rothstein Behar publishes memoir *Now I'll Tell*. (May)
- George and Stephen McManus arrested on gambling charges. (July)
- Death of Dr. Philip M. Grausman at his West 58th Street office. (November 21)

1935

- Nat Evans dies in at New York Presbyterian Hospital; leaves a half-million-dollar estate, including various Saratoga Springs holdings. (February 6)
- Inez Norton's marriage to Chicago's Thomas C. Neal Jr. announced.
- Inez Norton's marriage to Neal called off. (September 12)

- Murder of Charles "Chink" Sherman. (September 25)
- Dutch Schultz and three sidekicks (Otto "Abbadabba" Berman, Bernard "Lulu" Rosencrantz and Abe "Abie the Accountant" Landau) are shot at Newark's Palace Chop House (12 East Park Street). Rival gang leaders, nervous over Schultz's plans to assassinate Thomas E. Dewey, are suspected. They include: Lucky Luciano, Frank Costello, Louis Lepke Buchalter, and Meyer Lansky. (October 23)
- Death of Dutch Schultz at Newark City Hospital. (October 24)
- To combat organized crime's (and Ciro Terranova's) control of the city's artichoke trade, Mayor La Guardia bans their sale or display. (December 21)

1936
- Death of New York Giants owner Charles A. Stoneham in Hot Springs, Arkansas. (January 6)
- Charles A. Stoneham's former mistress Margaret Leonard's lawsuit against his estate is made public. (April 1)
- Maurice Cantor enters a guilty plea on behalf of his client Jack Eller, on trial with Lucky Luciano on prostitution charges. Representing two other defendants is James D. C. Murray, formerly defense counsel for George McManus in the Rothstein murder trial. (June 1)
- Lucky Luciano is convicted on sixty-two counts relating to prostitution trafficking. (June 7)
- Luciano is sentenced to thirty to fifty years at Dannemora. (June 18)
- Death of Bridgie Webber in Passaic, New Jersey. (July 30)
- Trial of Jay Thorpe, Inc. versus Carolyn Rothstein Behar in City Court. (October 6–8)
- Body of "Chink" Sherman found in a barn near Monticello in Sullivan County. (November)
- Judge rules in favor of Carolyn Rothstein Behar and grants her $81.80 in court costs.

1937
- "Tough Willie" McCabe detained for questioning regarding the slaying of "small-time Brooklyn hoodlum" John Spellman. The two had argued earlier in the day. "Spellman," noted a press report, "each morning went to the Clarendon Restaurant, 1135 Flatbush Avenue, for his breakfast. Today, after ordering, he started to read his paper. The door opened and a masked man walked in. He went directly to Spellman and fired five shots into Spellman's back and head. Then he walked out." (March 8)

- Gambler Mike Best wounded in the chest over a $4,000 gambling debt on West 53rd Street. (March 8)
- Jimmy Meehan and a confederate rob Mrs. Diana Lanzetta (widowed sister-in-law of a former Democratic congressman) of $2,250 in jewelry at her ninth-floor Ansonia Hotel apartment. (September 23)

1938

- Ciro Terranova dies penniless in Manhattan following a stroke. (February 20)
- Jack Rothstone files an accounting of his brother Arnold's estate, lists no assets. (March 1)
- Former Rothstein attorney Isaiah Leebove shot to death in Clare, Michigan. (May)
- Jimmy Meehan found guilty of a September 1937 robbery of Mrs. Diana Lanzetta. (June 6)
- Jimmy Meehan sentenced to Sing Sing for ten to twenty years. (June 22)
- Police raid the headquarters of George McManus's interstate gambling syndicate; he is not indicted. (July)
- Tammany's James J. Hines arrested regarding his involvement in the numbers racket. (July 11)
- Fanny Brice divorces Billy Rose. (October 27)

1939

- James J. Hines convicted of "contriving, proposing and drawing a lottery." (February 26)
- Judge Crater declared legally dead. (June 6)
- Death of Frenchy DeMange at the Hotel Warwick (September 18).
- Former Communist Party member Maurice L. Malkin testifies before the House Committee on Un-American Activities that during a 1926 furriers strike Rothstein lent to the Communist-dominated Furriers Union $1,175,000, of which $110,000 was used to pay off the police. (October 13)
- Dapper Don Collins sentenced to fifteen to thirty years in Sing Sing for extorting an immigrant.

1940

- Death of George "Hump" McManus of heart disease at his Sea Girt, New Jersey, summer home. (August 28)
- Death of Sidney Stajer. (December 11)

1941

- Death of Rose Cantor, mother of Maurice Cantor. (January 5)
- Death of Helen Morgan of cirrhosis in Chicago. (October 9)

1944

- Jimmy Meehan arrested for robbery in New Rochelle; receives a suspended sentence.
- Jimmy Hines paroled from Sing Sing. (September 12)

1946

- Lucky Luciano deported to Sicily. (February 9)
- Death of Damon Runyon at Memorial Hospital (now Memorial Sloan Kettering). (December 10)
- Jimmy Meehan implicated in the embezzlement of $734,000 from Brooklyn's Mergenthaler Linotype Company.

1947

- Joe Bernstein arrested on gambling charges at San Francisco's Seals Stadium; charges are later dropped. (July 4)
- Isadore Rapoport sentenced to two and a half to five years for his part in the Mergenthaler Linotype Company embezzlement case; suffers a heart attack. (October 7)
- Damon Runyon's former wife, now Mrs. Richard N. Coffin, robbed of $200,000 in jewels at her Dartmouth, Massachusetts, home. The three thieves drive off in her new husband's new convertible. (November 18)
- Harry Sitamore paroled.

1948

- Gay Orlova commits suicide in her Paris apartment. (February 12)
- Frank Tinney's former mistress Imogene Wilson (now known as Mary Nolan) commits suicide in Hollywood. (October 31)

1949

- Harry Sitamore pardoned.

1950

- Death of Dapper Don Collins at Attica Prison. (June 18)

1951

- Jimmy Meehan is shot by police and arrested during botched robbery of David's Fur Couture at 50 West 57th Street. (January 21)
- "Dandy Phil" Kastel indicted for contempt of Congress. (March 28)

- Waxey Gordon convicted of selling narcotics; sentenced to twenty-five years. (December 13)

1952
- Waxey Gordon dies at Alcatraz. (June 24)

1953
- Maurice and Helen Cantor are implicated as receiving suspicious revenue from Roosevelt Raceway parking and program concessions. (October)

1956
- Harry Sitamore arrested at Bal Harbor while in possession of seventy master keys to various local hotels.

1957
- Police detain George Uffner and gambling kingpin Frank Erickson (another former Rothstein associate) for questioning regarding Albert Anastasia's recent murder at the barbershop of the Park Central Hotel. (December 4)

1960
- Harry Sitamore named on the FBI's "Most Wanted" list.
- Harry Sitamore imprisoned.

1961
- Premiere of Rothstein biopic *King of the Roaring 20s* based on Leo Katcher's *The Big Bankroll,* starring David Janssen as Rothstein. Also featured, albeit in a small role, was veteran character actor William Demarest, best known for his role of "Uncle Charley O'Casey" on the popular television series *My Three Sons.* Demarest claimed to have been introduced to Rothstein on the night of his shooting.

1964
- Harry Sitamore released from prison.

BIBLIOGRAPHY

INDEX

Carolyn Holding Co., 272

Carroll, Earl, 123, 124, 189

Carroll, Renée (Rebecca Shapiro), 58–60, 189

Carter, Ed (Edwin J. Jerge, E. Jack Kayton, Harold Atwater, Edward Mack), 76–77

Caruso, Enrico, 200, 209

Casa Blanca, 165, 287

Caseri, Garbino, 132

Casseres, Ben De, 100

Cassidy, William "Red," 73, 159–160

Cedar Point Golf Club, 111

Cedar Point Realty Corporation, 178, 281

Chadbourne, Tom, 27, 278

Chadbourne, William M., 276

Chafetz, Henry, 104, 106

Chanin Brothers, 63–64

Chaplin, Charlie, 13, 144

Charles A. Stoneham & Co., 164, 271, 275

Charm Club, 107

Chase, Hal "Prince Hal," 65, 163, 211

Chateau Madrid, 158–159

Chez Florence, 107–109, 143

Chez Morgan, 280, 281

Chiaramonte, Frank, 180

Chicago Tribune, 101–102, 208, 271

Chicago White Sox, 64, 65, 209–210, 273, 274

Childs Restaurant, 189

Christy, Howard Chandler, 200

Church of the Ascension, 235–236

Cicotte, Eddie, 210

Cincinnati Reds, 64, 273

Cipollini, Christian, 217

Circle Theatre, 193–194

Cirofici, Francesco (Dago Frank), 16, 22, 271

Claire, Ina, 50

The Clarendon, 228–229

Clark, Arthur "Chick," 95–96

Clarke, Donald Henderson, 102, 176, 179–180

Clarke, Grant, 100

Clarke, Mae, 108

Club Abbey, 121, 154, 155

Club Anatole, 109

Club Dover, 107

Club Durant, 185–186

Club Florence, 282

Club Frivolity, 107, 139–140, 282

Club Hilda, 181

Club Intime, 152–158

Club La Vie, 112

Club Maurice, 132

Club Moritz, 109–110

Club Napoleon, 165

Club Richman, 109

Coffin, Mrs. Richard N., 291

Cohan, George M., xxiii, 20, 39, 71, 120, 163, 185

Cohen, Hyman, 274

Colgate, Gilbert, 218

Colin, Margot, 152–153, 154–155, 287

Coliseum Convention Center, 194

Coll, Vincent "Mad Dog," 147, 282, 286

Collier's Eye, 275

Collins, "Dapper Don," xxii, 18, 114, 142, 209, 275, 290, 291

Collins, John, 243, 255, 258, 266

Collyer's Eye, 276

Colonial Bank, 201, 226

Colonial Hotel, 226

Columbia Burlesque, 86

Columbia Theatre, 85–87

Columbus Circle Roller Rink, 194

Compton, Betty, 27, 32, 49, 58, 62

Comstock, William, 18

Conaway, Jack, 100, 101, 270

Congress Apartments, 147–150

Conrad, Con, 178

Considine, Bob, 6

Considine, George F., 14, 38, 195–196

Considine, John R., 14, 195

Considine, John W., Jr., 6

Considine, John W., Sr., 6

Considine, William F., 14, 38, 195

Continental Baths, 213

Coppa, Ignatius, 138

Corbett, James J. "Gentleman Jim," 21, 105, 120, 195

Cordes, John H., 250, 251, 257–258, 266

Corrigan, Jos. E., 113

Costello, Frank, xxiii, 119, 204, 283, 289

Cotton Club, 140

Coughlin, John D., 245–246, 248, 250, 251–252, 253, 265

Coward, Noel, 200

Crain, Thomas C. T., 284

Crater, Joseph F., 49, 62, 63, 74–75, 152, 156, 273, 285, 290

Crater, Stella, 285

Crawford, Joan, 119

Cree Club, 54

Criminal Lawyer, 86–87

Cripple Creek, 84–85

Cuff, James I., 267–268

Curry, John F., 286

Curry, Joseph, 21, 275

Curtis, James, 125

Grant, Bonny, 231, 282
Grant, Cary, 143
Grant, Jane, 100
Grausman, Philip M., 184–185, 226, 288
The Great Gatsby (Fitzgerald), 190
The Great Temptations, 108
Greb, Harry, 278
Green, Abel, 85, 87
Green, John, 244, 248, 266
Greenpoint People's Regular Democratic
    Organization, 54
Greenthal Arnstein, Carrie, 135, 236
Greenwald, Meyer, 77
Greenwich Social Club, 107
Gresheimer, Frederick "Freddie Gresham," 33,
    34, 46, 75, 102, 271, 272, 273
Grey, Joel, 200
Griffith, D. W., 219
Guimares, Alberto Santos, 138, 181
Guinan, Mary Louise Cecilia "Texas," xxiii, 56,
    57, 58, 69–70, 93, 107, 109, 119–120, 147,
    152–158, 200, 275
Guinan, Tommy, xxiii, 56, 57, 58, 107, 119, 143,
    165, 281, 282
Guys and Dolls, 82

Haas, Billy, 74–75
Hackett Theatre, 32–33
Hall, Mordaunt, 23, 125
Halpers, Irving "Little Itch," 231
Hammerstein, Oscar, 21–23, 46–47
Hammerstein, William, 185
Hammerstein's Victoria, 21–23
Hanson, Nils, 234
Harding, Warren, 57
Harold Ross Residence, 100
Harris, Sam, 21, 185
Hart, Flo, 25
Having, A. R., 179
Hawley, Joyce, 123, 276
Healey, Ted, 31
Hearst, Millicent Veronica Wilson, 228
Hearst, William Randolph, 25, 41, 142,
    143–144, 187, 188, 201, 228, 276
Heenan, Frances Belle "Peaches," 205–206
Held, Anna, 209, 271
Helen Hayes Theater, 80
Helen Morgan Club, 146–147
Helen Morgan's Summer Home/House, 109,
    147
Hellinger, Mark, xxiii, 26, 60, 79, 229–230, 231
Hell's Bells, 32

Helman, Louise, 157
Henry, Dominick, 183, 274
Hepburn, Audrey, 81
Herbert, Hugh, 31
Herbert, Victor, 13, 21
Herman Rosenthal's Gambling House, 68–69
Higgins, Vannie, 220, 286, 287
Highbridge Regular Democratic Club, 54
Hill, Percival S., 271
Hines, James J. "Jimmy," xxiii, 236–237, 290,
    291
Hoff, Max "Boo Boo," 116
Hoffman, Abbie, 37
Hoffman, Dr., 244
Holy Name of Jesus Church, 233
Homicide Squad, 246–247, 265
Hooper Realty Corporation, 178
Horowitz, Harry "Gyp the Blood," 15, 16, 271
horse racing, 10–11, 71, 213, 287, 288
Horwitz, Jake, 58
Hotel Albany, 9–11
Hotel Almanac, 203–204, 277
Hotel Astor, 64–67
Hotel at Times Square, 75
Hotel Belleclaire, 223–224, 279
Hotel Cadillac, 35–36
Hotel Claridge, 55–56
Hotel Consulate, 122
Hotel Des Artistes, 200
Hotel Diplomat, 37
Hotel Dorset, 142–143
Hotel Franconia, 207
Hotel Gerard, 51
Hotel Grenoble, 174–175
Hotel Harding, 281
Hotel Imperial, 103
Hotel Jefferson, 11
Hotel Knickerbocker, 17
Hotel Langdon, 280
Hotel Langwell, 50–51
Hotel Metropole, 14–15, 16, 17, 38–40, 269,
    270
Hotel Normandie, 8
Hotel Oxford, 231
Hotel Patterson, 75, 76
Hotel Plymouth, 117
Hotel Portland, 91
Hotel President, 112–114
Hotel Prisament, 213–215
Hotel Rand, 117–118
Hotel Rector, 56
Hotel Richmond, 76–77

Rugro Holding Corporation, 178
Runyon, Damon, xxiii, xxiv, 82, 110, 112,
   121–122, 123, 130, 185, 215, 291
Runyon, Ellen Egan, 121
Rush, Robert J., 243–244, 255, 259–260, 267
Ruth, Babe, 185, 204, 209–210
Ruttenberg, Nelson, 267

Salon Royale, 109
Sardi, Vincenzo "Vincent," 10, 21, 60
Sardi's Restaurant, 58–61
Saunders, Albert, 35
Scandals, 32
Scarne, John, 148–149, 168–170
Schaffer, Clifford B., 280
Scher, Abe, 125, 126–127, 245
Schoellkopf, C. P. Hugo, 136
Schoellkopf, Irene, 136–137
Schoellkopf, Mrs. Hugo A. C., 276
Schornstein, David, 139
Schultz, Dutch, xxiii, 82, 121, 154, 283, 286, 289
Scribner, Sam S., 87
Seabury, Samuel, 285
Seiden, Mary "Mickie of the Rendezvous,"
   111, 138
Seidenshner, Jacob (Whitey Lewis), 16, 22, 271
Self, Clifton, 32
Selwyn, Arch (Archie), xxiii, 29, 30–32, 49,
   185, 272
Selwyn, Edgar, xxiii, 29, 30–32
Selwyn, Ruth, 120
Selwyn Theater, 30–32
Sex, 196
Shade, Dave, 278
Shanley, Tom, 40
Shanley Building, 40–41
Shapiro, Gurrah, 280
Sharkey, Jack, 280
Shaughnessy, 103
Shea, William, 19, 270, 285
Sheerin, Doris (Mrs. Mary Elizabeth Dilson),
   76, 77
Sheridan, Andrew J., 282, 283, 284
Sherman, Charles "Chink," 121, 122, 154, 155,
   286, 289
Sherman, Henry, 121, 288
Sherman Billingley's Social Club, 107
Shor, Toots, 111
Show Boat, 81, 141–142, 280
Shubert Organization, 82
Shubert Theatre, 56–58
Shuffle Along, 196

Silver, Joe, 133
Silver Slipper, 107, 111–112, 282
Sinatra, Frank, 81, 134
Sinclair, Harry, 103
Sitamore, Harry, xxiii, 1–3, 4–5, 203–204, 220,
   271, 277, 278, 288, 291, 292
Sitamore, Mildred, 1–3, 4–5, 170–171
Skolsky, Sidney, 158
Slavin, John C., 52
Sloan, Alfred P., 185
Sloan, Tod, 19
Smith, Alfred E., 21, 27, 278
Smith, James E., 183
Smith, Moe, xxiii, 98–100, 278
Smith, Red, 238
Snitkin, Leonard, 279
Sobel, Irving, 278
Somerville, Charles, 98
The Sound of Music, 134
Speak Easily, 120
Spellman, John, 289
Spitale, Salvatore, 18, 76, 287
Spooner, Jack, 110
The Spotlight Café, 136
Stack, Robert, 82
Stahl, Rose, 32, 33
Stainkamp, Francis A., 255, 259, 266
Stajer, Sidney, xxiii, 18, 51, 214, 217, 218, 274,
   277, 282, 290
Stanwyck, Barbara (Ruby Stevens), 60, 69, 108,
   110–111
Star Democratic Club, 54
Stark, Irving H., 215, 216
Starrett, Goldwin, 49
State's Attorney, 86
The Steamer Club, 54
Steinhart, Charles, 37
Stern, Harry, 231
Still, William Grant, 196
St. Malachy's Church, 119–120
Stokes, William Earl Dodge, 208
Stoneham, Charles A., xxiii, 52, 67, 103, 145,
   161–165, 235, 237, 271, 272, 274, 275, 276,
   277, 278, 280, 288, 289
Stoneham, Jane Elizabeth, 162
Stoneham, Russell Charles, 162
Stotesbury, Edward T., 114
Strasmick, Marion (Kiki Roberts), 78, 79, 141,
   160, 197
Stravinsky, Igor, 209
Street of Chance, 23
Streisand, Barbra, 64

INDEX

ABOUT THE AUTHOR

Critics have hailed award-winning historian David Pietrusza as "America's preeminent presidential historian," "the undisputed champion of chronicling American Presidential campaigns," and "one of the great political historians of all time."

His books include studies of the 1920, 1932, 1936, 1948, and 1960 presidential elections and biographies of gambler Arnold Rothstein (an Edgar Award finalist) and baseball commissioner Kenesaw Mountain Landis (a CASEY Award winner).

His *Roosevelt Sweeps Nation* captured the Independent Publisher Book Awards Gold Medal for U.S. History, earned a rare *Kirkus* Starred Review (his third) as well as nominations for the Kirkus Prize and the New Deal Book Award.

His *TR's Last War: Theodore Roosevelt, the Great War, and a Journey of Triumph and Tragedy* won the Independent Publisher Book Awards Silver Medal for U.S. History and was a finalist for the Theodore Roosevelt Association Book Prize.

His *1932: The Rise of Hitler and FDR—Two Tales of Politics, Betrayal, and Unlikely Destiny* captured the Independent Publisher Book Awards Silver Medal for World History.

He served as editor-in-chief of Total Sports Publishing and coauthored the late Ted Williams's autobiographical *Ted Williams: My Life in Pictures*.

Pietrusza has appeared on NPR, C-SPAN, MSNBC, The Voice of America, The History Channel, AMC, ESPN, and the Fox Sports

Channel. He has appeared in the documentary film *American Rackets* and on such television series as *The Making of the Mob* and *Mafia's Greatest Hits*.

He has also spoken at the JFK, FDR, Truman, and Coolidge presidential libraries, the National Baseball Hall of Fame, and various universities, libraries, and festivals.

Visit davidpietrusza.com.